# WORLD OF LITERACY
## Yellow Level

READING COMPREHENSION BOOK

**General Editor:**
Miriam Shulamis Eisemann

**Editorial Project Manager:**
Rabbi Yitzchock Friedman

**Project Director:**
Rabbi Mordechai Resnick

**ELA Director:**
Esther Schwarz

**Project Coordinator:**
Miriam Shulamis Eisemann

**Design and Layout:**
Glenna Daniel
LeeZohar Lasry

**Contributing Authors:**
Shoshana Barron
Racheli Chalk
Miriam Shulamis Eisemann
Gitty Flohr
Chaya Hausmann
Adina Rosen

**Contributing Proofreader:**
Miriam Shulamis Eisemann

**Contributing Editor:**
Ellen Appelbaum

©2023 by Achievements Educational Services. All rights reserved. No part of this book may be reproduced or utilized in any form or by electronic or mechanical means, including photocopying, without permission in writing from the publisher.

Printed in the USA in August 2023.

ISBN: 978-1-948241-43-4

# Table of Contents

1. Frogs and Toads: Hopping Around ............................................................. 9
2. Seeing-Eye Dogs: The "Eyes" of Their Partners ....................................... 13
3. Cloudy Skies ................................................................................................ 17
4. High-Flying .................................................................................................. 21
5. Sea Otters: Just Floating Around ............................................................... 27
6. Alan Shepard: America's Best Pilot ........................................................... 31
7. Mountain Climbing: Race to the Top ......................................................... 37
8. Solids, Liquids, and Gases .......................................................................... 41
9. Glassblowing: Mesmerizing and Magical .................................................. 45
10. Ships and Subs: Above and Below Water ................................................. 49
11. Clara Barton: How One Shy Girl Changed the World ............................... 53
12. Weird and Amazing ..................................................................................... 59
13. Airplanes and Helicopters: Flying High ..................................................... 63
14. Tightrope Walkers: The Most Careful Stroll ............................................. 67
15. Recycling: Giving It a New Life .................................................................. 71
16. Say Cheese! ................................................................................................. 75
17. Born to Soar: The Amazing Story of John Glenn ..................................... 79
18. Ancient Shipbuilding: Marvels of Engineering ......................................... 85
19. Pigeon Post: A Different Kind of Airmail .................................................. 91
20. Julius Caesar and the Fall of the Senate .................................................. 95
21. People Who Fly: Trapeze Artists ............................................................... 101
22. Parakeets: Parroting Words ....................................................................... 105
23. The Great Basin Desert .............................................................................. 109
24. History of Checkers .................................................................................... 113
25. Snake Charmers: Swaying to the Music ................................................... 117
26. Yo Ho, Me Hearties! .................................................................................... 121
27. Telescopes: Exploring the Sky ................................................................... 125
28. Sea Explorations: Across and Beneath the Oceans ................................ 129
29. Neil Armstrong: Man on the Moon ............................................................ 133
30. Living Off the Congo River ........................................................................ 137
31. Stamps and Coins: Collecting History ...................................................... 143
32. Everglades National Park ........................................................................... 147

# Table of Contents

| | | |
|---|---|---|
| 33. | Davy Crockett: The Lion of the West | 151 |
| 34. | Stop Bugging Me! Ladybugs and Spiders | 157 |
| 35. | Zookeepers: Keeping the Animals Happy | 161 |
| 36. | Are You Afraid of Heights? | 165 |
| 37. | Yellowstone National Park | 169 |
| 38. | Woodpeckers: Pecking All Day | 173 |
| 39. | 'Listen, My Children, and You Shall Hear of the Midnight Ride of Paul Revere' | 177 |
| 40. | The North Pole and the South Pole | 183 |
| 41. | Wet and Thrilling: Go with the Flow | 191 |
| 42. | Shipwrecked at Sea: The Story of Robinson Crusoe | 195 |
| 43. | LEGO: Building a Business Brick by Brick | 201 |
| 44. | Electric Eels: Hunters of the Amazon! | 205 |
| 45. | Funny Visitors: Medical Clowns | 211 |
| 46. | Buffalo Bill and the Wild West | 215 |
| 47. | The Suez Canal: Gateway to Trade Between Europe and Asia | 219 |
| 48. | Elephant Building of Bangkok, Thailand and Other Skyscrapers | 225 |
| 49. | Deep in the Sea: Deep Sea Divers | 229 |
| 50. | Welcome to Anchorage, Alaska | 233 |
| 51. | Winemaking: From Vineyard to Market | 239 |
| 52. | Amazon: From Mocked to Amazing | 243 |
| 53. | How Dimes Defeated Polio | 247 |
| 54. | Something Fishy: The Fishing Industry | 253 |
| 55. | Balloonists: Smooth Sailing | 257 |
| 56. | Origami: Crafty Folds | 261 |
| 57. | The Legend of Johnny Appleseed | 265 |
| 58. | Bicycles, Unicycles, and Tandem Bikes | 269 |
| 59. | Signatures and John Hancock | 273 |
| 60. | Chess: A Thousand-Year-Old History | 277 |
| 61. | The Immune System: Fighting Foreign Invaders | 283 |
| 62. | Port Lockroy, Antarctica | 287 |
| 63. | Riding with Sally Kristen Ride | 293 |
| 64. | Geysers and Volcanoes: Eruptions From Deep Underground | 297 |

# Introduction - Yellow Level

### Isn't being in fourth grade exciting?

Your growing reading skills allow you to explore and appreciate all kinds of topics and ideas. You are able and eager to learn about things you may never have thought about or heard of before. For example, how are wine and cheese made? How are hot air balloons controlled? Who invented LEGO? And what on earth is a "John Hancock"? You'll find all these topics and many more waiting for you in the *World of Literacy*.

These lessons were written specifically for children your age. In addition to reading about a wide variety of topics, you will be able to comprehend them. Comprehension means the ability to understand information, add it to the knowledge you already have, and store it away for future use. As you make your way through this book, you will constantly be adding more and more facts and information to what you have previously learned. Things you may have wondered about before will become clearer to you. You will become more aware of things around you that you might not have noticed before. So pack your bags, and get ready for an exciting trip through the *World of Literacy*.

### You're sure to have a wonderful time!

# Frogs and Toads: Hopping Around

Walking along the river, you hear bushes rustle, a deep croak, and a splash. You rush to the stream and peer into the **murky**[1] water. What was that? Was it a frog? A toad? Can you tell the difference?

## Are Frogs and Toads the Same?

Frogs and toads are **amphibians**.[2] They both live on land and in the water. These slimy creatures might look the same to you and me. Maybe some have more **warts**,[3] some look more grumpy, and some are more colorful. They both croak, jump, and find bugs tasty.

*A fire-bellied toad.*
**Credit:** *Marek Szczepanek, Wikimedia*

So, are they actually different, or are these names just there to confuse us?

The reason you cannot decide whether you are staring at a frog or a toad is that they belong to the same family. These close cousins look extraordinarily similar. They both lay eggs in the water, and the eggs of both hatch into tadpoles. But surely there must be some differences because they have different names! Let's take a closer look.

## Skin

Take out your magnifying glass. Whether you like it or not, we are going to get awfully close to this jumping **figure**.[4] First, look at the skin. Does it look wet or dry? Is it smooth or lumpy? If its skin looks wet and smooth, it is a frog. Toad skin looks dry and warty.

---

1 **murky** – cloudy; muddy
2 **amphibians** – animals that need water or moist areas to live
3 **warts** – lumps or hard growths on the skin
4 **figure** – body shape

## Habitat

This leads us to our second clue. **Survey**[5] your surroundings. Do you spot a pond or river? Frogs stay close to water because they need to keep their skin wet. Toad skin can last longer out of water. So, if you are not near any water, you are probably staring into the face of a toad.

*Notice the toad's bumpy skin.*

## Legs

Lean in to look at their legs if you are brave enough to get closer. Frogs have long legs. These powerful legs allow them to leap far in a single hop and to swim quickly. Toad legs are shorter, making them look round and a lot less **elegant**[6] and be less **streamlined**.[7] There are no graceful leaps from our toad; rather, small little hops or even a lazy crawl.

*Frogs use their long, powerful legs to leap.*
**Credit:** Brian Gratwicke, Wikimedia

## Color

We cannot discuss frogs and toads without discussing their color. You can probably picture a bright and colorful frog, but you certainly cannot imagine a colorful toad. Frogs can have much brighter skin colors than toads. Poisonous dart frogs are particularly bright. Their skin can be a **vivid**[8] yellow, red, or even blue.

*A colorful poison dart frog.*
**Credit:** V2, Wikimedia

---

5 **survey** – look closely; examine
6 **elegant** – graceful; sophisticated
7 **streamlined** – shaped to allow easy movement through water
8 **vivid** – bright

Toads are generally dark green or brown. Don't worry if you still cannot tell the difference between toads and frogs. Sometimes scientists can't either! Here is one example. The Brazilian gold frog is also called the Izecksohn's toad. Hmm.

## Fun Frog Facts and Toad Tidbits

Frogs and toads may be small, but they are extraordinary.

*A flying frog. Look at its large, webbed feet that allow the frog to glide.*
**Credit:** *Rushenb, Wikimedia*

Humans need to breathe. We breathe with our lungs. Frogs and toads also need to breathe. However, they breathe through their lungs *and* their skin! In addition to their interesting breathing **technique**,[9] they have some odd eating habits. These amphibians use their eyes to help swallow their food. That sounds too silly to be true, but it is. Frogs and toads push their eyeballs down onto the top of their mouths to force their food down. It looks like they blink every time they swallow. And that is not all. They enjoy tasty snacks of flies, creepy crawlers, and their own skin. Eating skin sounds horrible, but in reality, this is a clever **tactic**.[10] Frogs and toads **shed**[11] their skin. If they left their skin lying around, **predators**[12] would spot it and know they were there. So, they eat their skin to destroy any **evidence**[13] of them hopping around.

We cannot talk about frogs without mentioning two frogs that seem to do the impossible. We have flying frogs! Yes—you read that correctly. Fearless frogs leap from a tree and spread out their enormous, webbed feet to glide down. The webbing acts as a parachute.

Another incredible frog is the wood frog. This frog does something unbelievable to survive the freezing winter. It freezes! It freezes to **hibernate**[14] and thaws when the weather warms.

9 **technique** – method; way of doing something
10 **tactic** – plan; strategy
11 **shed** – discard
12 **predators** – animals that kill and eat other animals
13 **evidence** – sign; indication
14 **hibernate** – "sleep" or be inactive for a long period of time

 # Questions

1. Circle the vocabulary word that best fits the sentence.

   *The police couldn't find any (**elegant/evidence**) of a crime being committed.*

2. Place a check mark next to each statement that correctly describes frogs.

   ___ They need to keep their skin wet.

   ___ They move in small hops or lazy crawls.

   ___ Their skin is generally dark green or brown.

   ___ Their skin looks wet and smooth.

3. What do frogs and toads do to fool predators?

   A. They breathe through their lungs and skin.

   B. They push their food down with their eyeballs.

   C. They hibernate during the winter.

   D. They eat the skin that they shed.

4. Which of the following sentences from the section titled *"Color"* best supports the idea that it can be difficult to tell the difference between frogs and toads?

   A. You can probably picture a bright and colorful frog, but you certainly cannot imagine a colorful toad.

   B. Don't worry if you still cannot tell the difference between toads and frogs.

   C. Poisonous dart frogs are particularly bright.

5. What do wood frogs do that is so unbelievable?

   _____

   _____

   _____

# Seeing-Eye Dogs: The "Eyes" of Their Partners

Seeing-eye dogs help blind people travel independently. This man is blind, and he rides the train with the help of a seeing-eye dog.
**Credit:** *John Robert McPherson, Wikimedia*

Chloe has an important job to do. She has to keep people alive and protect them. She works full-time. Chloe needs to be alert and **attentive**.[1] She looks for danger in the street. When Chloe does a good job, she is paid with hugs and food. Can you guess what Chloe's job is? Here is a hint: Chloe is a dog.

## A Seeing-Eye Dog

Imagine walking down the street with your eyes closed. You cannot see if there are **obstacles**.[2] You cannot see the cars in the street. Taking a simple walk, going to the store or to school, getting on an bus—these are all difficult for someone who cannot see.

Chloe works as a seeing-eye dog, or **guide**[3] dog. Chloe has to watch out for obstacles, not just those that **affect**[4] her. She is the "eyes" of her partner. Chloe must pay careful attention. Her partner holds on tightly to Chloe's **harness**[5] and feels Chloe pull right, left, forward, and back. They feel safer with Chloe in charge.

---

1 **attentive** – alert and watchful
2 **obstacles** – things that block the way
3 **guide** – show the way
4 **affect** – make a difference
5 **harness** – straps for fastening people or animals in place

### Learning to Be a Guide Dog

Chloe started life as a tiny puppy. For three weeks, her mother fed her and took care of her. During that time, people came to visit her, pet her, and give her many toys. They were trying to get her used to being around humans. A guide dog must be comfortable in a crowd of people.

*This man is blind. He holds onto his guide dog's harness as she leads him around the mall.*
**Credit:** *Antonio Cruz Abr/Agencia Brasil, Wikimedia*

By two months old, Chloe could walk, run, and play on her own. It was time for her to leave her mother and be adopted by a human family. This family loved and cared for her. They took her to the vet for checkups. They gave her lots of healthy food, exercise, and toys. Each day, Chloe took an **obedience**[6] class. She learned to listen to commands. She learned to stop, sit, and shake hands. When Chloe did a good job, her family would pet her and give her treats. Chloe wanted to please them and get more treats and attention. She learned quickly.

When Chloe was 16 weeks old, it was time to start guide dog school. Chloe's adoptive family missed her, but they knew she would learn and be happy. At school, Chloe's trainers taught her how to walk around the neighborhood. As they walked, they showed Chloe how to stop for obstacles, look around for low-hanging branches, and cross the street. As Chloe learned, her trainers gave her more responsibility. Over time, they let Chloe take over on walks. She was leading them. Chloe learned to follow directions. She was even taught that sometimes she had to avoid listening to directions. For example, suppose her blind owner would tell her, "Go." He might want her to walk into a street, but Chloe would have learned not to listen. She learned to disobey orders and let her partner know when there was danger.

Finally, Chloe was ready. Just before graduation, Chloe was tested. Her trainer put on a blindfold. Now her trainer couldn't see at all. It was all up to Chloe. Another trainer followed the two around as Chloe led the blindfolded trainer. She passed the test with flying colors! Now she was a guide dog.

6 **obedience** – following rules and commands

## A New Partner

It was time for Chloe to get a partner. The guide dog **agency**[7] called Richard. Richard's name was on a list of blind people waiting for guide dogs. They told him, "We have a dog for you!" When Richard met Chloe, it was immediate love between them. Richard loved petting Chloe's soft fur, and Chloe enjoyed how he scratched her neck.

*A blind boy meets his guide dog for the first time.*

The agency told Richard he needed to stay at school with Chloe for three weeks to learn to work with her. The trainers also came to Richard's neighborhood. They showed Chloe around. They showed her some of the obstacles outside Richard's home. Finally, after three weeks, Chloe officially became Richard's guide dog. They were a team.

### Service Animals

*Service animals are those that guide and help people with disabilities. There are dogs who help people in wheelchairs or who have difficulty moving. There are dogs to guide people with autism. Some dogs support people with epilepsy, a disease that causes seizures. They keep their partners safe. Some of these dogs can even be taught to call 9-1-1 if necessary. Dogs can help people with hearing loss by showing them if the phone is ringing or if someone is speaking to them.*

*Although service animals are usually dogs, other animals can act as service animals as well. Monkeys, parrots, miniature horses, potbelly pigs, ferrets, and even boa constrictors have been service animals.*

*Not all service animals are dogs. A miniature horse guides this man around the airport.*
**Credit:** *DanDee Shots, Wikimedia*

7 **agency** – an organization that provides a service

 **Questions**

1. Circle the vocabulary word that best fits the sentence.

   *To get good marks, you should be (obedience/attentive) in class.*

2. Mark each statement as T (true) or F (false).

   ___ Seeing eye dogs must only be on the lookout for obstacles that affect them.

   ___ Seeing eye dogs are trained to always obey their partner no matter what they say.

   ___ Seeing eye dogs and their partners train together for three weeks before they go home.

   ___ Seeing eye dogs must be able to cross a street blindfolded.

3. Number the following events in the order in which they took place.

   ___ Chloe started going to guide dog school.

   ___ Chloe trained with Richard for three weeks.

   ___ Chloe stayed with an adoptive family.

   ___ Chloe was tested before she graduated guide dog school.

4. Circle the choice that has the same meaning as the following sentence from the lesson: *Chloe passed the test with flying colors!*

   A. Chloe's trainers waved a brightly-colored flag when she passed the test.

   B. Chloe was given a colorful collar to wear when she passed her test.

   C. Chloe passed her test very successfully.

5. What do you think you should or should not do if you saw a guide dog and its partner walking down the street together?

   _____

   _____

   _____

## Cloudy Skies

Clouds are interesting **phenomena**.[1] Sometimes, if you're outside on a sunny day, you can see fluffy white clouds floating up above in the friendly blue skies. But on other days, you might shiver under the gray, angry clouds that warn you of a coming storm. Are both kinds of clouds made of the same things?

*What do these clouds tell you?*
*Credit: Alan LIght, Wikimedia*

### What Are Clouds?

Do you know what happens if you hang up a wet towel on a sunny day? All the water seems to disappear. Where does it go? The answer to that is that the liquid water in the towel changes into a gas. It turns into water vapor. Water vapor is water as a gas. The water vapor floats in the air, and you don't see it. Liquid water also turns to vapor when lakes and streams heat up from the sun's energy. Part of the water turns to vapor. There is always water vapor in the air.

The water vapor in the air keeps rising up and cooling off. When the air cools off, the water changes from a gas (vapor) into liquid droplets. These droplets are tiny, and they stay in the air, for now. Many water droplets join together to **form**[2] clouds. All clouds are made of water droplets in the air. Clouds can be all different sizes, sometimes even weighing more than an airplane! They are hundreds or thousands of feet above ground. Other times, clouds hang close to the ground, and that is called fog.

1 **phenomena** – marvels
2 **form** – develop; grow; take shape

When the clouds are heavy and full of lots of water vapor, less light passes through them and they appear darker, usually gray. You might be wondering how something so heavy can stay up, floating thousands of feet in the air. The warm air beneath it is what helps. Because the warm air from down below keeps rising, pushing upward, it keeps the clouds up in the air. It is as though the warm air is holding the clouds up.

*Clouds seem to be different shapes every day.*
**Credit:** Novoklimov, Wikipedia

When clouds are very full of water, the water droplets get too heavy for the cloud to hold, and it starts to rain, snow, or hail. This is called precipitation.

## Types of Clouds

There are many different types of clouds, and each one shows different things. Scientists study the clouds to figure out the coming weather based on how the clouds look.

*When clouds hang very low, that is called fog.*
**Credit:** Htm, Wikipedia

Some clouds are high up in the air, others hang low, and some are in between. There are even some clouds that have a long, **vertical**[3] shape. Vertical clouds are long clouds that stretch from high to low. Some clouds are very fluffy, while others are thin and **wispy**.[4] Sometimes clouds look like cotton balls and other times they look like tiny dots. There are big, fat ones and small, flat ones. You probably have also seen large clouds that seem to cover the entire sky.

Scientists divided all the clouds into groups to make it simpler. They have special names for each type of cloud, depending on how high it is and what shape it is. Clouds can be big and high or big and low. Sometimes they are flat and dark or flat and thin.

---

3 **vertical** – up and down; upright
4 **wispy** – light and delicate; fine and feathery

High, flat clouds show that it will probably rain the next day. The big, dark ones show that rain is coming very soon. The sweet, fluffy clouds usually mean the nice weather will last all day. The vertical clouds can warn of a big storm coming. Thick, low clouds can mean rain or snow.

## Water Cycle

A cycle is something that **repeats**[5] itself over and over. The way clouds are formed and then turn into rain is called the water cycle. Water stays on the ground until it turns into water vapor. The water vapor forms clouds, but sooner or later the clouds produce rain. The rainwater collects in ponds, rivers, and oceans until some of it turns into vapor.

There always seem to be clouds around. Now that you know so much about them, maybe you can try **predicting**[6] the weather!

*Vertical clouds go up and down.*
*Credit: Jessie Eastland, Wikimedia*

*When clouds are low and thick, it usually means that rain or snow is coming.*
*Credit: Helloserenityhere, Wikipedia*

---

5 **repeats** – happens over and over
6 **predicting** – foreseeing; foretelling; telling in advance

# Questions

1. Choose the vocabulary word that best fits the sentence.

   *He **(repeats/forms)** the same story every time he comes to visit us.*

2. Mark each statement as T (true) or F (false).

   ____ High, flat clouds show that it will probably rain the next day.

   ____ Sweet, fluffy clouds usually mean there is a big storm coming.

   ____ Big, dark clouds show that rain is coming the next day.

   ____ Thick, low clouds can mean rain or snow is coming.

3. Number the following events in the order in which they take place.

   ____ Clouds drop rain.

   ____ Water vapor forms clouds.

   ____ The rainwater collects in ponds, rivers, and oceans.

   ____ Liquid water turns into water vapor.

4. Which of the following statements best summarizes the section titled "Water Cycle"?

   A. The way clouds are formed and produce rain is called the water cycle.

   B. The water cycle means that it rains in the summer and snows in the winter.

   C. When clouds are very full of water, the water droplets get too heavy for the cloud to hold, and this is the water cycle.

5. You wake up in the morning and see big, dark clouds hanging in the sky. Do you think this morning is a good time to meet your friends in the park? Why or why not?

   _____

   _____

   _____

20   Lesson 3: Cloudy Skies

# High-Flying

Do you ever stretch out your arms and imagine you can fly? For most of history, people could only dream of flying. Today, we do not need to dream anymore! We did not learn how to grow wings. Instead, we built airplanes.

*An eagle in flight*

## Dreams of Flight

People cannot fly, but that did not stop us from trying! Inventors cleverly tried to copy birds. They looked at bird wings and tried to create something **similar**[1] that would allow them to fly. Although it may seem **bizarre**,[2] people even tried using bird feathers to create wings they could wear. Unsurprisingly, this did not work, and these efforts did not always end well. After all, birds and people are very different. So, inventors moved on. They built **gliders**[3] and airplanes. Let's discover the similarities and differences between the flight of airplanes and birds.

## Wing Shape

One obvious similarity between birds and airplanes is their wings. Look closely at different types of birds. Interestingly, their wings are not all the same. Bird wings can be either big or small, narrow or wide. A bird's wing shape is not **random**.[4]

---

1 **similar** – alike; close to
2 **bizarre** – very strange; odd
3 **gliders** – small, light aircraft that fly without engines
4 **random** – without thoughtful design

The wings are suited to the bird's needs. Birds that fly long distances over the sea have long, narrow wings to help them **soar**.[5] Hummingbirds have tiny wings that move very, very quickly and allow them to **hover**.[6]

An airplane's wing shape depends on the airplane's use. The wings of passenger planes are different than the wings of army jet airplanes. Gliders will have long **rectangular**[6] wings. Speeding jets have short, narrow wings.

## Feathery Wings and Flaps

Feathers do more than look pretty and keep a bird warm. They help the bird to fly. Birds flap their wings up and down. Each downward flap, called a downstroke, pushes the bird higher. After each downstroke, the bird lifts its wings. The wings' design makes it easier for the bird to do that. The bird can spread its feathers out like fingers, and air passes through the gaps. The wings are pushing against less air. Try this at a swimming pool. Move your hand through the water with your fingers closed. How does it feel? Then, open your fingers and try again. It will be much easier to move your hand through the water.

*A seagull's wings help it soar over the sea.*

*Hummingbirds can hover because their short wings move very quickly.*

*Notice the wings of this passenger airplane.*
**Credit:** Laurent ERRERA, Wikimedia

---

5 **soar** – fly without flapping wings
6 **hover** – hang in mid-air
7 **rectangular** – having four sides

**Lesson 4:** High-Flying

Birds have another great way to make flying easier. Air passes over a bird's wings as it flies. This air movement helps the bird fly. Birds **tilt**[8] their wings to change how air moves over them. Tilting the wings will change how much lift the bird has. Lift is the force that pushes the bird upward.

Airplane wings do not have feathers, but they do have flaps. Airplane flaps can move to change how the air moves over the wings, just like birds' wings. These moving flaps create lift during takeoff. Pilots also move the flaps to slow the plane during landing.

*The Concorde's wing shape allowed it to be the fastest passenger airplane.*

## Take off!

Both airplanes and birds need power to take off. We do not blink twice when a bird takes off. It is so natural and yet so amazing. Birds use their legs to push off the ground and take off. Some birds jump from high spots to take off. Once the birds are in the air, powerful flapping keeps them flying.

*Airplane flaps during landing*
**Credit:** *Trick on, Wikimedia*

Engines give an airplane its power. Air rushes past the wings as the airplane drives faster and faster. Soon, the airplane is driving fast enough for the air to lift it up into the sky.

## Streamlined!

There is a reason an airplane is not shaped like a hippopotamus. Airplanes and birds are both **streamlined**.[9] They are specially designed to move easily through the air.

---

8 **tilt** – lean; slant
9 **streamlined** – designed to move through air or water easily

## Weight

Another big difference between birds and airplanes is their weight. Airplanes are heavy, while birds are not. Bird bones are **hollow**[10] and extremely light. Light bones make it easier to fly. Airplanes are built with metal. They also carry passengers or heavy cargo. Each piece of luggage—stuffed with food, clothing, and entertainment—adds to the airplane's weight. Airplanes are incredibly heavy, but airplane **designers**[11] try to make them as light as possible.

---

10 **hollow** – empty
11 **designer** – creators; inventors

# Questions

1. **Circle the vocabulary word that best fits the sentence.**

   *People say that my brother and I look very **(bizarre/similar)** to each other.*

2. **Mark each statement as T (true) or F (false).**

   ___ All airplanes have the same shaped wings.

   ___ Birds tilt their wings to change how the air moves over their wings.

   ___ An airplane's engine is what gives it power.

   ___ Once birds are in the air, they move their feet to keep flying.

3. **What is the function of birds' feathers?**

   A. To look pretty

   B. To keep the birds warm

   C. To help the birds fly

   D. All of the above

4. **What was the author's purpose in including the section titled *"Streamlined"*?**

   A. To explain why bird bones are hollow

   B. To explain why birds and airplanes are shaped the way they are

   C. To explain how birds and airplanes get their power

5. **List a few similarities between the flight of birds and airplanes.**

   _____

   _____

   _____

   _____

# Sea Otters: Just Floating Around

*A sea otter*
**Credit:** Marshal Hedin, Wikimedia

Cute, fun-loving, and with the most amazing hair you have ever seen. Nope, not your friends. Sea otters! Like your buddies, these guys are both smart and friendly. Let's learn some fun facts about sea otters.

## What Do Sea Otters Look Like?

Sea otters belong to the weasel family. (Badgers, otters, ferrets, and wolverines are also in this extended family.) They spend most of their time at sea, thereby earning their name. These small animals have a few tricks to make a water-based life easier. Their **webbed**[1] feet help them swim. Their ears and nostrils close when they dive underwater. Their thick fur keeps them warm—and even keeps them dry. Sea otters' thick, **glossy**[2] fur is quite impressive. In fact, it is the thickest fur of any animal. Every day, they carefully lick and clean it.

The fur even helps mother sea otters look after their babies. How? Well, sea otters often dive far down into the ocean to collect food for themselves and their young. But what if a mother sea otter has a new baby? Where should she leave it while she searches for their meal? No need to worry; newborn sea otters are born wearing a life jacket. Their fur is so thick that they float right on top of the water. Their thick fur does not allow them to sink. Problem solved for mommy sea otters! Mothers can safely dive down and then find their baby still bobbing along on the waves when they **resurface**[3].

---

1 **webbed** – connected with a skin-like tissue
2 **glossy** – shiny
3 **resurface** – come back up to the water's surface

## Sea Otters' Diet

Sea otters are hungry. They need to eat one-quarter of their body weight each day. Luckily, they are comfortable in the sea and can swim quickly in the water. This is their **habitat**.[4] They dive down to collect their food from the ocean floor. Sea otters have enough time to find their food with each dive, because they can hold their breath for around five minutes. Sea otters collect **shellfish**[5] like mussels, clams, and sea urchins. They even collect octopuses.

*Sea otters floating together in a group called a raft*

Today, Shelley the sea otter dives to the sea floor and spots a pile of shellfish. Yum! (If you're an otter, anyway.) She picks up a mussel with her paw. Now, where should she put it? Shelley does not want to go up to the water's surface after catching only one mussel. But she is well prepared with her own personal "handbag." Shelley stores the mussel under a flap of skin. Then she continues to pick up the next one, and the next. When her **pouch**[6] is almost full, she also collects a small rock. It may be useful; you never know.

*A mother sea otter carrying her pup while floating on her back*
**Credit:** "Mike" Michael L. Baird, Wikimedia

## Sea Otters' Table Manners and Afternoon Naps

Shelley reaches the surface and is ready for lunch. She takes a mussel out of her pouch. Wait, how will she open the shell to **access**[7] the food hidden inside? Look at her paw! She is holding the rock she collected. Shelley lies on her back, balances the rock against her body, and uses it to crack open the mussel. Sea otters are one of only a few animals that use tools.

> 4 **habitat** – an animal's natural home
> 5 **shellfish** – fish whose bodies are covered in a shell
> 6 **pouch** – a pocket-like piece of skin that an animal uses for storage
> 7 **access** – reach

Sea otters also use seaweed as a tool. How? Sea otters like to rest in large groups, called "rafts." Resting in the ocean can be difficult. Sea otters do not want to float away from the group while they sleep. So, they have a clever solution. Sea otters tangle themselves in seaweed to **anchor**[8] themselves to the rest of the "raft." They can now rest peacefully.

Sea otters are incredible animals. They are **resourceful**,[9] **sociable**,[10] and look like your cuddliest teddy bear. But, if you see a sea otter, stay back! They also have a nasty bite. They're wild creatures, after all.

*A sea otter using a rock to open a shell*
**Credit:** Brocken Inaglory, Wikimedia

*A sea otter anchored with seaweed*
**Credit:** Mike Baird, Wikimedia

8 **anchor** – tie into a position
9 **resourceful** – able to think of ways to solve problems
10 **sociable** – friendly

# Questions

1. Circle the vocabulary word that best fits the sentence.

   *I became friendly with my new roommates quickly because they are very **(sociable/glossy)**.*

2. Place a check mark next to the statements that correctly describe sea otters.

   ___ They do not need much food because they don't get very hungry.

   ___ Their babies swim to shore while the mother is searching for food.

   ___ They can hold their breath for about five minutes underwater.

   ___ They use rocks and seaweed as tools.

3. What is the main reason you might not want to have a sea otter as a pet?

   A. They eat too much.

   B. Seaweed is too messy to have in your house.

   C. They can have a nasty bite.

   D. Their fur would shed all over the carpet.

4. What was the author's purpose in including the information in the third paragraph of the section titled *"What Do Sea Otters Look Like?"*

   A. To explain how mother otters can leave their babies while they hunt for food.

   B. To explain how sea otters can easily stay under water for up to five minutes.

   C. To explain how mother otters care for their thick, glossy coats.

5. How do sea otters keep from floating away while they're resting?

   _____

   _____

   _____

Lesson 5: Sea Otters: Just Floating Around

# Alan Shepard: America's Best Pilot

Alan Shepard became the first American to travel to outer space.

Do you have goals for your future? Alan Shepard was a boy who grew up in America in the 1930s. His goal was to be the best pilot. Alan Shepard worked hard and practiced as much as he could. Finally, he was chosen to become the first American astronaut in space. Let's read about his journey from East Derry, New Hampshire, to outer space.

## Alan Shepard's Childhood

Even as a small boy, Alan Shepard felt he was the best. He was smarter than most boys in his hometown of East Derry, New Hampshire. He even skipped two grades. Alan wasn't just smart; he was also **competitive**[1] and liked to win. Alan didn't like being told what to do. Despite his brains, he didn't always get good grades. After all, Alan had more interesting things to do than study, like building model airplanes or hanging out at the airfield.

After he finished high school, Shepard joined the **navy.**[2] There he learned to sail and won swimming and boating races. Shepard fought fearlessly in World War II. After the war ended, Shepard immediately signed up to be a pilot. He quickly became the top pilot in his class. Shepard felt he was one of the best pilots in America. Soon, he would have a chance to prove that he was.

1 **competitive** – wanting to be more successful or better
2 **navy** – the branch of the military that fights at sea

## Becoming an Astronaut

The chance came when the United States and Russia started competing. They wanted to see which country could explore outer space first. Both countries raced to build rockets and spaceships. NASA (National Aeronautics and Space Administration) is the organization that led America's space exploration program. NASA needed brave men willing to risk going to outer space. Nobody had ever gone into outer space before. It could be dangerous, even deadly. NASA needed tough, strong, and skilled men.

*These seven men were chosen by NASA for the first manned space program. Shepard is standing second from the right.*

NASA started with a list of 110 pilots. They chose Shepard and 31 others. NASA put them through difficult tests. These tests showed who was stronger, smarter, and braver. Shepard **focused**[3] on the tests. He just had to win. Would he succeed?

*Shepard wore this space suit during his 1961 flight.*

Finally, NASA announced the winners. They chose Shepard and six other men to become America's first astronauts. The seven astronauts would take turns traveling into outer space.

## The First Man in Space

But which of them would go first? NASA's first spacecraft could fit only one man at a time. Who would it be? NASA's leaders called all the men into a room. They had made their decision. Everyone waited, holding their breath. Then, NASA announced Shepard's name. He would be first. He would soar beyond Earth and make history. But, before launching Shepard into space, NASA wanted to test the spaceship. They put Ham the chimpanzee inside and sent him into the sky. Shepard couldn't believe he had to compete with an ape to be the first in space!

3 **focused** – paid attention

On April 12, 1961, a few weeks before Shepard's flight, America got terrible news. Yuri Gagarin, a Soviet astronaut, had successfully **orbited**[4] the Earth. Shepard had been excited to be first, to be the winner. He was supposed to be the first man in space. Now it seemed that the Soviet Union had won!

## A Successful Mission

But Shepard still achieved part of his dream. On May 5, he stepped into NASA's tiny capsule. The **capsule**[5] was so small he could only move his hand and nothing else. At any moment, NASA would **ignite**[6] the rocket, and his capsule would fly 113 miles into the sky.

*Shepard sat in this small capsule at the top of a large rocket. When the rocket was lit, it flew into the air, propelling the capsule into space.*
**Credit:** *HrAtsuo, Wikimedia*

*Cameras took pictures of Shepard inside the capsule during the flight. They also took pictures of what he saw outside the window.*

NASA started the countdown. Then, they stopped. A **mechanical**[7] issue had been found. Workers quickly rushed to the rocket to fix it. Shepard sat in the capsule, waiting. Then there was a weather **delay**.[8] Shepard waited. He felt terribly **cramped**.[9] Finally, at 9:34 a.m., after four hours of waiting, the rocket shot into the air in a burst of smoke. As he flew toward space, Shepard spoke about what he saw and felt. Radio stations **broadcast**[10] his voice across the country.

---

4 **orbited** – circled around
5 **capsule** – small spacecraft, often part of a larger one
6 **ignite** – set on fire
7 **mechanical** – the working parts of a machine
8 **delay** – set back; hold back
9 **cramped** – tight; crowded; confined
10 **broadcast** – transmission on radio or television

High up in the sky, the capsule separated from the rocket as planned. Shepard felt himself falling towards Earth fast. He waited and held his breath. Then parachutes opened, and the capsule floated to safety, landing in the Atlantic Ocean near the Bahamas. Shepard felt proud and **relieved**.[11] He had become the first American in space.

*Ten years after his first space flight, Shepard got to return to outer space aboard the Apollo 14 mission. This time he went to the moon.*

### Meniere's and the Moon

*Alan Shepard loved flying. He loved being an astronaut. When he returned from his first space flight, he couldn't wait to go again. Shepard was scheduled to fly on another NASA mission. Then, one day he woke up with his ear ringing. He felt dizzy and sick. Shepard's condition became worse and worse. Finally, a doctor told him he had Meniere's disease.*

*Meniere's disease isn't dangerous. But Shepard couldn't fly to outer space with the condition. He felt disappointed that he could no longer do what he loved. In 1969, Shepard contacted a doctor who said that a new, experimental operation might help him. The doctor didn't know if the surgery would work. Did Shepard want to try?*

*He did. Shepard had the experimental surgery. Luckily, it was a success, and the ringing and dizziness stopped. NASA permitted him to fly again. NASA scheduled Shepard for a mission taking place in 1971. The mission, Apollo 14, was headed for the moon.*

*Shepard was thrilled to return to outer space. But this time, he took along some entertainment. The spaceship traveled to the moon, and Shepard stepped onto the moon's surface. With millions of Americans watching, Alan Shepard pulled out a golf bag. Then, he played the first game of golf on the moon.*

11 **relieved** – no longer worried

# Questions

1. **Circle the vocabulary word that best fits the sentence.**

   *The driver kept his attention **(broadcast/focused)** on the road.*

2. **Number the following events in the order in which they took place.**

   ___ Alan Shepard played golf on the moon.

   ___ Alan Shepard signed up to become a pilot.

   ___ Alan Shepard joined the navy.

   ___ Alan Shepard was chosen as the first astronaut to travel into outer space.

3. **Why did the seven astronauts have to take turns traveling into outer space?**

   A. NASA couldn't afford to pay more than one person at a time.

   B. The capsule could hold only one person at a time.

   C. More than one person in the capsule would make it too heavy.

   D. Ham the chimpanzee was afraid to have more than one person with him.

4. **Which of the following statements best summarizes the lesson?**

   A. Alan Shepard was upset that a Soviet astronaut traveled into space before he did.

   B. Alan Shepard worked hard to achieve his dream of becoming the best pilot.

   C. Alan Shepard built model airplanes because he wanted to be the best pilot.

5. **Why was Yuri Gagarin's orbit terrible news for the United States?**

   _____

   _____

   _____

# Mountain Climbing: Race to the Top

A mountain climber
**Credit:** Mountaineer, Wikimedia

Perhaps you sometimes go for walks in your neighborhood or enjoy strolling on the beach. But have you ever climbed a mountain? Not a small slope in the park, but a towering mountain that reaches for the sky! Climbing mountains is hard work! It is fun and adventurous. It can also be dangerous. Let's discover how to climb these tall mountains and race to the top!

## What Is Mountain Climbing?

Mountain climbing is a sport. This sport is simple—pick a tall mountain and climb to the top. This sport is for people who love a challenge, the outdoors, and **extreme**[1] exercise. People who climb mountains are called mountaineers. Mountain climbing is both exciting and dangerous. Mountaineers may climb steep cliffs, **clamber**[2] over giant rocks, and battle ice and deep snow. Mount Everest is the tallest mountain on Earth. It takes about two months to climb Mount Everest! This is not a hike – it is mountain climbing.

## Let's Go Mountain Climbing!

David jumped out of bed. He had barely slept because he was so excited. Today he would finally climb Mont Blanc. He dressed in his special clothes for mountain climbing, slurped down a coffee, and gobbled up a filling breakfast.

---

1 **extreme** – most difficult
2 **clamber** – scramble; climb

37

David looked through his **rucksack**[3] for the hundredth time. Everything was there! After months of training, he was ready for the challenge. David joined the climbing group. They were off! A guide led the way. At first, Mont Blanc was not too difficult to climb. They reached a hut that climbers use to rest. David enjoyed the break. He went to bed early, ready for the big day ahead.

*Mountain climbers on a steep, snowy mountain.* **Credit:** *Chripell, Wikimedia*

The next morning, they started walking at 4:30 a.m. It was pitch-black outside. Only their **headlamps**[4] allowed David to see the rocky mountainside. David was grateful he was following an **experienced**[5] guide as he clambered up the awkward rocks. David concentrated on each step. A few hours later, his leg muscles were in great pain. Thankfully, there was another hut around the next bend. The group rested for a few minutes before the hardest climb began.

David attached crampons to his mountain boots. Crampons are **spikes**.[6] They are attached under boots to grip the snow and ice. This stops climbers from slipping. David tightened his helmet. His helmet would

*Mountaineers tie themselves together with a rope.* **Credit:** *Noclador, Wikimedia*

protect him from falling rocks or snow. The climbers stood in a line with the guide at the front. The guide helped them tie a rope to connect them all together.

---

3 **rucksack** – backpack
4 **headlamps** – lights attached to the front of a helmet or head
5 **experienced** – skilled
6 **spikes** – sharp nails

David felt safer with the rope on. If he slipped, the rope would hopefully stop him from falling down the steep mountain. And Mont Blanc definitely was steep—it was steeper than you can imagine and covered in a snowy blanket. Cracks in the ice were so deep they could not see the bottom. Then, it became even scarier. David felt like a tightrope walker as he carefully walked along the snowy ridge. A ridge is a narrow part of the mountain with steep drops on either side. David could not enjoy the stunning views. He was too focused on not falling!

Finally, the group reached the summit, the top of the mountain. The scenery was **dreamy**.[7] David had never seen anything like it. Soon the cold was too hard to ignore, and they started the climb down.

*Crampons help mountain climbers walk on ice and snow.* **Credit:** *Clayoquot, Wikimedia*

*Crampons help mountain climbers walk on ice and snow.* **Credit:** *Clayoquot, Wikimedia*

## Equipment

Every day before school, you pack notebooks, pens, and pencils. You peek outside and check if you need gloves or an umbrella. Mountaineers also make sure they have the correct equipment. Correct equipment keeps them safe. David took crampons, a headlamp, and a rope harness. He had **suitable**[8] boots and clothes for the cold, snowy weather. He carried a map to find the way, even though he had a guide. David's helmet protected his head. He also packed drinks and food for energy. Mountaineers need lots of equipment. But remember—whatever you pack, you have to carry!

---

7 **dreamy** – magical, unreal
8 **suitable** – appropriate; fitting

# Questions

1. **Circle the vocabulary word that best fits the sentence.**

   I didn't go to the wedding because I didn't have anything **(extreme/suitable)** to wear.

2. **Number the following events in the order in which they took place.**

   ___ The guide helped the group tie themselves together with a rope.

   ___ The group began to climb Mont Blanc.

   ___ The group reached the summit.

   ___ The group rested in a hut overnight.

3. **Place a check next to each statement that correctly describes mountain climbing.**

   ___ It is an easy sport that anyone can do.

   ___ Mountain climbers must be prepared with the correct equipment.

   ___ Mountain climbers often tie themselves together with ropes to prevent them from falling.

   ___ Climbers start at the summit and climb up from there.

4. **Circle the choice that has the same meaning as the following sentence:** *A few hours later, his leg muscles were screaming in pain.*

   A. After a few hours, his legs refused to move.

   B. After a few hours, he scratched his legs with his crampons.

   C. After a few hours, he needed to switch to a new pair of boots.

   D. After a few hours, his legs were terribly sore and painful.

5. **What is the meaning of the following sentence?** *David looked through his rucksack for the hundredth time.*

   _____

   _____

# Solids, Liquids, and Gases

Anything that takes up space is called **matter**.¹ A house is matter, a balloon is matter, and even a person is matter. Even the water you drink and the air you breathe are matter, as well.

## States of Matter

Matter can be found in different conditions. This is called its **state**.² The state can be solid, liquid, or gas. Objects that you can hold are solid, like toys, clothing, paper, and pens. **Liquids**³ can be poured, like oil, water, and milk. Gases fill the space between other objects, and they are often invisible, like air, helium, and carbon dioxide. Your bed is solid, your juice is liquid, and your breath is gas.

*This picture shows solid water, which is usually called ice.* **Credit:** *Sharon Mollerus, Wikimedia*

Matter can change which state it is in, depending on how hot or cold it is. Water, for example, is a liquid at room temperature. But when you freeze it, it becomes solid ice. And if you have ever watched a pot boil, you have probably seen **steam**⁴ rising out of it. That is the very hot water turning into its gas state. These are water's three states.

Other types of matter can also change their state, just like water does. It always depends on how hot or cold they are. For example, gold is usually solid but can be melted into liquid when heat is applied. (It can even turn into gas, but it would have to be really, *really* hot for that to happen.)

> 1 **matter** – anything that takes up space
> 2 **state** – condition; form of being
> 3 **liquid** – something that can be poured
> 4 **steam** – smoke; mist; fog

When we think of rocks, we usually think of something solid. That is how rocks are on Earth's surface. Deep underground, it is so hot that rock melts into its liquid state. When there is a volcano, there is a break in Earth's crust. Liquid rock pours out of the volcano through the break. The liquid rock that pours out is known as lava.

## Differences Between Solids, Liquids, and Gases

There are a few differences between solids, liquids, and gases. One difference is their shape. Solids always stay the same shape. You can put some sliced vegetables into a round bowl, and each vegetable slice will remain the same shape. Liquids and gases are not like that. When you pour some milk into a tall, thin glass, the milk takes on the shape of the tall, thin glass. When you blow air into a small, round balloon, the air fills the balloon. The air takes on the shape of the balloon.

Another difference between solids, liquids, and gases is the amount of space they take up. Solids and liquids have certain sizes. If you have a tiny chocolate chip, you can put it into a huge bag, but it will still be small. If you have too much juice, you can't **cram**[5] it into a small bottle. The amount of juice won't change to fit the size of the container. But gases are different.

*Here is water as a solid (ice cubes), liquid (water), and gas (steam).*
**Credit:** *Matthew Bowden www.digitallyrefreshing.com, Wikimedia (water)*
**Credit:** *Darren Hester, Wikimedia (ice cubes)*

5 **cram** – stuff in

Lesson 8: Solids, Liquids, and Gases

Gases can spread out or squeeze in, depending on the situation. One way to understand how gases spread is through your sense of smell. If you are baking a cake, the air in the oven will smell delicious. But the smell will not stay just in the oven. The delicious-smelling air will spread all over the kitchen and into other rooms. Air also takes up all the room it is offered. If you put a drop of helium into a large container, it will not all stay in one place. It will spread out all over the container. Of course, it will not be as strong if it is spread out. A slice of bread or a drop of milk won't spread all over. They would stay the same shape and size.

In other words, matter that has a certain shape and size is solid. Matter that has any shape, but a certain size is liquid. And matter that has no specific shape or size is a gas.

And that's the end of the matter!

*Hot liquid rock, called lava, pours out of a volcano.*

*Soups always take the shape of whatever they are poured into because soup is a liquid.*

# Questions

1. Circle the vocabulary word that best fits the sentence.

    The car was driving down the highway with a thick cloud of **(steam/state)** coming out from under the hood.

2. Mark each statement as T (true) or F (false).

    ___ Matter can change which state it is in, depending on how hot or cold it is.

    ___ Liquids only fit into a glass.

    ___ Gases fill up any space they are offered.

    ___ Solids change shape depending on what they are held in.

3. You put a container of ice cubes over a flame. Number the states they will go through in the proper order.

    ___ Liquid

    ___ Gas

    ___ Solid

4. What was the author's purpose in including the sentence *"The air and the smell spread all over the kitchen and into other rooms."*?

    A. To explain how we can tell when a cake is done baking

    B. To tell us we should always close the door when we go out of a room

    C. To give an example of how gases spread to fill the space they are offered

5. Old-fashioned engines and trains were powered by steam. What two things do you think were needed to produce the steam?

    _____

    _____

    _____

Lesson 8: Solids, Liquids, and Gases

# Glassblowing: Mesmerizing and Magical

Enter your favorite houseware store and walk past the plates, silverware, and pots. Pause to admire the rows of sparkling glassware. Notice the different shapes, sizes, and colors. Today, machines make most of our glassware. We will explore a time when each glass item was carefully formed by hand. Welcome to the art of glassblowing.

*A glassblower shapes glass using a metal table.*
**Credit:** Dbritta2, Wikimedia

## First Day at the Glassblowers

Jacob stood outside the workshop and peered through the door. He nervously entered and stood waiting near the entrance. It was his first day as an **apprentice**.[1] He had the honor of learning glassblowing from an expert glassblower. At first glance, the room looked like a regular workshop. Then Jacob noticed the bent figure inspecting a breathtaking bowl. Jacob took a minute to **marvel**[2] at the beautifully crafted piece of work and then cleared his throat. The figure straightened. The man gently put the bowl down before striding over and **vigorously**[3] shaking Jacob's hand. "Welcome. I'm Oliver. Let me introduce you to glassblowing."

## Collecting and Coloring

Jacob followed Oliver to a hot furnace. Oliver picked up a long metal rod. "See here, Jacob, the rod is hollow. This **ingenious**[4] design allows the magic to happen."

> 1 **apprentice** – a trainee learning from a skilled craftsperson
> 2 **marvel** – wonder; be amazed at
> 3 **vigorously** – energetically; forcefully
> 4 **ingenious** – original; clever

Oliver opened the furnace door. Heat blasted out. Sweat trickled down Jacob's face. Oliver carefully placed the end of the rod into the furnace and rolled it. "Rolling the rod picks up the molten glass from the furnace." Oliver carried the rod to a metal table. He continually rolled the rod, not stopping for a second. His brow tightened with concentration. "Keep it rolling, Jacob, always rolling." Oliver returned to the furnace several times to collect more

*Turning glass in a furnace.*
**Credit:** *Rhododendrites, Wikimedia*

**molten**[5] glass. "Looks like the right **quantity**[6] of glass for a vase. On to adding color," he murmured. Oliver dipped the molten glass into colorful crushed glass. He placed the rod back in the furnace. The glass **shards**[7] melted, giving the molten glass a beautiful blue shade.

## Shaping and Blowing

Shaping the vase was a **mesmerizing**[8] process. Oliver rolled the glass on the metal table. He **molded**[9] the **flexible**[10] glass using the table, tweezers, molds, and even a thick pile of wet newspaper. Oliver balanced the rod on a special stand. "Some people can blow glass without the stand. I find it is a bit like trying to juggle while walking on a tightrope," he chuckled. He blew through the tube of the metal rod.

*Crushed glass for coloring the molten glass. This is one of the ways you can make a colored glass object.*

5 **molten** – melted
6 **quantity** – amount
7 **shards** – bits; pieces
8 **mesmerizing** – fascinating; spellbinding
9 **molded** – formed
10 **flexible** – bendable

Jacob held his breath as he watched the glass **transform**.[11] Each blow forced air through the tube and into the glass. A bubble of air formed. The glass started to take shape. As Oliver blew, he kept turning the rod and the glass at the end of it. Oliver placed the rod back in the furnace to reheat the glass. He removed it and shaped it and blew again. Jacob watched, **transfixed**.[12] Time stood still. Glassblowing looked like a dance of heating, rolling, blowing, and shaping. Each puff blew the glass bigger and bigger. A vase took shape before his eyes.

*Glassblowing. Notice that one man is blowing the glass while the other is shaping the glass with the tweezers.*
**Credit:** *Tulane Public Relations, Wikimedia*

## Finishing the Vase

At last, Oliver finished. He removed the vase from the rod. This was a delicate job. One mistake and the whole vase could shatter. He carefully placed it in a special oven to cool down slowly. Jacob's head whirled with all the new information.

The next day Jacob thought he was ready to have a go. Smash! His first attempt shattered. So did his second and third. His tenth effort stayed whole, although it looked like it was made by a five-year-old. By the end of the day, Jacob felt hot but satisfied. He knew he had years of practice ahead. He hoped that one day he, too, would be able to pass on this **spellbinding**[13] artistry.

*Glassblowing produces glassware in all colors, shapes, and sizes.*
**Credit:** *Davidpatchen, Wikimedia*

---

11 **transform** – change
12 **transfixed** – frozen in place from amazement
13 **spellbinding** – fascinating

# Questions

1. Circle the vocabulary word that best fits the sentence.

    The magician performed a (**mesmerizing/molten**) show at my friend's birthday party.

2. Mark each statement as T (true) or F (false).

    ___ Glassblowing is a skill that can be learned without trying very hard.

    ___ A glassblower first shapes the object and then adds the color.

    ___ Glass-blown objects are shaped from bits of melted glass.

    ___ After being shaped and removed from the rod, the object is placed in a special oven to cool down slowly.

3. Number the following events in the order in which they took place.

    ___ Oliver carefully placed the vase in a special oven to cool down slowly.

    ___ Oliver carefully placed the end of the rod into the furnace and rolled it.

    ___ Oliver removed the vase from the rod.

    ___ Oliver dipped the molten glass into colorful crushed glass.

4. Which sentence in the section titled *"Finishing the Vase"* supports the idea that removing the vase from the rod was a delicate job?

    A. One mistake and the whole vase could shatter

    B. He carefully placed it in a special oven to cool down slowly.

    C. He knew he had years of practice ahead.

5. Why do you think most of our glassware today is made by machine?

    _____

    _____

    _____

48  Lesson 9: Glassblowing: Mesmerizing and Magical

# Ships and Subs: Above and Below Water

We live in a world of land and sea. Countries seem massive, and we can drive for hours over land. Amazingly, however big the land is, the sea is even bigger! Let us explore how to cross that watery world. Let us learn to live on the waves.

## Traveling the Seas

People have sailed the seas for as long as we know. They traveled to new lands, caught fish for food, and fought on the waters. The first boats were simple. Look no further than a tree: Cut it down, hollow out the trunk,

*A large ship*
**Credit:** *Tomasz Sienicki, Wikimedia*

and you have a boat! Easy! These boats were not complicated (or comfortable). Over time, improvements made these simple boats bigger and better.

Bigger boats are called ships. Today's ships can be larger than three football fields. Ships can hold airplane runways, swimming pools, rides, and ice-skating rinks. But that is not all. Some ships can also sink into the watery **depths**.[1] Submarines are ships that can dive down underwater.

## Ship and Submarine Uses

Ships and submarines are extremely useful. For centuries, ships carried **goods**[2] from one country to another. Ships are so great at carrying heavy loads that we still use them for this job today. Massive ships transport **cargo**[3] all over the world.

> 1 **depths** – distance down under something
> 2 **goods** – things to sell
> 3 **cargo** – goods; merchandise

The **military**[4] uses ships as well. These ships carry guns and sailors. But ships can have a fun side too. Cruise ships provide a vacation on a boat. People enjoy a **luxurious**[5] vacation with delicious food, shops, gyms, go-karting, and endless hours of fun. Well, as long as you don't get seasick!

Submarines are useful, not luxurious. Navy submarines are packed with deadly weapons like torpedoes and missiles. They are very cramped, and crewmembers take turns sleeping because there are more of them than there are beds to sleep in! Military submarines can hide underwater, ready to sneak up on the enemy. Submarines journey to a place that ships cannot reach: the sea floor. Scientists use submarines to explore the bottom of the ocean. These incredible submarines carry special equipment. Bright lights, cameras, and robotic arms help scientists collect information.

## Parts of a Ship

Ships have a hull and decks. The hull is the main **body**[6] of the ship, and the deck is the ship's floor. Most ships have more than one deck.

*This cruise ship, Oasis of the Seas, offers shopping, shows, gyms, and more.*
Credit: Baldwin040, Wikimedia

*A swimming pool onboard a cruise ship*

*This ship's hull is light blue. It has a cabin on top of the deck. The deck has a fence to prevent people from falling into the sea.*
Credit: Jpbazard, Wikimedia

---

4 **military** – army
5 **luxurious** – extremely comfortable and beautiful
6 **body** – main section of something

Lesson 10: Ships and Subs: Above and Below Water

The upper deck covers the hull like a lid on a tub. People enjoy standing on the upper deck, **gazing**[7] out at the beautiful ocean views. A ship's rooms are called cabins. Cabins are either in the ship's hull or on the deck. An engine room, not surprisingly, holds the engine! The engine provides all the power the ship needs. It turns the propellors, which pushes the ship forward. Ships have a rudder to help steer so they can avoid rocks and go in the right direction. Lastly, the all-important anchor drops down when the ship needs to stay in one place.

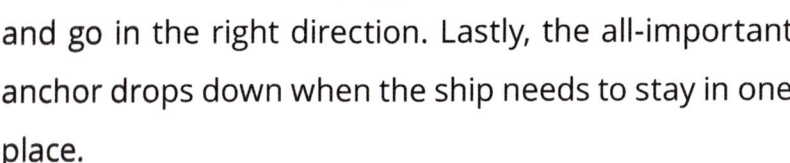

*A submarine at the water's surface. Most of it is still underwater.*

## Parts of a Submarine

Look closely at a submarine. Which parts do you recognize from a ship? The submarine's body is also called a hull, and submarines also have decks. However, submarines do not have a big upper deck. A big upper deck would be useless, as you cannot stand on top of a submarine when it is hundreds of feet underwater.

*Notice the submarine's propeller, which drives the submarine through the water.*
**Credit:** *Ido403, Wikimedia*

Submarines use engines, batteries, or **nuclear**[8] power to provide energy. Just like ships, propellors **drive**[9] the submarine forward. Submarines and ships carry water and food for their passengers. Submarines also need oxygen to make sure the passengers can breathe!

Did you ever wonder how submarines dive and come back up? Submarines use ballast tanks. A ballast tank is a compartment that fills with water when the submarine is ready to dive. All this water makes the submarine super-heavy, and it sinks. To rise back up, the ballast tank empties out all the water, and up floats the submarine.

> 7 **gazing** – looking steadily
> 8 **nuclear** – having to do with an atom
> 9 **drive** – push forward in a specific direction

#  Questions

1. Circle the vocabulary word that best fits the sentence.

   *Their big, new mansion was elegant and **(hollow/luxurious)**.*

2. Mark each statement as T (true) or F (false).

   ___ Ships can be luxurious as well as useful.

   ___ Submarines have plenty of beds for the crewmembers to sleep on.

   ___ Scientists use submarines to explore the bottom of the ocean.

   ___ The main body of a ship is called the hull.

3. Which of the following parts do ships and submarines NOT have in common?

   A. Hull

   B. Deck

   C. Ballast tank

   D. Propeller

4. What was the author's purpose in including the section titled *"Traveling the Seas"*?

   A. To describe how to build a boat

   B. To describe how boats have been improved over time

   C. To describe the differences between ships and submarines

5. List two differences between ships and submarines.

   _____

   _____

   _____

52  Lesson 10: Ships and Subs: Above and Below Water

# Clara Barton: How One Shy Girl Changed the World

*This towering sequoia tree is named in honor of Clara Barton.* **Credit:** *Marty Aligata, Wikimedia*

What do you do if you get hurt or sick? You can take medicine. You can visit a doctor or even go to a hospital. In some countries, like the United States, getting treatment isn't hard. During a war or a natural disaster, getting help can be a lot harder. Natural disasters are events that are out of human control. Some examples are earthquakes, floods, tornados, and other storms. There may be many injured people. Hospitals are overcrowded. Doctors may be extra-busy. Pharmacies may be damaged. Who takes care of people in those troubled times? There are organizations whose purpose is to provide supplies and first aid during wars and natural disasters. One of these organizations was founded, in part, by an unlikely figure. Let's read about how a shy young woman named Clara Barton changed the world.

## Childhood

Clara Barton was born in 1821. In the 1800s, women didn't usually have jobs as they do today. Most women stayed home, cared for their children, and kept their houses clean and neat. Some women worked as dressmakers or as maids. Clara Barton's parents thought she would be a homemaker as well. After all, as a child, Barton was very shy. She was afraid to speak up. Nobody imagined that she would become a world leader. Nobody thought she would change the world.

53

## Clara's First Job

Clara Barton was so shy that she rarely spoke. Her mother worried, and took her to a doctor for advice. The doctor examined Clara. Then, he turned to Mrs. Barton. "Your daughter is healthy," he explained. "She is just very shy. Maybe it would help if she got a job. Then, she would be forced to talk."

Clara Barton lived in this house in Maryland for the last 15 years of her life. Today it is a National Historic Site. **Credit:** Preservation Maryland, Wikimedia

At 17 years old, Barton took the doctor's advice. She found a job as a school teacher. At first, Barton felt scared to teach. She would need to talk in front of a class of students. Would her shyness allow it? To Clara Barton's surprise, she loved teaching! Her students loved her too. Many teachers were very strict, but Barton was not.

Barton went to a university. After she graduated, she looked for another teaching job. One day, Barton took a trip to Bordentown, New Jersey, to visit a friend. While there, she saw many poor children playing in the streets. Shouldn't those children be in school? Barton asked her

Injured Civil War soldiers being tended to on the battlefield

friend about the children. Her friend answered, "They are poor boys. They can't afford to go to school." Barton believed everyone should have the right to an education. So, she opened a school. It would be a public school that would be free for students. The people in charge of Bordentown gave Barton money to open her school.

## Earning Less Money Than Men

On the first day of school, there were six students **enrolled**.[1] By the year's end, Clara Barton had hundreds of students. She thought she would stay at the school forever. But the government of Bordentown hired a new principal, a man. They paid him twice as much as Barton made. Barton didn't think she should make less money because she was a woman. In **protest**,[2] she quit the school. She found a job as a clerk in Washington, D.C.

*An artist's drawing of the Civil War Battle of Antietam, the battle where Barton was almost hit by a bullet*

She was paid the same as the male clerks. Even so, Barton still missed teaching.

## The Civil War

Meanwhile, Americans were fighting over whether states had the right to allow people to own slaves. A war, called the Civil War, had broken out. Hundreds of thousands of soldiers were injured. Tens of thousands died. There weren't enough hospitals, medicine, or supplies to treat the soldiers. Barton was shocked! Quickly, she ran home to get food and medicine for them. The soldiers felt **grateful**[3] to Barton. They called her the "Angel of the Battlefield." This would become her nickname for the next six years.

## 'The Angel of the Battlefield'

After quitting her job as a clerk, Barton **devoted**[4] her life to helping soldiers. She took care of them and helped heal their wounds. She comforted the sick and injured soldiers. Sometimes Barton put herself in harm's way to save soldiers' lives. Once, she had been treating a soldier during a battle. Suddenly, a shot rang out. A bullet almost hit Barton in the arm! But instead, it ripped a hole in her dress sleeve. Then it hit Barton's patient. The soldier died. Barton never fixed the hole in her sleeve.

---

1 **enrolled** – signed up; registered
2 **protest** – an action showing disagreement
3 **grateful** – appreciative; thankful
4 **devoted** – gave over; dedicated

She didn't want to forget about the soldier, or how she had almost died as well. Even when the war ended, Barton didn't rest. Many soldiers were missing. Some had died, and their families had not been told. They continued to wonder if they would ever see their loved ones again. Barton started the Missing Soldiers Office.

The office worked to find out what had happened to 22,000 missing soldiers. Some had died. Their families had never been told, but now they knew. Other missing soldiers were now able to **reunite**[5] with their families again! Clara Barton could have stayed home and remained shy. Instead, she chose to help others. In doing so, she changed the world.

### The International Red Cross

*After the Civil War ended, Barton wanted to take a short vacation. She had worked very hard in those few years. She decided to visit Europe. She did not find rest and relaxation during her vacation. Instead, Barton came just in time for the start of the Franco-Prussian war.*

*Barton went back to the battlefield, this time in Europe. She started treating injured soldiers. While working with the soldiers, Barton learned about a new organization. It was called the International Red Cross. Its job was to help injured and captured soldiers on all sides during wartime. The International Red Cross also helped to gather supplies to care for the soldiers and to inform families when soldiers had died.*

*Barton thought the International Red Cross was an excellent idea. She wanted to open a branch in America called the American Red Cross. However, Barton changed the organization's role slightly. She also wanted it to help people during peacetime. Barton thought the organization could help people harmed by natural disasters like storms and earthquakes.*

*For the rest of her life, Barton worked to help the American Red Cross and the International Red Cross grow. She also taught people first aid. Barton had such an impact on the International Red Cross that it is probably only around today because of her.*

5 **reunite** – get back together again

# Questions

1. Circle the vocabulary word that best fits the sentence.

   *The man was very (**grateful/enrolled**) to the person who found his missing wallet.*

2. Number the following events in the order in which they took place.

   ___ Clara Barton found a job as a clerk in Washington, D.C.

   ___ Clara Barton started a school for poor children.

   ___ Clara Barton started the Missing Soldiers Office.

   ___ Clara Barton found a job teaching in a school.

3. Why did Clara Barton's doctor say she should get a job?

   A. So she wouldn't be bored

   B. So she would have extra money

   C. So she could help treat wounded soldiers

   D. So she would overcome her shyness

4. Which of the following sentences from the lesson supports the idea that Barton devoted her life to helping soldiers? Circle the correct answer.

   A. *Hundreds of thousands of soldiers were injured.*

   B. *Sometimes she put herself in harm's way to save soldiers' lives.*

   C. *Barton never fixed the hole in her sleeve.*

5. What was the effect of Clara Barton starting the Missing Soldiers Office?

   _____

   _____

   _____

57

# Weird and Amazing

*A blue dragon*
**Credit:** Sylke Rohrlach, Wikimedia

Picture all the different animals you know. There are thousands, from the tiniest ant to the towering giraffe. All these animals are **unique**[1] and special. Some are even a little weird. Let's discover six fascinating animals.

## Awesome but Creepy

Many animals are easy to admire. Everyone loves seeing a colorful parrot or a swinging monkey. However, other animals make people shiver. They are incredibly awesome and incredibly creepy. They are not animals we would like to meet on a regular morning.

Small, uninvited houseguests regularly crawl into our homes. We quickly **banish**[2] these hairy, eight-legged friends. Today, we will meet their bigger cousins—the bat-eating spiders. Although most spiders do not eat bats, some spider **species**[3] do enjoy an occasional bat snack. Weaving spiders are the most common **culprit**.[4] They can spin strong circle-shaped webs. The webs are strong enough to trap a bat. Large, tropical orb spiders weave webs that are almost five feet long! These are giant spiders. Large enough to take on a bat. Are you brave enough to catch a large tropical orb spider? They can grow to a size of four to six inches.

---

1 **unique** – one of a kind
2 **banish** – get rid of; send away
3 **species** – groups; types
4 **culprit** – guilty party; wrongdoer

Another fantastic and slightly gross animal is the Japanese spider crab. What a name! Is it a spider, or is it a crab? It is a crab. The name makes sense because its long, long legs and its body shape make it look like a spider. This crab is giant. It can grow as large as 12 feet. Massive! Although they look a little scary, these slow crabs do not usually hunt. They search the sea floor for plants or dead animals.

*A tropical orb weaver spider*
**Credit:** ggallice, Wikimedia

## Confusing Animals

Some animals look strange. They make you look twice. What are they? Here are two animals to puzzle over.

The first one has a beak and webbed feet. Nope, not a duck. Its body looks a little bit like an otter. Wait a minute; its tail looks like a beaver's! Are you able to guess what this animal is? You are meeting a platypus. They look bizarre. In fact, when Europeans first saw a picture of a platypus in the late 1700s,

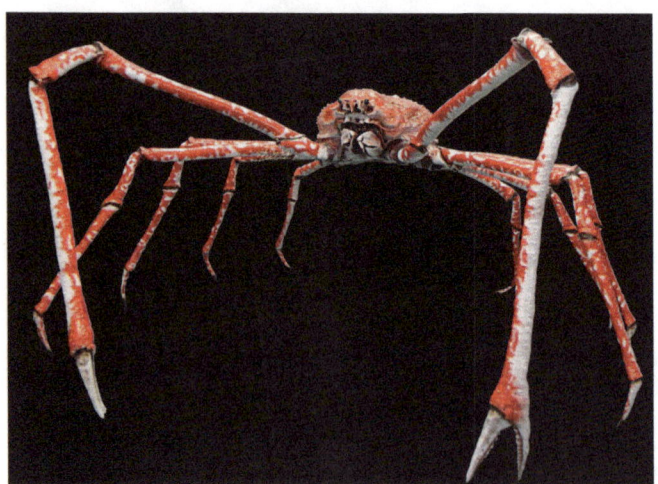

*A Japanese spider crab*
**Credit:** Lycaon (Hans Hillewaert), Wikimedia

they thought it was a joke. The platypus may look awkward, but they are fast swimmers and fantastic hunters.

The next animal, the okapi, is also fun to look at. Its striped legs look a lot like a zebra's, but it also looks like a deer. To make matters even more confusing, this weird-looking animal is not related to either zebras or deer. It is related to the giraffe. Okapis live in thick rainforests. Their unusual skin helps to **camouflage**[5] them from predators. Their fantastic hearing also helps to keep them safe.

5 **camouflage** – disguise; conceal

**Lesson 12:** Weird and Amazing

## Small but Fierce

Our last two animals remind us not to judge a book by its cover. These animals are small, but they pack a punch.

Honey badgers look cute, but do not be fooled. They are strong and they are not afraid to fight. They sometimes fight much larger animals, even lions! Their skin is loose and very thick. This makes it hard for a predator to bite through it. And, if a predator does bite, the honey badger's loose skin saves the day. It allows the creature to twist around, wiggle free, and bite back!

A blue dragon is a sea slug, but not an ordinary slug. It looks like it has come out of a storybook. This fascinating animal is not scared of the scary. It attacks an extremely poisonous type of jellyfish called the Portuguese man o' war. It steals the jellyfish's poison and saves it for later. It will use it on anything that dares to try and attack it!

*A platypus swimming in a creek*
**Credit:** *Klaus, Wikimedia*

*Notice the okapi's striped legs.*
**Credit:** *Raul654, Wikimedia*

*A honey badger*

# Questions

1. **Circle the vocabulary word that best fits the sentence.**

   *When the man saw the damage to his car, he wanted to know who the (camouflage/culprit) was.*

2. **Mark each statement as T (true) or F (false).**

   ___ Blue dragons are afraid to attack other animals.

   ___ Honey badgers have skin that is loose and very thick.

   ___ Japanese spider crabs are a type of spider.

   ___ Okapis have excellent hearing.

3. **Place a check mark next to each statement that correctly describes platypuses.**

   ___ Their bodies look like otters.

   ___ They are poor swimmers.

   ___ They are fantastic hunters.

   ___ They have no tail.

4. **Circle the choice that has the same meaning as the following sentence from the lesson:** *Our last two animals remind us not to judge a book by its cover.*

   A. Our last two animals remind us that animals don't always look the same in real life as they are shown on a book's cover.

   B. Our last two animals remind us that things aren't always the way they seem from the outside.

   C. Our last two animals aren't the only ones the book talks about.

5. **Have you ever seen a strange or weird-looking bird, fish, or animal? Write a little bit about it.**

   _____

   _____

   _____

62   Lesson 12: Weird and Amazing

# Airplanes and Helicopters: Flying High

A helicopter flies near an airplane in an airfield.

Have you ever traveled to a different country by plane? Imagine traveling by boat instead. How long do you think it would take? A **century**[1] ago, a trip to Europe by steamship took about two weeks. Today, it takes fewer than eight hours by plane. Air travel has made traveling faster and easier. Let's read about airplanes and helicopters. We're going to see how they fly and what they are used for.

## How Airplanes Fly

Have you ever wondered how airplanes fly? How can something so heavy rise up in the air and stay there? There are four **forces**[2] that make an airplane fly: lift, weight, drag, and thrust. Lift is the force that pushes an airplane up. An airplane's wings have a special shape. This makes the air move around them in a way that lifts the airplane up. Weight is the force that pulls the airplane toward the ground. For an airplane to take off, the lift needs to be stronger than the weight. Thrust is the force that pushes an airplane forward. Thrust comes from the engine. Drag is the force that pulls on the airplane and tries to slow it down. For an airplane to move forward, the thrust must be stronger than the drag. When all of these forces are working together, an airplane can take off and fly!

---

1 **century** – one hundred years
2 **forces** – pushes or pulls on something

## Types of Airplanes

Did you know that airplanes can be used for many different things? The most common is to fly people between two places. These are called commercial airplanes. Commercial airplanes can also be used to transport goods, or cargo. Cargo planes carry many different things, including mail, animals, clothes, and cars. Military planes are used by an army in battle or to transport soldiers and goods where they are needed. There are also people who buy their own airplanes. These are called private airplanes. They are usually smaller than commercial planes, and the inside looks very different than commercial airplanes too.

*There are four forces that work together to make an airplane fly.*

*A DHL cargo plane. Cargo planes do not have windows.*

## How Helicopters Work

Helicopters don't have wings, so the lift force is made with their blades. These blades are called **rotors**.[3] When the rotors spin, a helicopter can fly up. There are also smaller rotors at the back of the helicopter, called tail rotors. They allow the helicopter to move forward, backward, and sideways. Without tail rotors, a helicopter would just spin around in circles!

Helicopters are slower and noisier than airplanes, but they are very useful. For example, helicopters can do many things that airplanes can't. Helicopters don't need a runway to take off or land. They just fly straight up or down. This means they can land anywhere. They can fly sideways, backward, and spin around in the air. Helicopters can also hover, which means to stay in one spot in the air without moving.

3 **rotors** – the blades on a helicopter

Lesson 13: Airplanes and Helicopters: Flying High

## How Helicopters Help

Helicopters can land in hard-to-reach places. They are used to rescue people stuck on a mountain or in the water. The helicopter hovers in the air as the person is lifted into it. Helicopters can also be used as ambulances to fly sick people to a hospital. They can land on the roofs of some hospitals. Helicopters can help with forest fires by carrying loads of water and dropping them on the fire. The police sometimes use helicopters to search for people or cars. Helicopters direct police cars where to go. And some people like to fly in helicopters just for fun!

*A helicopter flies by creating lift with its rotors.*

*Helicopters can land without a runway, so they are used to rescue people in hard-to-reach places.* **Credit:** *Dachris, Wikimedia*

# Questions

1. Circle the vocabulary word that best fits the sentence.

   *The helicopter was flying so low that we could hear its **(rotors/forces)** spinning.*

2. Mark each statement as T (true) or F (false).

   ___ Helicopters can do things that airplanes can't.

   ___ Helicopters need runways to take off and land.

   ___ Helicopters move just as quickly as airplanes.

   ___ Helicopters can be used to rescue people in hard-to-reach places.

3. Which of the following is the force that pushes an airplane forward?

   A. Lift

   B. Weight

   C. Thrust

   D. Drag

4. What was the author's purpose in including the section titled *"How Helicopters Work"*?

   A. To tell us why helicopters don't land on runways

   B. To tell us why helicopters are slower and noisier than airplanes

   C. To tell us how helicopters work and some ways they are different than airplanes

5. List a few differences between airplanes and helicopters.

   _____

   _____

   _____

# Tightrope Walkers: The Most Careful Stroll

*A tightrope walker*

Did you ever see a tightrope walker? They walk so carefully on a thin cable, usually very high above the ground. Children can tightrope, too. They may do it in their yard, on a rope tied between two trees.

## How to Become a Tightrope Walker

Tightrope walking can be learned from a young age. It can be learned through afterschool lessons or in a summer program. Even some colleges offer courses in tightrope walking. Of course, learning such a **skill**[1] takes a lot of practice and plenty of focus. The tightrope walker must concentrate the whole time. To lose focus for even one moment could lead to a fall.

Most tightrope walkers carry long, heavy poles in their hands while they walk. This helps them to balance. **Posture**[2] is important, too. Once the tightrope walker knows how to balance well, he can try other tricks. Some tightrope walkers lay down on the wire as if they are asleep. Others balance different items on their nose while performing. They may balance a stick, or even a chair. Some acrobats act out entire stories on the **highwire**.[3] If you're lucky, you might get to see a tightrope walker flip in the air and then land back neatly on the rope.

---

1 **skill** – ability; expertise
2 **posture** – way of standing
3 **highwire** – the cable that tightrope walkers walk on

## Performing

Not too many people only walk a tightrope for a living, but there are a few. These people usually work for a circus or a show. A tightrope walker's main task is to give the audience a good time and great entertainment.

*Performing in a show*

Some tightrope walkers are their own boss. They open a show and advertise. People call them to **book**[4] shows for parties, camps, or schools. They pack up all the equipment they need and travel to the show's location. They set up the ropes, **secure**[5] them in place, and begin the show. Some tightrope walkers have other jobs by day. They do shows at night and during vacations.

Experienced tightrope walkers can walk in many different locations. They can walk between two mountains or between two buildings. In 1974, a red-headed acrobat named Philippe Petit snuck into the Twin Towers in Manhattan. He strung a cable 1,350 feet above ground, between the two towers. He had spent months planning the activity. Petit even hired a helicopter to get an **aerial**[6] view of where he would walk. He didn't ask anyone's permission before his walk. Police arrested Petit as soon as he got off the wire. Another man, Nathan Paulin, **recently**[7] did the longest walk ever on a tightrope. He did it in France, and it took two hours!

*In 1974, acrobat Philippe Petit walked a tightrope between the Twin Towers high above ground.* **Credit:** *Chrisa Hickey, Wikimedia*

---

4 **book** – reserve; sign up for
5 **secure** – attach in place; fasten
6 **aerial** – operating in the air
7 **recently** – a short time ago

*Step by step, the tightrope walker makes his way across the rope.* **Credit:** Rhett Sutphin, Flickr

## Try It At Home

Tightrope walking is fun and entertaining. If you want to learn how, you need a strong rope and a place to hang it. If you asked tightrope walkers for tips, most would say the same few things: Focus on one spot ahead of you, like a tree or a mountain. Focus on something that is not moving. While tightrope walking, you should also move slowly. Feel with your foot for the rope before fully putting your foot down. And if you feel shaky (you will!), bend your knees to help you balance better. Don't get discouraged. Remember, practice makes perfect!

 # Questions

1. Circle the vocabulary word that best fits the sentence.

    *Speaking politely is an important **(posture/skill)** to have.*

2. Mark each statement as T (true) or F (false).

    ___ Learning to be a tightrope walker takes a lot of practice.

    ___ Tightrope walkers often work for circuses or other shows.

    ___ Tightrope walkers all have red hair.

    ___ Tightrope walkers often carry poles to help them balance.

3. What do all tightrope walkers probably have in common?

    A. They are all men.

    B. They practice a great deal.

    C. They work for themselves.

    D. They all begin training when they are children.

4. Which of the following statements best summarizes the lesson?

    A. Tightrope walking is an entertaining skill requiring lots of concentration.

    B. The longest tightrope walk ever lasted two hours.

    C. Tightrope walkers can work for themselves or for others.

5. What is one of the most important skills a tightrope walker must have?

    _____

    _____

    _____

70  Lesson 14: Tightrope Walkers: The Most Careful Stroll

# Recycling: Giving It a New Life

This picture shows plastic bottles that were used once but can be recycled.

Just about 100 years ago, plastic wasn't used much. Dolls were made of wood or cloth. Cups were china or metal. Bags were paper. Hard to imagine, isn't it? As plastic was developed, things became cheaper and more convenient. Plastic could be shaped however you wanted. Since it is cheap to make, people can throw it out. It is light and can be made in any color. Plastic sounds perfect, doesn't it? Plastic is not perfect for a few reasons.

## Save Oil

First of all, did you ever wonder where plastic comes from? It is made from oil **pumped**[1] out from deep inside the earth. There is a **limited**[2] amount of oil down there. Oil doesn't grow. Although there is a lot of oil deep in the earth, many people also use a lot of plastic. Many people are worried that the oil will be used up **eventually**.[3] That is why we should try to **reduce**[4] how much plastic we use—to save oil. Plastic can also be made from something else, and that is old plastic. Old plastic can be melted down and shaped into new plastic items. That would definitely save oil. To make old objects into new ones is called recycling.

1 **pumped** – sucked out of
2 **limited** – has a certain amount; doesn't last forever
3 **eventually** – after a while
4 **reduce** – make less; cut down on

## Too Many Landfills

There are also other reasons why it is important to recycle. Many of the things we use can **decompose**.[5] To decompose means to break down slowly and disappear over time. Fruits, for example, decompose. Other materials, like wood, decompose more slowly. Can you guess if plastic decomposes easily? If you guessed no, then you are correct. It takes many years for even a small plastic item to decompose. Meanwhile, all the plastic that people use is filling up the landfills. Landfills are places where all the garbage is dumped. There are many landfills in the United States, and the government keeps making new ones because the old ones are full. The landfills smell, attract lots of bugs, and sometimes leak unpleasant liquids that are bad for the people who live around the landfills. Also, the animals living around the landfills have less space to live in because of all the trash. If we used less plastic, we would need fewer landfills.

*Pumping oil from deep in the earth*

*Landfills are overflowing with garbage.*
**Credit:** *Cezary p, Wikimedia*

## Dirty Oceans

A third reason we all need to cut down on plastic is that it is bad for animals. A lot of plastic gets blown into the oceans and lakes. Every year, hundreds of animals die from swallowing plastic or from plastic bags covering their heads. Scientists cut open a dead whale's stomach and found many pounds of plastic in it. The whale thought the plastic was food and ate it. That blocked real food from entering its stomach. Sometimes small fish swallow tiny pieces of plastic, and then big fish eat the small ones.

> 5 **decompose** – break down

The big fish end up with a lot of plastic from inside the small fish. Then the plastic can reach humans who eat a fish with plastic in its stomach.

## Recycling Solves a Lot of Problems

There are so many ways to reduce the amount of plastic we use. Recycling is great because we can still enjoy plastic items and reuse them afterward. We can also try not to use plastic items made to be used only once, like plastic cups, straws, and bottles. We can try to use other items besides plastic whenever possible, and we can reuse plastic items before getting rid of them.

Many different materials can be recycled. Glass, metal, paper, and cardboard are just some of them. When you put those items in the recycling bin, you are giving them a new life!

*The oceans are full of plastic, which harms the fish.*

*It's important to take the time to put trash in the right bin. Many communities have separate bins for paper, plastic, glass, and other recyclable materials, as pictured above.*

# Questions

1. Circle the vocabulary word that best fits the sentence.

   *Most citizens want the government to **(reduce/decompose)** taxes.*

2. Mark each statement as T (true) or F (false).

   ___ Plastic decomposes quickly.

   ___ Many animals die from swallowing plastic or having it get stuck over their heads.

   ___ Plastic is made from kerosene pumped from underground.

   ___ Plastic is filling up landfills.

3. Which of the following things can plastic be made from?

   A. Used plastic

   B. Used paper

   C. Used wood

   D. Used glass

4. Which of the following statements best summarizes the lesson?

   A. Plastic items are more convenient than wooden or paper items.

   B. It is important to reduce the amount of plastic we use for several reasons.

   C. Plastic can be found inside large fish that eat smaller fish.

5. What plastic items in your house can you think of that can be recycled?

   _____

   _____

   _____

# Say Cheese!

*A variety of cheeses on display.*
**Credit:** Silar, Wikimedia

It could be a pizza topping. It could be mixed with your pasta. It could be a salad ingredient. It could be eaten by itself as a healthy, filling snack. It may come in a square box. It might come wrapped in paper, perfectly round. We're talking all about cheese! Have you ever wondered what happens to cheese before it gets to your pizza bagel? Listen up, it's fascinating!

## How is Cheese Made?

Milk is cheese's star ingredient. But how does watery milk turn into a piece of hard, yellow cheese?

In this lesson, we're going to explore the exciting **process**[1] of cheese making.

Beginning on a dairy farm, milk is collected from cows, sheep, and goats. Usually, cow milk is used for cheesemaking. Sheep and goat milk are also used, often to make special and unique types of cheese.

At the **dairy**[2], the milk is poured into a large container called a cheese vat. Before anything, the milk needs to be heated to get rid of any harmful **bacteria**.[3] This is called pasteurizing.

Now, how is the milk made to harden? At this point, good bacteria are added to the milk.

1 **process** – method; way to do something
2 **dairy** – place where milk and cream are made into cheese and butter
3 **bacteria** – germs

The bacteria cause the milk to thicken into clumps. The clumps are called curds, and the liquid that is left around them is called whey.

Next, the curds are cut into smaller pieces and heated. Salt is added to dry out and **preserve**[4] the curds. At this point, some of the curds are removed from the vat. These curds are ready to be packaged and sold as cream cheese or cottage cheese.

Caption: Pasta and cheese, a favorite supper
**Credit:** Vancouver Bites! From Vancouver, Canada, Wikimedia

The remaining curds are pressed into molds. To harden, the cheese needs to be left in a cool place to age. Some cheeses are left to age for a few weeks. Others are left for years! Cheese will taste very different depending on how long it was left to age.

## Popular Types of Cheese

When you think of cheese, you probably think of the simple kind in your fridge. But as cheese lovers will tell you, there are hundreds of different cheeses to try.

In this section, we'll read about four of the most popular types of cheese.

**Mozzarella cheese:** Mozzarella wins the prize for being America's favorite cheese! And guess why? Because mozzarella is used as the topping for the world's favorite food—

A cheese vat in action. **Credit:** James.folsom at English Wikipedia, Wikipedia

pizza! Mozzarella is named after the Italian word "mozzare," meaning "to tear." Perhaps it was given this name due to its stringy, stretchy nature that Americans love.

4 **preserve** – protect from spoiling

**Cheddar cheese:** The name "Cheddar" **originates**[5] from the English town Cheddar in Somerset. This is where Cheddar cheese was first made. But today it is made in many countries. A super-popular cheese, cheddar can be found in almost every American fridge. That doesn't mean it's easy to make, though! Cheddar must age for at least two to four months before it is ready. During that time, it is checked for quality often by professional cheese graders. Cheddar cheese is very **versatile**.[6] It can be melted into dips, sprinkled on casseroles, and even used in desserts. It is usually a pale to deep yellow color.

*Blue cheese.* **Credit:** *smial (talk), Wikimedia*

**Parmesan cheese:** Parmesan cheese has been described as tasting like many things. Some say it tastes nutty, some say it's tangy, and others claim it tastes fruity. Overall, it has a **savory**[7] taste and a **gritty**[8] texture. Parmesan cheese is **typically**[9] enjoyed on foods like pasta and salads.

**Blue cheese:** What makes blue cheese look blue? It sounds yucky, but the blue color actually comes from mold. Usually, we avoid mold when it comes to food, since it's not good for our health. Blue cheese, however, is made using a safe type of mold called Penicillium. If you're brave enough to try it, you'll find it tastes spicy and slightly salty. Blue cheese is often melted into grilled cheese sandwiches, made into dips, added to salads, eaten with chips, or used to make macaroni and cheese.

---

5 **originates** – comes from
6 **versatile** – good for many uses; all purpose
7 **savory** – salty; spicy
8 **gritty** – sandy; grainy
9 **typically** – usually

 **Questions**

1. Circle the vocabulary word that best fits the sentence.

    The sand felt very **(savory/gritty)** when we walked barefoot on the beach.

2. Mark each statement as T (true) or F (false).

    ___ Usually goat's milk is used for cheesemaking.

    ___ The process of heating milk to get rid of any harmful bacteria is called pasteurizing.

    ___ Milk thickens into clumps, called whey.

    ___ Most cheeses harden overnight.

3. Number the following events in the order in which they take place.

    ___ The milk thickens into clumps.

    ___ The milk is pasteurized.

    ___ The curds are cut into smaller pieces and heated.

    ___ Milk is collected from cows.

4. Which of the following sentences from the section titled *"Cheddar Cheese"* supports the idea that Cheddar cheese is very versatile?

    A. A super-popular cheese, cheddar can be found in almost every American fridge.

    B. It can be melted into dips, sprinkled on casseroles, and even used in desserts.

    C. It is usually a pale to deep yellow color.

5. Why is blue cheese safe to eat if it contains mold?

    _____

    _____

    _____

# Born to Soar: The Amazing Story of John Glenn

John Glenn was a dreamer, pilot, soldier, astronaut, senator, and American hero.

John Glenn had a happy childhood in New Concord, Ohio. Although his town was small, John had big dreams. Airplanes were a brand-new invention, and John dreamed of flying in one. When John was young, his father took him for a ride in an airplane. John felt the wind rush past his face. He was thrilled. This is what he wanted to do with his life. John Glenn spent the rest of his life making his dreams come true. Let's read about Glenn's adventures in the sky and space.

## A Pilot Career

World War II broke out in Europe when Glenn was 18 years old. When the United States joined the war, Glenn signed up to fight. He signed up to be a pilot because he loved airplanes.

After two years of training, Glenn went to war, fighting Japanese pilots. He faced many dangers and adventures. After the war, Glenn came home to his family.

But Glenn's "vacation" didn't last long. Five years after World War II ended, the United States fought another war—the Korean War. Glenn was a pilot in the Korean War. He became known as a brave fighter and skilled pilot. Glenn even won medals for his war **service**.[1]

1 **service** – fighting for the army

After the war, Glenn continued to work for the army and fly airplanes. In 1957, Glenn broke a record! He flew a jet across the United States from New York to Los Angeles. This airplane was supersonic, which means it went faster than the speed of sound. Glenn was the first to make this flight. It took him three hours and 23 minutes.

*John Glenn flew this airplane during the Korean War.*

## The Mercury 7

John Glenn loved adventure. He liked flying, taking risks, and trying new things. He wanted to go beyond the limits of what was possible. Glenn wasn't the only person interested in adventure and flight. Many scientists and leaders were excited about going to outer space. The United States and the Soviet Union were enemies. The two nations started a "Space Race" to see who would be the first to explore beyond Earth.

*The Mercury 7 team wearing space suits. John Glenn is in the front row, second from the right*

Glenn imagined how it would feel to leave Earth and see it from above. NASA, the government agency in charge of getting America to outer space, was looking for pilots. Glenn **eagerly**[2] volunteered. NASA chose him and six other army pilots to become the first American astronauts. Overnight, this group of brave men became **national**[3] heroes. Newspapers started writing about them. They nicknamed the group "the Mercury 7." Photographers followed them around. Everyone wanted to know more about these seven men.

## Into Orbit

The country was getting **discouraged**.[4] Scientists had been working for years and hadn't gotten a man into orbit yet.

> 2 **eagerly** – full of interest and excitement
> 3 **national** – relating to a country
> 4 **discouraged** – losing hope; disappointed

Lesson 17: Born to Soar: The Amazing Story of John Glenn

Meanwhile, Soviet astronaut Yuri Gagarin had become the first man in outer space almost a year before. However, America was not far behind. NASA had worked for three years to build a rocket that could hold a rider.

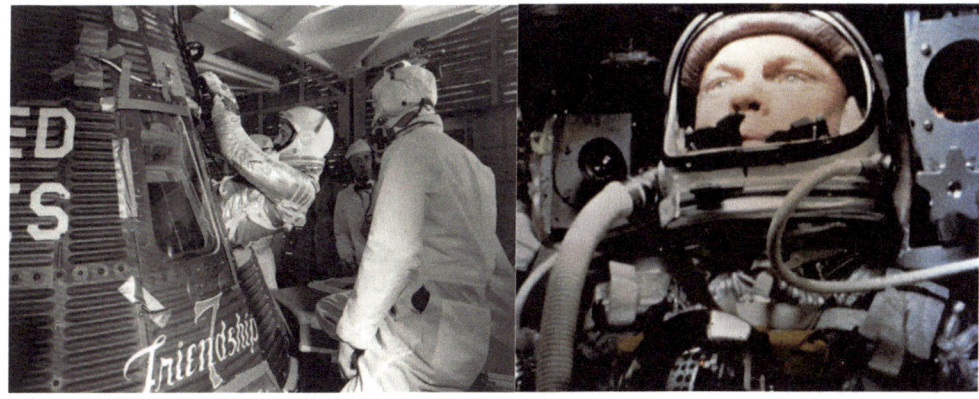

*John Glenn climbed into the small capsule. The entire capsule was only six feet across and ten feet tall. A camera inside the capsule took a picture of Glenn as he flew through space.*

They created a space suit to help an astronaut survive outside Earth's **atmosphere**.[5] They worked, **calculated**,[6] and tested. In 1961, NASA sent an American, Alan Shephard, into outer space. Next, it was John Glenn's turn to soar. He would be the first man in orbit. His spaceship, Friendship 7, was ready to **launch**.[7]

It was February 20, 1962. Everyone felt excited and scared. The entire country was listening or watching live as Glenn climbed into the tiny **cockpit**[8] wearing a stiff space suit and a helmet closed over his face. Glenn buckled up. The door was shut. What would happen next? Nobody knew.

Glenn's family watched nervously. The countdown began. "3, 2, 1.... LIFT OFF!" The rocket launcher shot out a blaze of flame and smoke, **propelling**[9] the spaceship into the air. Up, up, up, 160 miles into the air, outside the Earth's atmosphere. Glenn looked out the window and saw the entire Earth stretched below him.

*This is how the rocket looked when it launched the Friendship 7 capsule into outer space. The space capsule where John Glenn sat is near the top of the rocket.*

5 **atmosphere** – the gases surrounding planet Earth
6 **calculated** – planned; worked out
7 **launch** – send into orbit
8 **cockpit** – area where the pilot sits
9 **propelling** – pushing something forward

He orbited the planet three times, traveling five miles per second.

Mission completed, Glenn directed the spacecraft back to Earth. This was the tricky part. When re-entering Earth's orbit, the spaceship would be heated to 3,000 degrees. It had a heat shield to protect Glenn. But would it work? Everyone watched and waited, holding their breaths...

The spaceship **hurtled**[10] towards Earth and entered the atmosphere. A parachute opened, slowing its fall. Glenn's capsule landed safely in the Atlantic Ocean, where a ship waited for him. He stepped out of the **capsule**,[11] and everyone cheered! He had made it. His childhood dream of flying and adventure had come true.

*After John Glenn's adventures as an astronaut, he ran for office as a United States senator. At age 77, the aging John Glenn went into outer space again and became the oldest astronaut at the time.*

### John Glenn's Later Years

*John Glenn continued to lead an exciting life after becoming the first American in orbit. In 1964, he ran for a seat in the U.S. Senate. However, after a bad fall, he had to withdraw from the race. In 1974, he ran again and was elected. In 1984, he even tried to run for president of the United States but wasn't nominated.*

*Even during his job as senator, John Glenn still loved flying. He really wanted to go back to outer space again. Finally, in 1998, when Glenn was 77 years old, NASA let him fly on the space shuttle Discovery. At that time, he was the oldest man in outer space. After an exciting life as a pilot, military hero, astronaut, and senator, John Glenn died in 2016 at age 95.*

---

10 **hurtled** – moved at a high speed
11 **capsule** – the small compartment of a spacecraft where the astronauts live

# Questions

1. Circle the vocabulary word that best fits the sentence.

    I **(hurtled/calculated)** exactly how much money I would need to buy a new bicycle.

2. Number the following events in the order in which they took place.

    ___ Yuri Gagarin became the first man in outer space.

    ___ John Glenn fought in World War II.

    ___ John Glenn orbited Earth in Friendship 7.

    ___ John Glenn fought in the Korean War.

3. The Space Race was between which two countries?

    A. The United States and Japan

    B. The Soviet Union and Korea

    C. The United States and the Soviet Union

    D. The United States and Korea

4. Which of the following sentences from the section titled *"Into Orbit"* supports the idea that America was getting discouraged about sending someone into outer space?

    A. *Scientists had been working for years and hadn't gotten a man into orbit yet.*

    B. *However, America was not far behind.*

    C. *In 1961, NASA sent an American, Alan Shephard, into outer space.*

5. Why was it so important for the heat shield to work properly?

    _____

    _____

    _____

# Ancient Shipbuilding: Marvels of Engineering

What are some common forms of transportation? For local travel, people walk or use bikes, cars, and buses. For longer trips, they may take trains or airplanes. When it comes to moving large amounts of goods to faraway places, many countries and companies rely on ships. Ships have been used for thousands of years for traveling, fishing, and fighting. What did ancient ships look like? And how did they change over time?

European shipbuilders in the 16th century put together a ship's rounded hull by nailing boards together.

## Early Ships

The first ships were small canoes or flat rafts. They were made by cutting down large trees. The thick tree trunks were hollowed out to make small canoes. Canoes were also sometimes made with big pieces of tree bark or animal skin. Logs made from tree trunks were tied together into flat rafts. Small canoes and rafts couldn't travel far into the ocean. They couldn't be used to fight battles. They could only carry small loads of goods. They could bring fishermen out to sea, just far enough to fish.

Ancient empires, like that of Egypt, usually used more **complex**[1] ships as they spread out and developed. An **archaeological**[2] discovery of an ancient ship in Egypt showed historians how these ships were made.

---

1 **complex** – complicated
2 **archaeological** – the process of studying history by digging up old ruins and remains of earlier civilizations

## Pharoah's Ship

In 1954, an Egyptian archaeologist dug underneath the massive pyramid in Giza. There, buried in a huge stone **tomb**,[3] he was shocked to find an entire ancient ship! This had been a royal ship belonging to the pharaoh named Khufu. It was 4,600 years old!

*Khufu's ship was found in pieces.* **Credit:** *Bradipus, Wikipedia*

The ship was in sad shape after being underground for 4,600 years. Kamal el Mallakh, the archaeologist who found it, took out all 1,224 pieces. Then a team worked to put them together. The archaeologists learned that instead of using one piece of wood or bark for the **hull**,[4] the ship had 30 boards of wood. The wood **planks**[5] had been bent into a curved shape. They were fitted together like puzzle pieces to make a solid ship where no water could enter. The longest board was 76 feet long! It must have come from a very tall tree. The planks, which had carvings, were sewn together with rope.

*Parts of Khufu's ship were stitched together with rope.* **Credit:** *Thesevenseas, Wikimedia.*

After piecing the hull together, the builders used planks to build a ship **deck**.[6] Pharoah Khufu and the ship's captain could go on the deck, see the ocean, and sit in a small room called a deckhouse.

## Moving the Ship

A modern canoe only needs one person **paddling**[7] with one oar to move it through the water. But Khufu's huge ship had 12 oars, each carved from a piece of wood.

---

3 **tomb** – underground burial chamber
4 **hull** – body of a ship, including the rounded bottom and sides
5 **planks** – long flat pieces of wood, used for construction
6 **deck** – upper level of the ship
7 **paddling** – rowing with oars

The oars were attached to the ship and rowed by a group of sailors sitting inside. On some ancient ships, drums were used to pound out a beat. This kept all the rowers rowing in rhythm.

There were five oars on each side and two in the back for steering. A large **crew**[8] was required to move the ship through the water. It's unknown if Khufu ever actually used the ship, but it did teach archaeologists about ancient shipbuilding.

*Khufu's ship has been put together and is on display in a museum.*
**Credit:** *Olaf Tausch, Wikimedia*

## Using Sails

Oars worked well to move a ship quickly through the water. But ships needed a full crew to move them. Shipbuilders quickly realized they could get nature to do this work for them. The same wind that made dangerous waves appear in the water could also **propel**[9] a ship forward.

As early as 4,000 years ago, shipbuilders built **masts**[10] on ship decks and attached large sheets of cloth to them. The cloth sheets were called sails. They caught the wind and used it to push the ship forward. By rolling up some or all of the sails, sailors could change the ship's speed.

*The Vikings were an ancient people known for being great sailors. They built fearsome-looking ships with shields, rams, and dragon heads. They attacked cities located on the shores. This model of a Viking ship shows oars attached to the inside.*

Over time, shipbuilders designed newer and better sails. Some ships had dozens of sails in different shapes and sizes. Shipbuilders starting using different support beams to hold the hulls together. Shipbuilders added metal to their ships.

---

8 **crew** – group of people who work together
9 **propel** – drive; push forward
10 **masts** – tall ship poles that hold sails

They used metal nails and naval **rams**.¹¹ These made ships stronger, better at fighting, and longer lasting.

In more modern times, shipbuilders started using engines to propel ships. They began to power the engine using wood, coal, oil, and gas instead of relying on sails and oars. Warships were **upgraded**¹² with cannons and, later, guns.

Even though ships today are very different from the ones in ancient times, they still have hulls and decks. Some still have masts and sails as well. Most are still made from wood and metal. A lot has changed in shipbuilding, but some things have stayed the same.

*An ancient coin from India showing a ship with masts and a sail*

*Modern ships, like this one, come in many shapes and sizes. They are different than ancient ships, but they still have hulls and a power source, and they still move people and goods along by water.*
**Credit:** *Frila, Wikimedia*

11 **ram** – type of weapon
12 **upgraded** – improved

88    Lesson 18: Ancient Shipbuilding: Marvels of Engineering

# Questions

1. Circle the vocabulary word that best fits the sentence.

   *Putting the many pieces of the new bicycle together was a difficult and **(upgraded/complex)** procedure.*

2. Mark each statement as T (true) or F (false).

   ___ Ancient civilizations often used small canoes and rafts when fighting battles.

   ___ A team of archaeologists rebuilt Khufu's ship after it was discovered underground.

   ___ Modern ships have engines to help propel them.

   ___ Archaeologists are sure that Pharoah Khufu sailed on his ship many times.

3. How were the planks on Pharoah Khufu's ship held together?

   A. They were nailed together.

   B. They were sewn together.

   C. They were glued together.

   D. They were stapled together.

4. Which of the following sentences from the section titled *"Using Sails"* supports the idea that ancient and modern ships have some features in common?

   A. *In more modern times, shipbuilders started using engines to propel ships.*

   B. *Some ships had dozens of sails in different shapes and sizes.*

   C. *A lot has changed in shipbuilding, but some things have stayed the same.*

5. Why were drums used on some ancient ships?

   _____

   _____

   _____

# Pigeon Post: A Different Kind of Airmail

*A homing pigeon.*
**Credit:** *Monandowitsch, Wikimedia*

"Pigeons are fun to chase," giggles your younger brother. "Pigeons are pests," moans your dad. "Pigeons bring me the news." ....Wait, what was that? You read that right. There's more to pigeons than just eating yesterday's stale bread. Generations of people have used pigeons' special skills.

## What Are Homing Pigeons?

Homing pigeons are a **specific**[1] type of pigeon. They have a special ability. Humans can feel objects. We can feel a cool floor tile, a soft coat, and pieces of **coarse**[2] tree bark. Homing pigeons can feel which direction they are going! They have a homing **instinct**[3]–a sense that tells them how to get home. You cannot trick a pigeon in this matter. Pigeons can find their way home even if you release them somewhere they have never been before. No one is fully certain how pigeons can do this. But we all agree—it is impressive. And useful.

## How to Make a Homing Pigeon Useful

This skill is amazing. Better than Waze. So how can it help us? We have worked out how to **utilize**[4] a pigeon's homing instinct. We can train a pigeon to return to its **loft**[5]. It will return to its loft if we release it down the road.

> 1 **specific** – certain; particular
> 2 **coarse** – rough
> 3 **instinct** – natural behavior
> 4 **utilize** – make use of
> 5 **loft** – where pigeons live

It will return to its loft if we release it across the country. It may take time to train a pigeon, but it is worth it. You will have a reliable messenger. A postal carrier who will not give up. Homing pigeons have proved their worth. Let's see how.

## Cher Ami

War medals are a great honor. They are a way of showing respect to people who fought bravely and **selflessly**.[6] What about a pigeon? Can a pigeon deserve a medal? You decide.

*A pigeon has a small tube attached to its leg. This is where the message is placed.* **Credit:** *Crocodile2020, Wikimedia*

Cher Ami was a homing pigeon during World War I. In 1918, Cher Ami traveled with the "Lost Battalion" **unit**.[7] This American unit found itself surrounded by Germans. The soldiers were stuck. They could not easily escape. To make matters worse, American **troops**[8] were bombing the area by mistake. The unit needed to get a message to the troops. It was urgent. Major Charles W. Whittlesey quickly scribbled the message. It read, "We are along the road parallel to 276.4. Our own artillery is dropping a **barrage**[9] directly on us. For heaven's sake, stop it." He attached it to Cher Ami's leg and sent him off. Cher Ami took to the skies. He flew through bombs and flying bullets. A bullet hit him. The brave bird somehow managed to complete the rest of the journey. He arrived back at his loft and delivered the message. The American unit was now safe.

*A London bus was converted into a pigeon loft for use during World War I.*

---

6 **selflessly** – doing for others rather than yourself
7 **unit** – army group
8 **troops** – soldiers
9 **barrage** – large number of guns firing at an area

## Winkie

During World War II, on February 23, 1942, a damaged British army plane had to land in the North Sea. The crew was stuck in the freezing water. There was no way to radio for help. Thankfully, there was a shred of hope. They had brought Winkie the pigeon on the mission. They could not write a message, but Winkie was their last chance for survival. They released Winkie. Winkie managed to fly back to her loft. Now the British air force realized that the crew was still alive and knew to rescue them. Winkie received a well-deserved award for saving the day.

*Crew members in bomber planes would take pigeons along. The pigeons could send messages if the plane crashed or their radio broke.*

## Pigeon Photography

Looking for a photographer for your sister's wedding? We have a great selection of pigeons to choose from. No, I am not joking. Think of it as an old-fashioned drone.

Julius Neubronner had used pigeons before. He had already used pigeons to carry medicines. Now he had another fantastic idea. He attached a timed camera to a pigeon. The pigeon could now take pictures from the air. Great idea! Before ditching your photographer, please remember that these photographers are not the most artistic. You may not receive the exact shots you ask for.

*Julius Neubronner's invention—a camera attached to a pigeon that takes pictures using a timer*

 # Questions

1. Circle the vocabulary word that best fits the sentence.

   *The books aren't organized in any **(coarse/specific)** order.*

2. Place a check mark next to each statement that correctly describes homing pigeons.

   ___ They are a specific type of pigeon.

   ___ They only return to their lofts if the lofts are close by.

   ___ They can be trained quickly.

   ___ They have been used to help soldiers during wars.

3. How are homing pigeons able to find their way home even when released from places they've never been before

   A. They have very sharp eyesight.

   B. They communicate with other pigeons, who give them directions.

   C. They have a very specialized sense of smell that guides them.

   D. No one really knows exactly how they do it.

4. Which of the following sentences from the section titled "What Are Homing Pigeons?" supports the idea that homing pigeons have an instinct that tells them how to get home?

   A. They have a special ability.

   B. Pigeons can find their way home even if you release them somewhere they have never been before.

   C. No one is fully certain how pigeons can do this.

5. Do you think Cher Ami deserved a medal for serving during World War I? Why or why not?

   _____

   _____

94  Lesson 19: Pigeon Post: A Different Kind of Airmail

# Julius Caesar and the Fall of the Senate

One of many statues of Julius Caesar in Italy
Credit: Georges Jansoone (JoJan), Wikimedia

Imagine if you were the most powerful person in your country. What choices would you make? How would you rule? What would you do to fight against enemies? Think about these questions as you read about the life of a Roman ruler, Julius Caesar.

## A Republic

Ancient Rome began as a **republic**.[1] That meant that there was not an individual ruler. Instead, a small group of people called the Senate shared power. The Senate was made up of rich and powerful Romans called senators. In Rome, the wealthy people made laws for the whole empire. The senators chose a consul to lead the Senate. Every year, there would be a new consul. Sometimes there were two consuls at once.

## Caesar Gains Power

Julius Caesar was born into a rich family in the Roman Republic. Unfortunately for Caesar, civil war broke out during his childhood. A civil war is where people in the same country fight against each other. In the war, Caesar's family lost its money. Caesar had to run away from Rome. When he came back, he joined the Roman army to earn wealth and power. Caesar became known for winning wars and taking over lands. His **slogan**[2] was "Veni, vidi, vici," which means "I came, I saw, I conquered."

> 1 **republic** – a country that elects a group to rule it
> 2 **slogan** – a saying used by a person or group

95

Caesar used wars to gain power. At age 40, the Senate chose him to be the consul. Caesar made an **alliance**[3] with two other senators. They called their alliance a Triumvirate (try-UM-vir-rit), which means an alliance of three. This helped him and his friends, Pompey and Crassus, rule the Senate. It also helped Caesar become the governor of a place called Gaul.

## Crossing the Rubicon

Caesar continued to take over lands in Gaul. His wars made him one of the richest men in Rome. Caesar was also very popular among ordinary Romans who were not powerful or rich. Caesar helped these Romans out. He gave land to soldiers and to poor people. Back in Rome, Pompey, the new consul, watched Caesar's power grow. It made him uncomfortable. Eventually, Pompey called Caesar back to Rome. Caesar was worried. He knew Pompey wanted to get rid of him. Pompey could have had him jailed or killed. Caesar chose to return to Rome anyway. However, he brought his army with him. This too was risky, because there were laws against armies coming into Rome.

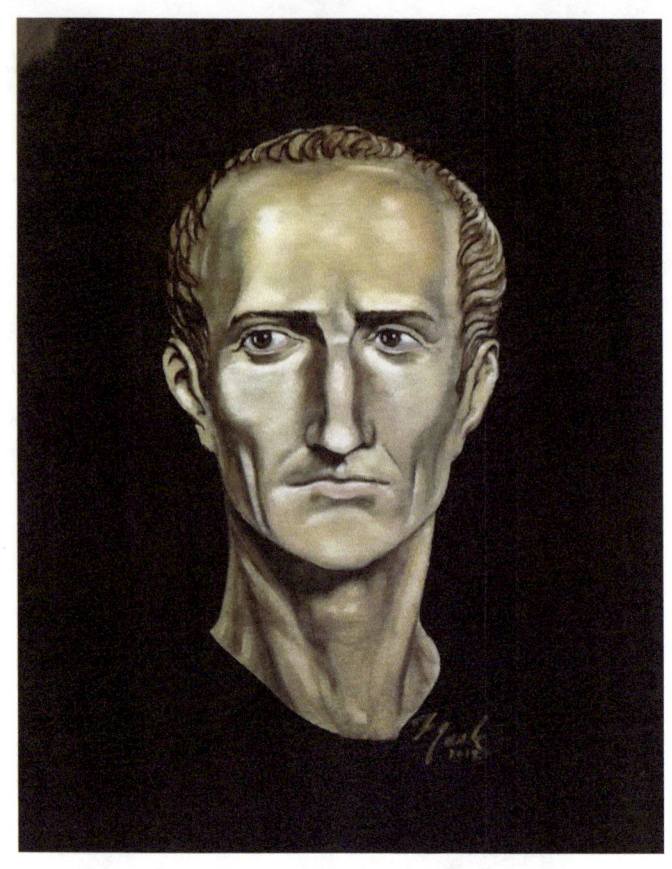

*An artist has used information from statues of Caesar to make a picture of what his face probably looked like.*

*This map of the ancient Roman empire shows Gaul ("Galli" on the map). Today, the country of France is in the land once called Gaul.*

3 **alliance** – a treaty or joining together of a group

Lesson 20: Julius Caesar and the Fall of the Senate

Caesar took a **legion**[4] of Roman soldiers and crossed the Rubicon River into Rome. He marched in with his army and challenged Pompey. Pompey ran away, and Caesar chased after him. The civil war between Caesar and Pompey finally ended when the leader of Egypt killed Pompey. In response, Caesar had the Egyptian ruler killed. Then he **pardoned**[5] most of those who had fought against him. This helped Caesar by turning his enemies into friends.

## Caesar's Death

Back in Rome, Caesar became dictator. Dictator was a title the Senate gave to consuls during war. It gave them emergency powers and was meant to last only a short time. But Caesar got the Senate to make him dictator perpetuo, dictator for life!

*A 19th century artist painted Caesar crossing the Rubicon River. The phrase "crossing the Rubicon" has come to mean "the point of no return" because Caesar's decision to cross with his army changed world history.*

Caesar was rich. He was liked by ordinary Roman people, but many others worried that he had too much power. Sixty senators made secret plans to end Caesar's rule. On March 15, in the year 44 BCE, Caesar returned to the Senate. Suddenly, many senators surrounded him. They stabbed him with **daggers**.[6] Caesar fought back. Then, he saw Brutus in the crowd. Caesar had pardoned Brutus. He had been close with Brutus and had treated him like his son. When Caesar saw how Brutus had **betrayed**[7] him, he lost his will to struggle. After Caesar's death, many Romans were very angry. Caesar's killers hadn't realized how much the ordinary people liked Caesar. Mark Antony (Caesar's co-consul), the new ruler of Egypt, and a mob of angry Romans began to fight the senators.

4 **legion** – troop; army unit
5 **pardoned** – forgave
6 **daggers** – knives
7 **betrayed** – was disloyal to

The civil war led to the Senate **dissolving**[8] and an emperor taking its place. The emperor was an individual. He ruled as a king without a Senate. The Roman Republic was no more.

Historians today argue about Caesar. Was he a bad ruler who wanted power? Or was he a good ruler who helped ordinary Romans? Did Brutus betray Caesar to gain power? Or did he betray Caesar to save the republic? Should the senators have killed Caesar? What do you think?

### Kidnapped by Pirates

*Julius Caesar was known for his bravery. One story told is about the time pirates kidnapped Caesar. The pirates said they would let him go if his friends and family paid them 20 marks, the money used in Rome. Caesar was outraged! He said 20 marks was way too little for a man like him. He told the pirates to ask for at least 50 marks.*

*While Caesar's friends and family were getting the 50 marks together, Caesar acted as if he were in charge. Even though he was a captive of the pirates, Caesar still bossed them around. He even made them listen to his speech and poems. Caesar also told the pirates that he would have them killed when he was free.*

*Just 38 days later, Caesar's family paid, and he became a free man. Shortly after, he found a new ship and crew and sailed to the pirates' island. Caesar's crew captured the pirates, and true to his word, he executed them.*

8 **dissolving** – breaking up; ending

## Shakespeare's Play

*Julius Caesar's story became famous when Shakespeare wrote a play about him, more than a thousand years after he died. The play, Julius Caesar, highlights the events that led to Caesar's death. Then it tells about the war that followed.*

*People are familiar with many lines from this play. For example, at the beginning of the play, an old woman warns Caesar to "beware the ides of March." (The ides refer to the 15th of March). True to her words, Caesar died on the 15th of March.*

*Later in the play, Shakespeare writes Caesar's last words. Famously, Shakespeare has him say, "Et tu Brute?" (You too, Brutus?) Because of the play, many people think those were really Caesar's last words.*

*Another famous moment in the play comes after Caesar's death. Many Romans attend Caesar's funeral. Mark Antony wants to get the crowd angry. He wants to turn them into a mob and have them attack Caesar's killers. Shakespeare has Mark Antony give a very dramatic speech that begins with "Friends, Romans, countrymen, lend me your ears." When he says, "lend me your ears," he means "listen to me."*

# Questions

1. Circle the vocabulary word that best fits the sentence.

   The company made up a new **(slogan/legion)** to advertise their products.

2. Mark each statement as T (true) or F (false).

   ___ Julius Caesar was born into a poor family.

   ___ His wars made Julius Caesar one of the richest men in Rome.

   ___ Julius Caesar was made dictator for only a short while.

   ___ Julius Caesar died when the senators decided to hang him.

3. Number the following events in the order in which they took place.

   ___ Caesar joined the Roman army and earned wealth and power.

   ___ Caesar had to run away from Rome after his family lost their money.

   ___ Caesar became the Roman dictator.

   ___ The Senate chose Caesar to be the consul.

4. Which of the following sentences from the section titled *"A Republic"* supports the idea that there was not an individual ruler in ancient Rome?

   A. *In Rome, the wealthy people made laws for the whole empire.*

   B. *Ancient Rome began as a republic.*

   C. *Every year, there would be a new consul.*

5. What was the effect of Caesar pardoning most of those who had fought against him after the civil war between him and Pompey?

   _____
   _____
   _____

# People Who Fly: Trapeze Artists

*Trapeze artists perform at dizzying heights.*

The first known trapeze artist lived almost 200 years ago. He was a man named Jules Leotard, and his family owned a gym in France. He would practice flying and flipping over their pool. While flying high above the ground, trapeze artists are often seen as **extraordinary**.[1] Their moves almost look magical, and many people dream of trying them out. Did you ever wonder what it is like to be a trapeze artist? How does one become a trapeze artist?

## Becoming A Trapeze Artist

Being a trapeze artist is exciting, but it comes with a lot of hard work. Trapeze artists have worked hard to **achieve**[2] their dreams, and they continue to work hard every day. They perform even when they are not feeling well or if their muscles are sore.

Trapeze artists can fly really high, but they have to keep calm. Sometimes they perform before thousands of people. If they get nervous, they can ruin the show or make a dangerous mistake. They have to trust themselves that it will be okay.

People who become trapeze artists have to be strong and **flexible**.[3] They have usually been good at such moves since they were small.

---

1 **extraordinary** – very special; exceptional
2 **achieve** – reach; accomplish; succeed
3 **flexible** – able to bend and stretch easily

Many trapeze artists took gymnastics or dance classes when they were younger. But it is not enough just to know how to make the moves. Trapeze artists must keep **training**[4] to stay in shape. All of them still do lots of exercises. They train at least a few times a week. They stretch often so they can stay flexible.

Trapeze artists travel a lot and perform in many places. Some performers find that to be fun. Other trapeze artists don't enjoy traveling as much, especially if they have a lot of family or young children.

Some trapeze artists grew up in families that lived with a circus group. Such families live in **trailers**[5] and travel with the circus from place to place to perform. Children in these families may start performing when they are as young as two years old! Other trapeze artists decide to follow this career when they are older. They take trapeze classes and then apply for jobs

You might think these skilled performers make a lot of money, but that is usually not the case. Even though trapeze artists are greatly admired, the reason people become trapeze artists is not to become rich. People who become trapeze artists do it because they love **acrobatics**[6] and want to feel like they are flying.

Trapeze artists may work backstage when they get too old to perform. They can direct performances or set up shows.

*Jules Leotard.*

*Trapeze artists perform skilled acrobatic tricks in the air.*

---

4 **training** – doing exercises to keep fit
5 **trailer** – a big vehicle that is usually used for moving large items, like boats
6 **acrobatics** – spectacular gymnastics moves

Lesson 21: People Who Fly: Trapeze Artists

## Performing

A producer is in charge of the show. The producer chooses music and costumes for the performers. The producer also chooses a message or story that the show will tell the audience.

*At trapeze school, students learn to flip and fly.*
**Credit:** *Santanu Chandra from Kolkata, India, Wikimedia*

Trapeze artists often have some specific moves that they always perform. Their routine includes those moves in every show. They may change the order and the timing of the moves according to the music.

Before a performance, trapeze artists come to the theater early in the day. They warm up and then put on their costumes and makeup. Right before the show, they attach their safety harnesses and get onto the stage.

Trapeze artists wear harnesses to protect them if they fall. A harness is a strong belt clipped to the performer and to a strong **beam**.[7] A harness is great for both new trapeze artists and for experienced ones.

All that training and traveling means that these performers work very hard. When it is time for a show, though, all the hard work pays off. The audience claps and cheers when the lights go down and the music begins to play. It's exciting! And that excitement gives the trapeze artists even more energy to perform well and enjoy the show.

*This man has a harness around his waist.*

7 **beam** – bar

103

# Questions

1. Circle the vocabulary word that best fits the sentence.

   His **(training/trailer)** session lasts for half an hour every morning.

2. Mark each statement as T (true) or F (false).

   ___ Trapeze artists earn a lot of money.

   ___ Trapeze artists often have some specific moves that they always perform.

   ___ Trapeze artists wear harnesses to protect them if they fall.

   ___ Trapeze artists have to keep training even after they have a job.

3. Number the following events in the order in which they take place.

   ___ Trapeze artists come to the theater.

   ___ The lights go down and the music begins to play.

   ___ Trapeze artists attach their harnesses.

   ___ Trapeze artists put on their costumes and makeup.

4. Which of the following sentences from the section titled *"Becoming a Trapeze Artist"* supports the idea that trapeze artists keep training to stay in shape?

   A. They perform even when they are not feeling well or if their muscles are sore.

   B. Many trapeze artists took gymnastics or dance classes when they were younger.

   C. They train at least a few times a week.

5. Why might some trapeze artists not enjoy having to travel a lot?

   _____
   _____
   _____

# *Parakeets: Parroting Words*

Sit down with a friend. How do you share a funny story? How do you share your feelings? How do you work together? We communicate with each other in so many ways. Our faces can tell a story. We can even use our bodies to show how we feel or what we want. Of course, we are human and can speak. Most people like to chat, some more than others. But have you ever had a bird join in your conversation?

One type of parakeet found in Australia
Credit: Josh Berglund, Wikimedia

## What Is a Talking Bird?

It would be incredible to have a bird that can chat with you. Maybe it could join your lesson and answer that tricky question for you! Unfortunately, talking birds are not that clever. They probably don't understand what they are saying. These birds only **mimic**[1] what they hear.

Some birds that can talk are easy to understand and can learn hundreds of words. Parakeets are one kind of bird that can talk. They are in the parrot family. This means that they share some physical **traits**[2] with other parrots. Small and colorful, these noisy birds are fun to watch. They are very sociable. In the wild, they usually live in large groups.

These active copycats need room to fly. Aside from flying around your living room, they can make terrific pets. In fact, many people do have pet parakeets because they are cute and entertaining!

> 1 **mimic** – copy
> 2 **traits** – features; characteristics

Just remember that although they can talk—almost like us—they do not eat like us. You may love sharing your mom's delicious chocolate cake, but make sure to feed only **nutritious**[3] seeds to your bird.

## Finding a Parakeet

Where are parakeets found? If we want to find a parakeet, we drive to the **local**[4] pet store. But where are parakeets found in the wild?

Parakeets live in lots of different places all over the world. They **thrive**[5] best in areas that are warm, and they avoid cold weather. You will not find a wild parakeet in the Arctic! Parakeets live in India, Sri Lanka, Australia, the Pacific Islands, and more. Parakeets are native to Australia, where the climate is hot and dry most of the year. Those conditions are perfect for parakeets. In the wild, they live in rainforests, grasslands, woodlands, **scrublands**,[6] and even deserts. They also live in parks and gardens.

Parakeets in different countries can sound different, just like people. People living in the United States have a different accent than people in England. Parakeets also have different accents.

*A male and female parakeet pictured in India*
**Credit:** *Karthik Easvur, Wikimedia*

*Brightly colored parakeets in an aviary*
**Credit:** *Bidgee, Wikimedia*

---

3 **nutritious** – healthy; full of nutrients
4 **local** – close by; in the neighborhood
5 **thrive** – do well; develop well
6 **scrublands** – flat areas where low bushes, shrubs, and grass grow

Parakeets like to live in grassy areas and can actually become **pests**.[7] They love to live near grain fields because it means a delicious and easy meal is always nearby. Farmers are not too pleased with these neighbors, even with their cheerful chatter.

## Training a Parakeet

*A parakeet feeding on grain*
**Credit:** *Hari K Patibanda, Wikimedia*

You jump out of bed and race downstairs. Your pet parakeet has arrived! You sit eagerly by the cage and wait for the bird to say hello. Nothing. You wait a bit longer, and still nothing. Hmmm. It obviously has not learned any words yet. Over the next few weeks, you **concentrate**[8] on teaching your parakeet all the important words, like "Hello. Goodbye. Come again" and "**hodgepodge**."[9] How's that going for you?

Here are some tips for training a parakeet to talk:

- Buy a young bird. Young birds find it easier to mimic new words.
- You want your pet to be happy. Happy parakeets are happy to learn.
- Concentrate on teaching your bird one short phrase at a time. You can chat at your parakeet, but remember to keep repeating the phrase you want it to mimic. Give your parakeet an English lesson. Parakeets will learn the words better if you give them only one or two short lessons daily.
- Be patient. They will not mimic the entire dictionary in a day.
- Lastly, have fun and enjoy your pet (even if it decides never to mimic words).

## Parakeet Fun Fact

Parakeets can learn over 100 new words. Sparkie Williams was a famous parakeet. He could speak over 500 words and repeat nursery rhymes! Truly incredible.

---

7 **pests** – animals that attack crops or food
8 **concentrate** – focus
9 **hodgepodge** – random mixture

# Questions

1. Circle the vocabulary word that best fits the sentence.

   *My dresser drawer is filled with a **(scrubland/hodgepodge)** of items.*

2. Mark each statement as T (true) or F (false).

   ___ Parakeets are mostly found in the Arctic.

   ___ Parakeets have different accents.

   ___ Parakeets can be fed whatever food is left over from your supper.

   ___ Parakeets are very sociable.

3. Why wouldn't your pet parakeet be able to help you answer a question on your test?

   A. Birds are not allowed into the school building.

   B. The parakeet wouldn't sit still long enough.

   C. The parakeet only mimics words.

   D. None of the above

4. Which of the following sentences from the section titled *"Finding a Parakeet"* supports the idea that you will not find parakeets in the Arctic?

   A. *If we want to find a parakeet, we drive to the local pet store.*

   B. *Parakeets live in lots of different places all over the world.*

   C. *They thrive best in areas that are warm, and they avoid cold weather.*

5. What was it about Sparkie Williams that made him so famous?

   _____

   _____

   _____

# The Great Basin Desert

Have you ever heard of frost in the desert? What about a lake? Does that belong in the desert? Our amazing planet boasts many types of **landscapes**.[1] Even its deserts are not all the same. The Great Basin Desert is one such example. Together, we will enter the Great Basin Desert and take a quick peek at some of the world's wonders.

*The Great Basin Desert*
**Credit:** *Earth's beauty internet site, Wikimedia*

## Where Is the Great Basin Desert?

The Great Basin Desert is located in the United States of America. Most of the desert is found in Nevada. The rest lies in Utah and a few other states.

## Why Is the Great Basin a Desert?

The Sierra Nevada is a mountain range. This impressive wall of rock sits next to the Great Basin Desert. It blocks rain clouds from reaching the Great Basin. Only a small amount of rain reaches the area. There is so little rain that the area is called a desert. There are four deserts in the United States, and the Great Basin Desert is one of them. As we would expect, it has hot, dry summers, but it also has cold, snowy winters.

---

1 **landscapes** – views; scenery

109

## A Great Basin

You probably already know that rain usually flows into streams, which often flow into rivers. These rivers eventually reach an ocean. But interestingly, the Great Basin is different. Here the rainwater flows towards a few valleys, not an ocean. The water either **evaporates**,[2] sinks into the ground, or joins a lake. The "basin" part of Great Basin Desert really lives up to its name. The area acts like a big bucket catching all the rainwater. However, the desert is not one big giant basin. The area has several basins.

## Visiting the Great Basin Desert

Let us visit the Great Basin Desert. You can be **assured**[3] that there is more to see than sand, rock, and an occasional cactus. The Great Basin Desert has incredible landscapes—from mountains to lakes to rocky dry ground. It is rich in **minerals**,[4] including gold and mercury.

## World's Oldest Trees

It has stood for almost five thousand years. Think of the generations it has seen and the stories it could tell. For a long time, people thought a Great Basin bristlecone pine was the world's oldest tree. Today, there is a **debate**[5] about whether a different tree can claim this title.

*A map showing the Great Basin*
**Credit:** *Kmusser, Wikimedia*

*Bristlecone pine trees*
**Credit:** *Rick Goldwaser, Wikimedia*

---

2 **evaporates** – turns from water to vapor
3 **assured** – promised; guaranteed
4 **minerals** – inorganic substances that form naturally in the ground
5 **debate** – discussion of two sides of an issue

*Stalactites and stalagmites in Lehman Caves*
*Credit:* Famartin, Wikimediat

*The Great Salt Lake*
*Credit:* L. Ochmanski, Wikimedia

However, it is amazing how this bristlecone pine has thrived in a desert. Since it grows very slowly, its wood is very **dense**,[6] allowing it to live a long time.

## Lehman Caves

Rooms of crystals, fantastic mineral **structures**,[7] and bats. What else could you want when visiting a cave? It is damp inside Lehman Caves. Water drips slowly and steadily from the roof. Each falling water droplet leaves behind the tiniest bit of minerals. Slowly, over years and centuries, this changes the cave. Interesting structures form as the dripping water leaves these minerals behind. Stalactites and stalagmites develop and grow. Stalactites hang from above, and stalagmites reach upward from the ground. These dramatic shapes make the cave incredibly interesting. Thousands of visitors come to enjoy the great sights the cave offers.

## Great Salt Lake Desert

Come to the Great Salt Lake to visit a **massive**[8] lake that is saltier than the ocean. It is so salty that it is easy to float in. Pack suntan lotion and enjoy a relaxing day out. You may even spot some wildlife like bison or birds enjoying the Great Salt Lake's rich environment.

---

6 **dense** – thick
7 **structures** – formations; shapes
8 **massive** – huge

 **Questions**

1. Circle the vocabulary word that best fits the sentence.

   We saw many beautiful **(landscapes/debates)** while driving through the country.

2. Mark each statement as T (true) or F (false).

   ___ There is only sand, rock, and an occasional cactus to be seen in the Great Basin Desert.

   ___ The Great Salt Lake is easy to float in.

   ___ There is no wildlife near the Great Salt Lake.

   ___ There are stalactites and stalagmites inside Lehman Caves.

3. Number the following events in the order in which they take place.

   ___ Stalactites and stalagmites develop.

   ___ Water drips slowly and steadily from the roof of the cave.

   ___ Each falling water droplet leaves behind the tiniest bit of minerals.

4. Which of the following sentences from the section titled *"World's Oldest Trees"* supports the idea that there might be a tree even older than the bristlecone pine?

   A. *For a long time, people thought a Great Basin bristlecone pine was the world's oldest tree.*

   B. *Today, there is a debate about whether a different tree can claim this title.*

   C. *However, it is amazing how this bristlecone pine tree thrived in a desert*

5. If you were visiting the Great Basin Desert, what would you be most interested in seeing and why?

   _____

   _____

   _____

# History of Checkers

*A game of checkers.*
**Credit:** PartsnPieces, Wikimedia

How many board games do you have at home? Some board games have been around for hundreds of years. One game that has withstood the test of time is the game of checkers.

## What Is Checkers?

Checkers is a game played on a dark and light checkered board. Two players with 12 pieces each play the game. Players take turns moving their pieces, which are flat, round **disks**.[1] They capture the other player's pieces by jumping over them.

## Origins

Who were the first people to play checkers? A similar game was well established by the time of the ancient Greeks. Famous Greeks, like Plato, mention the game, so the origin of checkers appears to date back many centuries.

**Astonishingly**,[2] the checkers game sitting on your table may have its roots in ancient Egypt. That game is not identical to how we play now. We will possibly never know how the ancient world played the game. However, historians believe the ancient Egyptian game may be similar to checkers. Alquerque is an ancient Middle Eastern game that uses dark and light round pieces. Just like checkers today, Alquerque is played on a **grid**.[3]

---

1 **disks** – flat, circular objects
2 **astonishingly** – amazingly; surprisingly
3 **grid** – pattern of lines that cross to form squares or rectangles

113

Additionally, players need to capture their **opponent**'s[4] pieces. There are some differences between Alquerque and checkers. In Alquerque, diagonal lines run through the board, and the playing pieces move along the lines. An illustration in a Spanish book from the Middle Ages shows a game of Alquerque.

By the 1100s, checkers had become the game we recognize today. Someone, probably in France, combined Alquerque with a chessboard to create the game of checkers. The same 64-square checkboard was used. The French game was called "Fierges."

*A game of checkers on top of a barrel.*

## Additional Rules

An additional rule was added to the early checkers games by the 16th century. This rule **compels**[5] capture. A player must take his opponent's piece when he can. This rule transformed the game into the checkers we love to this day. It also helps keep the game of checkers different from chess. In chess, you can choose not to take a piece if you prefer to leave it.

*A picture from Libro de los Juegos, the book written in 1283, showing men playing Alquerque.*

Different countries have slightly different checkers rules. For example, American checkers is played on a checkerboard with 64 squares. But in other countries, checkerboards have 100 squares.

---

4 **opponent** – person playing against another
5 **compels** – forces

## Modern Checkers

Checkers is a popular game in many countries around the world. But if you travel to different countries and ask to play checkers, you may just get a confused look. Many countries call the game draughts. But you will still be able to play together. Checkers and draughts are different names for the same game.

*A painting of men playing draughts, circa 1824*
*Credit: Louis-Léopold Boilly, Wikimedia*

Over time, it became clear that when **experts**[6] played in tournaments, the games often ended in a draw. A draw is when neither player wins nor loses. Something needed to happen to make this situation change. In 1934, a new rule called the three-move restriction was introduced in America. The game's first three moves are now **randomly**[7] picked from a list of different options. There are only around 300 different ways to start the game because of this rule. The game is then played twice with the chosen three-move start. Each player gets a chance to start. Players now need to think hard to win and not repeat the same moves as in the previous game.

## Solving the Game

Computer scientist Jonathan Schaeffer successfully created the first computer program that could play a game of checkers against humans. Schaeffer called his program Chinook. In 2007, he claimed that he had solved the game of checkers. He tried to prove that the game always ends in a draw if players play perfectly.

*Jonathan Schaeffer*
*Credit: Scott Mair, Wikimedia*

---

6 **experts** – specialists; people knowledgeable in a specific area
7 **randomly** – without a method or system

# Questions

1. **Circle the vocabulary word that best fits the sentence.**

   The winner's name was picked from the box *(randomly/astonishingly)*.

2. **Mark each statement as T (true) or F (false).**

   ___ The way we play checkers today is identical to how it was played in ancient Egypt.

   ___ Alquerque is played on a grid and is similar to today's checkers game.

   ___ American checkers is played on a board with 100 squares.

   ___ Checkers and draughts are different names for the same game.

3. **Number the following events in the order in which they took place.**

   ___ The three-move restriction rule was introduced in America.

   ___ A rule to force players to capture pieces was added to the checkers game.

   ___ The ancient Greeks played a game similar to checkers.

   ___ Alquerque and chess were combined to create the game of checkers.

4. **What was the author's purpose in including the sentence** *"In Alquerque, diagonal lines run through the board, and the playing pieces move along the lines."*?

   A. To teach us how to play Alquerque

   B. To explain why Alquerque is so popular

   C. To give an example of how Alquerque is different from checkers

5. **Why was it necessary to make the three-move restriction rule**

   _____

   _____

   _____

116  Lesson 24: History of Checkers

# Snake Charmers: Swaying to the Music

Some things seem too tricky for humans to master. Yet, we can do more than we realize. People have achieved the (almost) impossible. Talented circus performers dance along a tightrope. Astronauts have stood on the moon. But we do have to admit that some things are downright impossible. Time travel? Impossible! Licking your elbow? Impossible. Controlling a snake? Impossible... Or is it?

*A snake charmer*

## What Is a Snake Charmer?

Hot gusts of wind swirled down the winding, **cobbled**[1] street. A thick smell of spices hung in the air. The **harmony**[2] of chatter became a whisper on the breeze. Children laughed; adults **bartered**[3] for goods. Then suddenly, everyone froze. A snake **emerged**[4] near the clothes-dealer's stall. It sat quietly, unaware of the terror it had caused. The crowds parted. A man carrying an instrument appeared. A snake charmer! He lifted his instrument to his lips. Musical notes floated through the marketplace. The snake began to sway along with the instrument. Is this creature **hypnotized**[5]?

---

1 **cobbled** – made of pieces of rock
2 **harmony** – combination of sounds
3 **bartered** – traded goods rather than purchased with money
4 **emerged** – came out; appeared
5 **hypnotized** – put into a trance or sleep-like condition

## How Does Snake Charming Work?

Snake charming is not magic, although it would be exciting if it were! The snake charmer's skill is his instrument. Traditional snake charmers use an instrument called a pungi (pronounced PUN-jee). A pungi is a wind instrument. Its insides are similar in some ways to a clarinet.

On the floor before the snake charmer lies a small basket that holds the snake. **Captive**[6] snakes are kept specifically for the performances. The snake charmer blows into the pungi and starts to play. Musical notes fill the air. But this does not hypnotize the snake. The snake cannot hear! Instead, the snake carefully watches the instrument. It reacts to the motion of the instrument and appears to sway along with the pungi's tune. It is not at all hypnotized.

*Snake charmers often use cobras in their performances.* **Credit:** *Ghorayr, Wikimedia*

*A pungi is a musical instrument commonly used for snake charming.* **Credit:** *Kareesa Tofa, Wikimedia*

## Where Is Snake Charming Practiced?

Snake charming is an unusual skill. Ask your friends if they have seen a snake charmer. Most certainly have not! Where can we find them? Snake charming probably began in India. From there, it spread to other Asian countries. It is still practiced today. Snake charmers perform for tourists. That is their job. Learning to be a snake charmer takes time and patience. If you wished to become a snake charmer, you would start practicing from a young age. You would take some good advice and train with a non-poisonous snake. Otherwise, your practice sessions would be spent avoiding **fangs**[7] filled with **venom**![8]

---

6 **captive** – caged; imprisoned
7 **fangs** – sharp teeth
8 **venom** – poison

Snake charming used to be an important job in India. As you can imagine, people in this trade became **adept**[9] at treating snake bites, a **hazard**[10] of the job. Snake charmers branched out and worked as healers. Today snake charming is a form of street entertainment. The spare change that tourists throw their way is not enough to live on.

*Snake charming in 1870*

## Modern Snake Charmers

Snake charming is hardly a popular career choice. These kinds of traditional jobs are disappearing fast. Young people do not often want the same jobs that their parents, grandparents, and great-grandparents had.

This is not the main reason that snake charming is dying out. A **drastic**[11] change occurred in the late 1900s. India, the capital of snake charming, outlawed the practice. Why would they do this? Snake charming is dramatic and looks fascinating! Sadly, though, snake charming can be very cruel for the snake. Of course, the snake charmer wants to avoid venomous snakebites. So, some go to great lengths to **dodge**[12] a bite. They remove the snake's fangs and sometimes even sew its mouth shut. How awful! Additionally, the snakes are often kept in dirty, cramped conditions. However, although snake charming is illegal, it is still practiced to this day.

*Snake charming is still practiced today. This picture was taken in 2017.*
**Credit:** *Biswarup Ganguly, Wikimedia*

9 **adept** – skilled
10 **hazard** – risk; danger
11 **drastic** – great; extreme
12 **dodge** – avoid

# Questions

1. Circle the vocabulary word that best fits the sentence.

   *Good swimmers are usually also (**adept/drastic**) at diving.*

2. Mark each statement as T (true) or F (false).

   ___ Snake charming is a type of magic.

   ___ Snake charmers earn a lot of money.

   ___ The snakes start to sway when they hear the music playing.

   ___ Learning to become a snake charmer requires time and patience.

3. Why did snake charmers often branch out into working as healers?

   A. They were bored.

   B. They wanted to help their snakes stay healthy.

   C. They became skilled at treating snake bites.

   D. There weren't enough other doctors.

4. Which of the following sentences from the section titled *"Modern Snake Charmers"* best supports the idea that snake charming can be very cruel? Circle the correct answer.

   A. *They remove the snake's fangs and sometimes even sew its mouth shut.*

   B. *Snake charming is dramatic and looks fascinating.*

   C. *However, although snake charming is illegal, it is still practiced to this day.*

5. What would you do if you were a snake charmer and wanted to avoid getting bitten without being cruel to your snake?

   _____

   _____

   _____

# Yo Ho, Me Hearties!

*A drawing of Blackbeard*

We have so many different methods of transportation. There are airplanes, trains, trucks, and cars. Another important form of transportation is by sea. You may think crossing the ocean on a ship is old-fashioned, but ships are still useful today. Ships carry heavy loads, and they are **essential**[1] for fishing. Can you think of any other ways we use ships?

*Two ships carrying goods*

In the 1600s, ships were the only way to cross the sea. Think of the sea as a highway. Ships brought all kinds of foods from across the world. They carried expensive goods across the ocean. People journeyed to other lands on ships. Countries fought wars with ships. But the waters were not safe. The money and **products**[2] crossing the seas were perfect targets. They were too tempting. Some less-than-honest people thought, why buy goods if you can take them? Pirates were all around.

---

1 **essential** – necessary; very important
2 **products** – goods; merchandise; things for sale

## Early Life

Edward Teach was born around the year 1680. We have very little information about Teach's life before he became a pirate. We do not even know his exact birth date or the exact spelling of his **surname**!³ What we do know is that he was born in England. People have tried to discover more details about this famous pirate. Some even believe he had an honest job in the English Navy before he became a pirate. We will probably never know the details of his early life for sure.

*A model of Blackbeard's ship, the Queen Anne's Revenge.* **Credit:** *Qualiesin, Wikimedia*

## Becoming a Pirate

How does a person become a "good" pirate? Obviously, there is no such thing as a pirate school, but Edward Teach still found the perfect teacher. He learned his pirating skills from Captain Benjamin Hornigold. Teach was a good student. He was very talented in the robbing and fighting **trades**.⁴ He became a pirate captain and "worked" in the West Indies. The West Indies is the region of the seas where the Caribbean Islands are located.

*Blackbeard holding a gun on a ship*

Teach looked for a ship of his own. He was not interested in buying one. After all, he was a pirate! One day Teach found the perfect match. He readied his men and captured the French slave ship La Concorde. He then chose a new name for the ship: *Queen Anne's Revenge*. Teach armed the ship with 40 guns and more than 300 men. Teach and his men **boarded**⁵ ships at sea and stole anything valuable, including food, gold, and money. News of his pirating adventures spread. He was now a famous and feared pirate.

---

3 **surname** – last name; family name
4 **trades** – jobs; careers; professions
5 **boarded** – got on a vehicle

## Blackbeard

Teach understood people. He knew that the more he terrified them, the quicker they would surrender. Teach did not want to fight if he didn't have to.

Teach was a tall figure with a thick, long, black beard. He became known as Blackbeard because of that feature. He twisted his long black beard and tied it around his ears.

*A cannon from a shipwreck near North Carolina. It may be a cannon from Queen Anne's Revenge.*

Blackbeard also lit little candles or small sticks in his hair. Smoke would come out of his hair. This made him look even more threatening. He encouraged all the frightening stories about him. Interestingly, we have no proof that Blackbeard himself acted **violently**.[6] However, his men were certainly not people you would want to meet!

Blackbeard's pirate life was dangerous. In 1718, Blackbeard based himself in North Carolina. This great spot allowed him to **plunder**[7] ships going to and from the **harbor**.[8] He even made a deal with North Carolina Governor Charles Eden so that he could rob the ships easily. However, constantly robbing the ships angered Alexander Spotswood, governor of Virginia. He sent Lieutenant Robert Maynard to find the pirates. Maynard found Blackbeard. Blackbeard died fighting Lieutenant Maynard in 1718.

Blackbeard has become somewhat of a hero in American **legends**.[9] But it is important to remember that he was a pirate who hurt many people. There are still rumors that Blackbeard buried his treasure. Divers discovered the wreck of *Queen Anne's Revenge* off the coast of North Carolina. The treasure has not been found. Maybe there is buried treasure; but maybe there isn't. Do you think Blackbeard buried his treasure?

---

6 **violently** – fiercely; forcefully
7 **plunder** – steal; rob
8 **harbor** – port; dock
9 **legends** – historical stories that are not necessarily true

# Questions

1. Circle the vocabulary word that best fits the sentence.

   The new store sells many **(plunder/products)** that we need.

2. Mark each statement as T (true) or F (false).

   ___ Blackbeard's real name was Edward Teach.

   ___ Blackbeard and his men captured the French ship named Queen Anne's Revenge.

   ___ Blackbeard lit little candles or small sticks in his hair.

   ___ Blackbeard's treasure was found in 1718.

3. Number the following events in the order in which they took place.

   ___ Lieutenant Robert Maynard was sent to find the pirates.

   ___ Blackbeard and his men captured the French slave ship called *La Concorde*.

   ___ Blackbeard learned his pirating skills from Captain Benjamin Hornigold.

4. What was the author's purpose in including the section titled *"Becoming a Pirate"*?

   A. To explain how Teach captured *La Concorde*

   B. To explain how Teach became a famous pirate

   C. To explain why Teach did not want to buy a ship

5. Why do you think Blackbeard's treasure has never been found?

   _____

   _____

   _____

# Telescopes: Exploring the Sky

Telescopes allow us to see stars and planets.
**Credit:** Ryan Wick, Wikimedia

Besides the sun, what's the furthest thing you can see when you're outside? Maybe some clouds, a passing jet, or a bird. And at night, you can see the moon and lots of stars. But do you know that there are many things in the sky that we can't see? There are planets, **galaxies**,[1] and many more stars. If we can't see them, how do we know that they are there? **Astronomers**[2] use a special tool called a telescope. It helps them discover things in the sky. Let's find out why telescopes help us see things that our eyes alone cannot!

## Refractor and Reflector Telescopes

Telescopes make distant things look bigger. How? They do this by collecting light and **magnifying**[3] objects. To understand better, we're going to explain how two different types of telescopes work.

The first type is the refractor telescope. This kind of telescope has glass lenses. The big lens at the front is called the objective lens. It collects light from a distant object. It **focuses**[4] the light in one area called the focal plane.

---

1 **galaxies** – system of stars, planets, gas and dust, held together by gravity
2 **astronomers** – scientists who study objects in space
3 **magnify** – make something look bigger than it is
4 **focuses** – causes to meet in one place

This light forms an image. The small lens that we look through is called the eyepiece. It magnifies the image to make the object look bigger.

The second type is the reflector telescope. This kind of telescope uses mirrors instead of glass lenses. A big mirror collects light. The light **reflects**5 from this mirror to the focal plane. The light forms an image. Another smaller mirror reflects the image to the eyepiece. The eyepiece makes the image look bigger.

*A man looks through a telescope.*

## Why We Need Telescopes

Why can't our eyes see distant objects? Why do we need telescopes to help us? Our eyes collect light, similar to how telescopes collect light. This light forms an image that we see. But our eyes have relatively small **apertures**.6 They can only collect a small amount of light. They are not big enough to see distant, **faint**7 objects.

*The aperture of a telescope. The bigger the aperture, the further it can "see."*
**Credit:** H. Raab, Wikimedia

Telescopes have bigger apertures and therefore can collect more light. This makes them able to "see" further than our eyes can. They can also improve the image of objects that are very **dim**.8

---

5 **reflects** – bounces off
6 **aperture** – opening
7 **faint** – very hard to see
8 **dim** – not bright

## Inventors of the Telescope

The telescope has allowed our knowledge of the universe to grow. It has helped us discover a lot of new things. Who invented the telescope? It wasn't just one person.

A Dutch **optician**[9] named Hans Lippershey invented the first telescope in 1608. He called his invention a Looker. It made objects look three times bigger than the eye could see. This telescope was mainly used to spot ships that were far away.

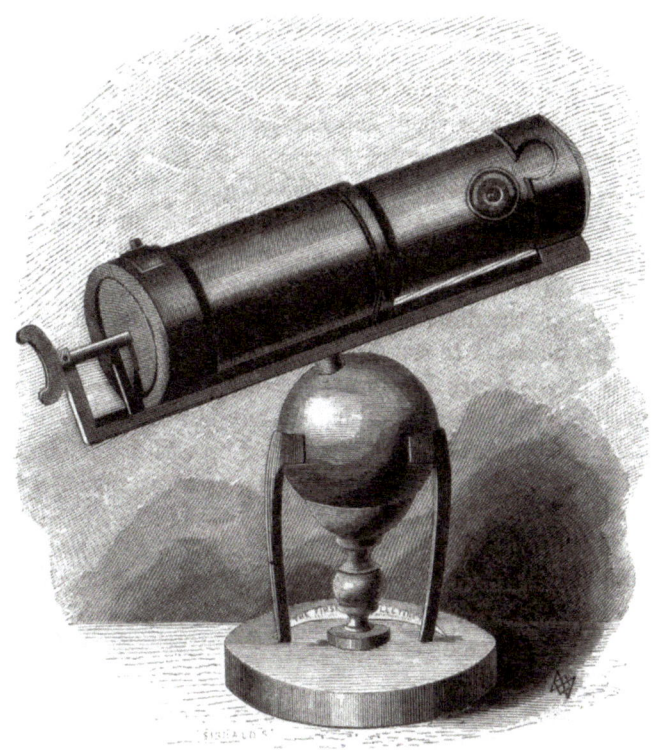

*A drawing of Sir Isaac Newton's first reflector telescope*

A scientist named Galileo Galilei heard about this invention a year later. He improved the design. His telescope made things look 20 or 30 times bigger than the eye could see. He was the first person to study astronomy using a telescope. He discovered new and interesting things about the sky, stars, and planets.

Many scientists tried to build their own telescopes after this. Johannes Kepler made a better refractor telescope in 1611. But it had a big problem: Its images were upside-down!

Sir Isaac Newton saw Kepler's telescope. He decided to improve it by using mirrors instead of glass lenses. He made the first reflector telescope in 1668. It was more powerful and more **portable**[10] than refractor telescopes. Most people use this type of telescope today.

9 **optician** – person who makes and sells glasses and contact lenses
10 **portable** – easy to carry around

# Questions

1. Circle the vocabulary word that best fits the sentence.

   The nightlight in my bedroom is very **(dim/portable)**, so it provides enough light without keeping me awake.

2. Number the following events in the order in which they took place.

   ___ Johannes Kepler made a better refractor telescope, but its images were upside-down.

   ___ Galileo Galilei improved the Looker's ability to magnify images.

   ___ Sir Isaac Newton made the first reflector telescope, using mirrors instead of glass lenses.

   ___ Hans Lippershey invented a telescope that he called the Looker.

3. Which of the following people invented the first telescope?

   A. Sir Isaac Newton

   B. Hans Lippershey

   C. Johannes Kepler

   D. Galileo Galilei

4. What was the author's purpose in including the section titled *Refractor and Reflector Telescopes*?

   A. To tell us who invented each kind of telescope

   B. To compare how each type of telescope works

   C. To help us understand how telescopes help us see distant objects

5. Why can't we see distant objects in the sky without using telescopes?

   _____

   _____

   _____

# Sea Explorations: Across and Beneath the Oceans

There is more sea than land in the world. People have sailed the seas for thousands of years. You would think that we have finished exploring the watery world surrounding us. In truth, we still know so little about the sea. Most of the ocean's depths are a mystery. Let's dive into some famous sea explorations that give us a glimpse of our blue world!

*An image of the horizon at sea.*

## Christopher Columbus (1452-1506)

We were not always able to open an **atlas**[1] and study a map of the world. People did not know what lay across the seas. North America and South America are huge, vast **continents**[2], and Europeans did not know they were there.

In 1492, Christopher Columbus set sail from Spain to find a new route to India. India had items, such as spices, that Europeans wanted to trade. Columbus sailed westward across the Atlantic Ocean from Europe, but he did not reach India. Instead, he made landfall on an island off the coast of North America.

*Historians believe this is a picture of Christopher Columbus.*

> 1 **atlas** – book of maps
> 2 **continent** – vast area of land, surrounded by ocean

129

## Ferdinand Magellan (1480-1521)

The Americas were now known to the Europeans. People understood how little they knew about what lay over the **horizon**.[3] There were continents they knew nothing about. What else was there? Could a person sail around the world? Ferdinand Magellan helped **provide**[4] the answer. He located an important crossing in South America connecting the Atlantic and Pacific Oceans. This was a major find. The crossing is named after him and is called the **Strait**[5] of Magellan. Magellan managed what no man had achieved before. He sailed all the way around the world.

*Notice the Strait of Magellan. This is the narrow strip of sea connecting the Atlantic and Pacific Oceans..*

## James Cook (1728-1779)

James Cook was an extremely skilled **cartographer**.[6] He did not have a computer or even a pen. He had no modern equipment because he lived about 300 years ago. However, his map making was **precise**.[7] The maps were so exact that they were even used in the 1900s. James Cook mapped out the east coast of Australia, New Zealand, and the Great Barrier Reef. The Great Barrier reef is the biggest coral reef in the world.

## Deep Sea Exploration

There were many more sea explorers. Some found new lands, and others mapped unknown areas. They opened up travel. They connected our world.

We knew how to sail and **navigate**[8] the seas. But what was happening beneath the surface? What if we dived down? We still had no idea of the world beneath the waves.

---

3 **horizon** – the line where it looks like the land and sky touch
4 **provide** – give; supply
5 **strait** – narrow waterway connecting two large bodies of water
6 **cartographer** – map maker
7 **precise** – exact; accurate
8 **navigate** – travel across

## Jacques Piccard (1922-2008)

Love of the sea was in Jacques Piccard's blood. It ran in the family. His father Andrew designed a special vessel called Trieste. Trieste was no ordinary boat. It could go down to the deepest part of the ocean.

*The Trieste is lifted out of the water.*

Let's understand why ordinary submarines cannot dive too far down. Fill a bucket with water. Can you lift it? It is heavy, but yes. Now fill the biggest tub you can buy. It is impossible to lift. The water is too heavy. Imagine swimming in the deepest part of the ocean. Think of the massive amount of water above. Water is extraordinarily heavy. Piccard built the Trieste to **withstand**[9] the crushing weight of the water.

In 1960, Jacques Piccard and Don Walsh used the Trieste to explore Challenger Deep, the deepest point of the ocean. It is miles deep. No one knew what was down there. Incredibly, Piccard saw that there is life, but there is no light. Amazingly enough, the water weighs too much for humans to survive outside of their specially made vessel.

*The Deepsea Challenger. This was used by James Cameron to reach the bottom of Challenger Deep.* **Credit:** *Raimond Spekking, Wikimedia*

Over 50 years later, James Cameron made this journey down by himself. It took him under two hours. Modern **technology**[10] allowed him to take videos and gather **samples**[11] from the depths of the ocean.

---

9 **withstand** – to last; not get damaged
10 **technology** – equipment; machinery; tools
11 **samples** – small bits taken to study

 **Questions**

1. Circle the vocabulary word that best fits the sentence.

   The sun setting on the *(cartographer/horizon)* was a beautiful sight.

2. Mark each statement as T (true) or F (false).

   ___ Christopher Columbus discovered a crossing connecting the Atlantic and Pacific Oceans.

   ___ James Cook used computers to draw his maps.

   ___ The Trieste was a special boat that could go down to the deepest part of the ocean.

   ___ There is no light in the deepest part of the ocean.

3. Number the following events in the order in which they took place.

   ___ James Cameron reached the bottom of Challenger Deep.

   ___ Columbus set sail and made landfall off the coast of North America.

   ___ Jacques Piccard and Don Walsh used the *Trieste* to explore Challenger Deep.

   ___ Magellan sailed all the way around the world.

4. Circle the choice that has the same meaning as the following sentence from the lesson: *Love of the sea was in Jacques Piccard's blood.*

   A. Piccard had a blood disease called "love of the sea."

   B. People in Piccard's family were interested and involved in sea travel.

   C. Piccard started bleeding whenever he went on a boat.

5. What would have happened if Magellan hadn't discovered the Magellan Strait?

   _____

   _____

   _____

# Neil Armstrong: Man on the Moon

*The Apollo 11 mission as it lifts off for space*

Everyone knows what the moon is. Each evening, children look up at the sky and search in all directions trying to spot the moon. People have been curious about the moon for thousands of years. What is it like there? Can we walk on the moon? Now let's read about the day that answered these questions.

## Neil Armstrong

Let us begin our trip to the moon with a man named Neil Armstrong. Armstrong was born in August 1930 in Wapakoneta, Ohio. At the young age of six, Armstrong took his first airplane ride, and he loved it. His life of flying had begun. Armstrong became a naval aviator in 1949. A naval aviator is someone who flies aircraft for the navy. Later, Armstrong started working at NASA. Have you heard of NASA? NASA stands for National Aeronautics and Space Administration. It is a United States government agency that is in charge of space **technology**.[1]

Armstrong learned new skills and worked in several different areas at NASA. Armstrong spent lots of time in aircraft. He flew jets, helicopters, gliders, and rockets. We can certainly **assume**[2] that he loved flying and was not afraid of heights! Armstrong did not have an ordinary job. He found a job that was out of this world – literally. In 1963, Neil Armstrong became an astronaut.

---

1 **technology** – practical application of knowledge
2 **assume** – decide without proof

133

## Apollo 11

Apollo 11 was a spacecraft with a special **mission**.[3] It was going to land on the moon. Although other spaceships had already flown to the moon, none had landed on it. Apollo 11 took off on Wednesday, July 16, 1969. On board were three astronauts: Neil Armstrong, Buzz Aldrin, and Michael Collins. The spacecraft also carried a lunar module called Eagle. A lunar module is a special vehicle with one purpose. It transports astronauts from a spaceship to the moon's surface, and back again.

*Neil Armstrong*

Armstrong and Aldrin were going to land on the moon. Michael Collins stayed behind to **operate**[4] the spaceship. Imagine being part of the first mission to land on the moon and not actually stepping foot on it!

## Landing on the Moon

Four days into their journey, Armstrong and Aldrin boarded the Eagle and landed on the moon. At least 600 million people were watching or listening to broadcasts all over the world. This was a day people had only dreamed of! It seemed more like a fairy tale than **reality**.[5] As Armstrong stepped out onto the moon, he said, "One small step for man, one giant leap for mankind." What an achievement! The astronauts **fixed**[6] a flagpole on the moon, flying an American flag. Armstrong and Aldrin got busy on the moon. They collected rocks and moon dust to study when they returned to Earth.

*The lunar module Eagle took Neil Armstrong and Buzz Aldrin to the moon's surface.*

---

3 **mission** – job; purpose
4 **operate** – to perform a function
5 **reality** – truth; actual occurrence
6 **fixed** – placed; positioned

The moon is different from Earth. There is no water, no rain, and no wind. Nothing to wash or blow anything away. So, if you go up to the moon today, you can still see Neil Armstrong's footprints.

## Returning Home

After 21 hours and 36 minutes on the moon, the astronauts began their long journey home. After they arrived back on Earth, they were placed in **quarantine**.[7] No one had been to the moon before. Scientists did not know if any dangerous germs had traveled back with the astronauts. After 18 days, they left quarantine and properly celebrated their amazing experience.

Incredibly, our cell phones today are more powerful than the computers used on Apollo 11. Would you be brave enough to fly to the moon using that **ancient**[8] technology?

*Armstrong and Aldrin set up the U.S. flag on the moon.*

*Armstrong and Aldrin set up the U.S. flag on the moon.*

7 **quarantine** – keep away from others to prevent the spread of disease
8 **ancient** – very old

# Questions

1. Circle the vocabulary word that best fits the sentence.

   It is safe to (**reality/assume**) that it will be hot tomorrow.

2. Mark each statement as T (true) or F (false).

   ___ Apollo 11 was the second spaceship to have landed on the moon.

   ___ Neil Armstrong and Michael Collins boarded the Eagle and landed on the moon.

   ___ A naval aviator is someone who flies aircraft for the navy.

   ___ If you go up to the moon today, you can still see Neil Armstrong's footprints.

3. Number the following events in the order in which they took place.

   ___ Neil Armstrong began working at NASA.

   ___ Neil Armstrong became an astronaut.

   ___ Neil Armstrong became a naval aviator.

4. What did Armstrong mean when he said the following?

   *"One small step for man, one giant leap for mankind."*

   A. There was only one step to go down when exiting the Eagle.

   B. Landing on the moon was a huge accomplishment for mankind.

   C. He would take small steps and Aldrin would take giant leaps as they moved around on the moon.

5. Why can Neil Armstrong's footsteps still be seen on the moon today?

   _____

   _____

   _____

# Living Off the Congo River

*The Congo River glows in the rising sun.*
**Credit:** Lkcl it, Wikimedia

What are some things you use water for? Drinking? Brushing your teeth? Washing your clothing? Cooking? The people who live near the Congo River rely on the river's water to live as well. But they use the Congo River for much more than just drinking and washing clothing. Let's discover how the Congo River helps people living near it.

## Fishing in the Congo River's Rapids

Even though Joseph is only ten years old, he already has a job. In the morning, he goes to school. His school only has one room in it and very few books. At noon, Joseph leaves school and runs to join his family for work. Joseph works as a fisherman. He lives in a **rural**[1] village in the Democratic Republic of the Congo, also called the DRC. The DRC is a country in Africa. The Congo River flows in a curved path around much of the country. The Congo River is the second-largest river in Africa and the ninth-longest river in the world. It is the deepest river in the world. Some parts of it are as deep as 720 feet. It is so deep that if 40 giraffes were stacked up on top of each other, they wouldn't reach the river's surface in some places.

Joseph's whole life **revolves**[2] around the Congo River. His village is near the river's powerful **rapids**.[3] Joseph's family uses the rapids to catch fish. His family builds wooden poles and ladders.

---

1 **rural** – countryside; not in the city
2 **revolves** – is concerned with; is focused on
3 **rapids** – fast-flowing parts of a river with strong currents

They use these **structures**[4] to hang over the rapids. Then they **cast**[5] wooden baskets into the water. The baskets are cone-shaped. The rapids push fish into these baskets. The fish cannot swim out because the water moves too fast, and they are trapped inside. Joseph's family pulls the baskets out of the water and takes the fish out of them.

Putting the baskets in the water and pulling them out of the water is dangerous. To do this job, the men must brave the rapids. As he climbs into the water to set up a basket, Joseph hangs on tightly to the wooden beams and vines. If he lets go, the fast-moving water could sweep him away.

People use the Congo River's rapids to help them catch fish.
Credit: Julian Harneis, Wikimedia

## The Congo River Basin

The Congo River helps Joseph's family in other ways, too. The land that the Congo River surrounds is watered by the river. This makes it a good place for plants and trees to grow. A river basin is where all the rainwater and other water in an area collects and then

The Congo River Basin covers a large part of Central Africa. The Congo River runs through the Congo rainforest.
Credit: MONUSCO Photos, Wikimedia

flows into a river. Nearly all of the DRC is in the Congo River Basin. The Congo River Basin is the second-largest river basin in the world. Its **runoff**[6] feeds the Congo rainforest. Joseph's family uses wood from the forest to build canoes and fish traps.

---

4 **structures** – buildings
5 **cast** – throw
6 **runoff** – draining water

## Riding the Congo River

The Congo rainforest is home to many different types of animals, including the lowland gorilla and the African forest elephant.
*Credit: Thomas Breuer, Wikimedia*

But sometimes, Joseph's family needs something they cannot get from the river. His mother sometimes needs new knives to prepare the fish the men have caught. Sometimes, his father needs oil to power the generator they use for electricity.

The river also comes in handy when Joseph's family needs to trade or travel. It is the fastest way to travel across the DRC. The Congo River connects villages that don't have roads. Some people travel the river on long wooden canoes called pirogues. Others travel by **barge**[7].

*Pirogues are traditional canoes used by people in the Congo.*
**Credit:** *Julian Harneis, Wikimedia*

The barges are sometimes called floating villages, and it's easy to see why. They **consist**[8] of a motor-powered tugboat at the front. The tugboat tows barges behind it. Sometimes a single boat can pull dozens of barges. The barges are piled with all sorts of goods. More than 2,000 passengers can live on the barge as well. They build tents and huts on the barges to sleep in and shade them from the hot sun. Sometimes the journey takes months.

---

7 **barge** – flat-bottomed boat
8 **consist** – made up of

## Facts About the River

Most of the Congo River is in the DRC, but parts run through other African countries. It runs through the Central African Republic, the Congo, Angola, Zambia, and Tanzania. The river begins on the west coast of Africa.

*Tugboats pull barges slowly along the Congo River.* **Credit:** *Julian Harneis, Wikimedia*

The Congo River feeds the Congo rainforest, the second-largest rainforest in the world. Some of the animals and plants in the forest are found nowhere else in the world! Chimpanzees, gorillas, and elephants are just a few animals living there. The Congo River Basin has three parts to it. The upper part of the river basin has fast-moving water called rapids. The middle part has calmer water, and the lower part has small waterfalls and deep gorges.

# Questions

**Circle the vocabulary word that best fits the sentence.**

*It is very relaxing to spend the summer in a (rural/runoff) setting.*

**Mark each statement as T (true) or F (false).**

___ The DRC surrounds the Congo River.

___ The Congo River is the second-largest river in Africa.

___ The Congo River Basin is the fastest way to travel across the DRC.

___ The Congo rainforest contains animals and plants found nowhere else in the world.

**Number the following events in the order in which they take place.**

___ Joseph's family casts wooden baskets into the water.

___ Joseph's family takes the fish out of the baskets.

___ The river rapids push fish into the baskets.

___ Joseph's family builds wooden poles and ladders.

**Which of the following sentences from the second-to-last paragraph of the lesson supports the idea that traveling by barge can be dangerous?**

*The barges are an inexpensive way to travel.*

*The extra weight means that they may not be able to stay afloat.*

*Sometimes the engine breaks down, and the barge is delayed.*

**Do you think it is easy to travel by barge? Why or why not?**

_____

_____

_____

141

# Stamps and Coins: Collecting History

Do you have a collection? Or do you know someone who does? People like to collect all sorts of things. From stickers to keychains, it's always fun to add something to a collection! Did you know that collecting things is not new? Let's discover two different things that people have been collecting for many years.

*There is great variety in a coin collection like this.*
**Credit:** *Udaykumar236, Wikimedia*

## Coins: Not Just Metal

Collecting coins is a **hobby**.[1] It is one of the oldest hobbies in the world. Collectors look for old or unusual coins. The coins are kept in an album. Some people enjoy collecting coins for fun. Other people have a collection because the coins can be **valuable**.[2] The value of coins depends on their **condition**[3] and how **rare**[4] they are. Rare coins or coins with mistakes can be worth a lot of money. Coins in good condition are much more valuable than coins with a **matte**[5] finish and **hairline**[6] scratches.

What kind of coins do collectors look for? Beginner collectors might collect all types of coins from all over the world. Serious collectors only collect one type of coin. Some collectors might only want ancient Greek coins. Some people only look for coins that have a picture of a famous ruler on them. There may also be collectors who only want coins from certain years.

---

1 **hobby** – something that people do for fun
2 **valuable** – worth a lot of money
3 **condition** – quality
4 **rare** – not often found; uncommon
5 **matte** – dull; with no shine
6 **hairline** – thin

## Stamps: More Than Paper

The first postage stamps were made in 1840, and collecting stamps has been popular since then. By 1860, there were already thousands of stamp collectors and **dealers**[7] around the world. At first, it was mostly children and teenagers who were interested in stamp collecting. Adults thought it was a childish thing to do. But not long afterward, they also got interested in collecting.

*Albums like this keep a collection neat and organized.* **Credit:** *Billjones94, Wikimedia*

Stamps are not just pieces of paper. Each stamp has a story, and collectors can learn a lot from their stamps. They can discover some history and learn about the country the stamp comes from.

Collectors only look for stamps in good condition. Stamps that are torn or **faded**[8] are not worth anything. There are so many stamps around that only rare stamps are valuable.

Stamp collectors usually collect one type of stamp. Some examples are stamps from one country, yellow stamps, or stamps with animals on them.

## What Stamps and Coins Have in Common

*A page from a stamp album showing stamps from Sweden.* **Credit:** *bomont57, Wikimedia*

Where do collectors find stamps or coins for their collections? Coin collectors used to find interesting coins in their pockets. Stamp collectors would find stamps on their own pieces of mail. Today, it is done differently. A lot of collectors buy from dealers on the computer.

7 **dealers** – people who buy and sell
8 **faded** – lost color

Collectors also go to stamp or coin shows. At these shows, there are many dealers selling stamps or coins. Collectors look around for things they can add to their collections.

Collectors also enjoy going to clubs, where they meet other collectors like themselves. They discuss and show each other their collections. They can also trade stamps or coins there.

*A booth at the large Stampex stamp show in London.* **Credit:** *Philafrenzy, Wikimedia*

Do stamp and coin collections need any special tools? Collectors who are beginning need just a few things. An album keeps the collection neat and organized. A magnifying glass is important for looking closely at the stamps or coins. Coin collectors use gloves, so they don't get fingerprints on the coins. Stamp collectors use special tweezers called **tongs**[9] to move their stamps. The tongs keep the stamps from tearing or bending.

## Stamps or Coins?

Collecting stamps is more popular than collecting coins. This is because stamps are not expensive and are easy to find. There are so many different stamps that there are enough for everyone. Although stamp collecting is not as popular now as it was in the early 1900s, about 200 million people still collect stamps today.

*A booth at the large Stampex stamp show in London.* **Credit:** *Philafrenzy, Wikimedia*

Collecting coins is becoming less common. Good coins are hard to find, and they can be expensive. Most coins need to be bought, and some of them cost a lot of money. But this also means that coin collections are more valuable than stamp collections.

No matter what a person is collecting, it's not only for the value. It's really all about the fun!

9 **tongs** – tweezer-like tool for gripping things

# Questions

1. Circle the vocabulary word that best fits the sentence.

    Some people use *(dealers/tongs)* to turn the hot dogs on the barbecue grill.

2. Mark each statement as T (true) or F (false)

    ___ Stamp collecting is one of the oldest hobbies in the world.

    ___ Coins with mistakes are not worth very much money.

    ___ People can learn about a country's history from its stamps.

    ___ Torn or faded stamps are not worth anything.

3. Which of the following are tools that collectors might use?

    A. Magnifying glass

    B. Gloves

    C. Tongs

    D. All of the above

4. Which of the following sentences from the section titled *"Stamps or Coins?"* supports the idea that coin collections are worth more than stamp collections?

    A. *Collecting stamps is more popular than collecting coins.*

    B. *Collecting coins is becoming less common.*

    C. *But this also means that coin collections are more valuable than stamp collections.*

5. If you decided to have a collection, would you rather collect stamps or coins? Why?

    _____

    _____

    _____

# Everglades National Park

*One of Everglades' entrances*
**Credit:** Ken Lund from Reno, Nevada, USA, Wikimedia

Where can you see alligators, dolphins, snakes, and hundreds of fish and birds in one place? *Clue: I don't mean the zoo.* Did you say Everglades National Park? That's right! Get ready for some fun... In this lesson, we're going to explore this incredible park from top to toe!

## Let's explore!

Everglades National Park is located in southern Florida. A whopping one and a half million acres in size, it's the third largest natural park in America. Over a million people come to see its beautiful landscape and wide **variety**[1] of wildlife every year.

One and a half million acres can't be explored in one afternoon! So, let's imagine we have a few days to spend in the park. In Everglades National Park, visitors are allowed to camp overnight. So grab your rucksack and sleeping bag, and let's go!

## Habitats

There are five different habitats in Everglades. On our tour, we'll start with the habitat called hammock. Moving on from there, we'll visit mangrove, pineland, sawgrass, and slough. During the summer months, these habitats look very different from how they look in the winter. Winter is the dry season. During the dry season, from December to April, visitors can see over 400 species of birds.

1 **variety** – selection

And with these birds come their predators: alligators, crocodiles, and **panthers**.² The summer, from May to November, is the wet season. During the wet season, there is a lot of rain and mosquitoes. Because of this, not as many activities are available for visitors.

*A bird silhouetted against the Everglades sunset*

## Hammock

Less than half a mile long, the hammock trail is one of the easier trails in the Everglades. Why is it called the Hammock Trail? A "hammock" in nature means a **dense**³ group of trees surrounded by water. The area where the trees grow is slightly higher than the surrounding water. Therefore, the area is like a hammock for the trees and vegetation. Don't leave this trail before you've seen the enormous 70-foot-tall mahogany tree!

## Mangrove

Trees that can survive in salty water are called mangroves. To explore this habitat, we're going to take a ride in an airboat. An airboat is a flat-bottomed boat powered by an airplane propeller in the back. The water in mangrove is very shallow and **marshy**.⁴ 

*An alligator makes its way into the water.*
**Credit:** *Wilafa, Wikimedia*

A regular boat can't drive through it, but an airboat can glide over it. Some of the mangrove trees have roots that stick out above the water. This gives them a special look, as if they're standing on the water. As we glide along the water, count how many bird species you can spot. Did you catch a glimpse of any birds of prey? The osprey, bald eagle, and kingfisher can be spotted swooping into the water to catch fish. Try to get a close-up look at the trees near the water. There are frogs, turtles, snakes, and even alligators sneaking around over there!

---

2 **panthers** – large American leopards, usually black
3 **dense** – crowded together
4 **marshy** – swampy; muddy

## Pinelands

Welcome to the pine forest trail!

This trail is in the shape of a loop. Look out for signs as we walk between the tall pine trees. Did you spot the sign with a picture of snails? If you look carefully at the pines, you'll see some beautiful Liguus tree snails. Like snowflakes, every Liguus snail looks slightly different.

Don't get too near those trees, though! The next sign warns us of poisonwood. The **sap**[5] of poisonwood trees is ten times more poisonous than poison ivy!

## Sawgrass

After seeing the sawgrass habitat, I think we'll decide to give it a skip! Do you know why it's called sawgrass? Along the side of every blade of grass are tiny, tooth-like **ridges**.[6] These teeth can give you cuts like paper cuts. And if you would step into a field of sawgrass, guess what? You would find that these scary blades are about the same height as a fourth-grader!

Let's get out of here!

## Slough

Pronounced slew, a slough is a slow-moving body of deep water. Even in the dry season, this trail can only be reached by a bridge. This marshy water eventually leads into Florida Bay. There, we might be lucky enough to spot some playful bottleneck dolphins! What an exciting way to end our day at Everglades National Park!

*Dolphins surf the waves.*
*Credit: Alessandro Caproni, Wikimedia*

---

5 **sap** – fluid that seeps out of trees
6 **ridges** – raised surfaces

# Questions

1. Circle the vocabulary word that best fits the sentence.

   *The cafeteria has a large **(variety/panther)** of food to pick from.*

2. Mark each statement as T (true) or F (false).

   ___ Everglades National Park is located off the coast of Florida.

   ___ Mangroves are animals that live in salty water.

   ___ Liguus tree snails can be seen on the pine forest trail.

   ___ A slough is a slow-moving body of deep water.

3. Why aren't there many activities available for visitors during the Everglades' wet season?

   A. The park workers don't want to come to work then.

   B. The birds all fly to Florida for the winter months.

   C. There is too much snow.

   D. There is a lot of rain and mosquitoes.

4. Which of the following sentences from the section titled *"Mangrove"* supports the idea that it is best to explore the Mangrove in an airboat?

   A. Trees that can survive in salty water are called mangroves.

   B. A regular boat can't drive through it, but an airboat can glide over it.

   C. Some of the mangrove trees have roots that stick out above the water.

5. Why is the Sawgrass habitat called that?

   _____
   _____
   _____

# Davy Crockett: The Lion of the West

*Davy Crockett was known for being a man of many adventures.*

They say he wore a cap of raccoon skin at all times. They say that he was the best hunter on the American **frontier**.[1] According to legend, Davy Crockett wrestled a bear at three years old—and won! He fought alligators and mountain lions by hand! Davy knew every tree in the forest! Or did he?

## Davy Crockett: An American Legend:

These stories are fun and exciting. But they are only legends. They are not necessarily true. However, Davy Crockett did really live. He was born in 1786, more than 200 years ago.

Davy led an exciting life. He also liked to tell stories, and he got people to listen to him. Because of this, Davy Crockett was a household name even during his lifetime. In 1831, when Davy was in his 50s, someone wrote a play about him. It was called "The Lion of the West." The play was full of fantastic stories. But who was the real Davy Crockett?

## Davy Crockett's Childhood

Shortly after the play came out, Davy Crockett wrote an **autobiography**.[2] He told about his own childhood. Davy was born to a large family. He had four older brothers and sisters and four younger brothers and sisters. Davy's family lived in Tennessee.

---

1 **frontier** – the last area of settled land before a wilderness
2 **autobiography** – story that one writes about one's own life

151

At the time, Tennessee was the American frontier. Places like New York, Boston, and Philadelphia were already cities. But Tennessee had just been **settled**[3] by American colonists. It had no post offices, banks, or shopping malls. As frontier settlers, Davy's family built a rough log cabin—by hand. They grew their own food and hunted for meat. Therefore, Davy learned to hunt at a very young age.

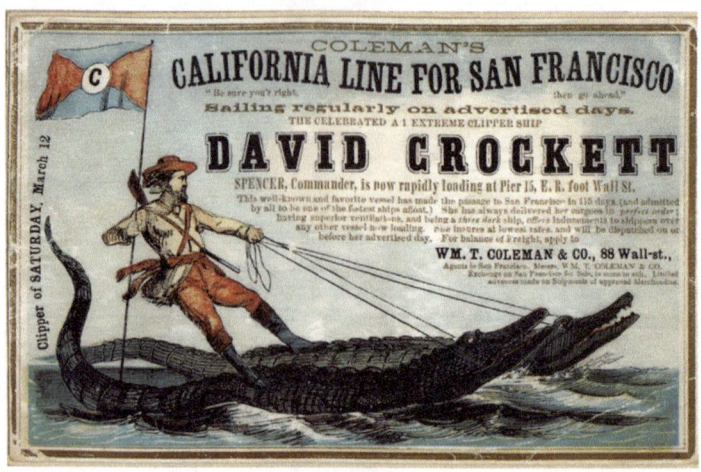

*This advertisement for a ship named after Davy Crockett shows the legends about the man.*

The Tennessee frontier town had a small schoolhouse. Davy's father didn't have a lot of money. Still, he thought it was important for his sons to go to school. Davy's father paid a lot of money to send Davy and his brothers to school.

*This drawing shows what it may have been like for frontier fur traders during Davy Crockett's time.*

Davy lasted in school for exactly four days. Then, he got into a fight with another boy. Davy worried that he would get into trouble for fighting, so he stopped going to school. Every morning, he would leave the house with his brothers. Instead of going to class, however, Davy headed for the woods. He spent the days hiking and learning about the frontier world. At the end of the day, the school bell rang. Davy met up with his brothers and returned home.

After a few months of skipping school and playing in the woods, Davy got caught. The school principal met with his father and asked why Davy hadn't been in school. Davy's father was **furious**![4] He had paid so much money to send Davy to school. Davy feared being punished, so he ran away.

---

3 **settled** – made into a permanent place to live
4 **furious** – very angry

At age 13, Davy started to travel on his own through rural Tennessee. He found different jobs, working as a **farmhand**[5] and as a cowboy. Finally, after three years away, Davy returned home. He started working for his father. He returned to school and learned to read and write.

*This is how Davy Crockett probably dressed when serving as a representative, not living as a frontiersman.*

## Davy Crockett: Frontiersman and Statesman

After he finished school, Crockett married and moved to a farm of his own. He worked many different jobs. He worked as a fur trader. He also fought for the United States Army against Native American tribes in the area. Crockett opened a mill and started a business. People really liked the frontiersman who told such colorful stories. Crockett decided to use this popularity to get involved in **politics**.[6] Eventually, Crockett was elected to the Tennessee state legislature. Then he was elected to **represent**[7] Tennessee in Congress. He headed to Washington, D.C.

As a congressman, Crockett became even more famous. He also made some enemies. For example, Crockett fought with the president of the United States, Andrew Jackson. He disagreed with Jackson's decision to force Native Americans to relocate in the Oklahoma territory. Crockett's choice was not a popular one, and he lost the next election.

*An artist painted what he thought the Battle of the Alamo looked like.*

## Davy Crockett Heads to Texas

Crockett was upset about losing the election. He wanted to stay in politics. But, after he lost, Crockett decided to move to Texas. A war was being fought there. American and Mexican soldiers were fighting for control of Texas.

---

5 **farmhand** – person hired to help with chores on a farm
6 **politics** – having to do with the process of government
7 **represent** – act on behalf of another, such as a group

Crockett fought in a battle known as the "Battle of the Alamo." He fought bravely, but the American side was greatly outnumbered. All the Americans in that battle lost their lives, including Davy Crockett. Much folklore spread about the man known as Davy Crockett. His real life was full of exciting adventures, too. He may not have hand-wrestled bears, but he did travel hundreds of miles as a cowboy at age 15. Which do you think is more interesting—the true story or the legends?

**Crockett's Death**

When Davy Crockett moved to Texas, it was even more of a frontier than Tennessee had been. It was also at war. Many Americans had moved to Texas over the years. However, the United States had not been in charge of the state. Instead, the Spanish ruled Texas.

Then the Spanish decided to give up some of their land. Control of Texas passed to Mexico. This made the Americans living in Texas very angry. They didn't want to be part of Mexico!

The Americans in Texas formed a small army, and Crockett joined up. He traveled with the army to a small fort near the Texas-Mexico border. The fort was called the Alamo. Crockett and the men with him were determined to guard the fort, no matter what. Meanwhile, Mexico was determined to take back the fort, no matter what. Mexican general Santa Anna sent a huge army to fight the Americans in the Alamo. The men in the fort did not have enough men to guard it. But they refused to give up.

On February 23, Santa Anna's men reached the Alamo. They started to attack using cannons and guns. The fort had thick walls, so at first, the men were safe inside. They climbed the walls and shot back at the Mexicans. The fort was surrounded by the enemy for 13 days. On the last day, the Mexican army was able to enter. They fought the Americans hand-to-hand. After a few hours, the battle was over. Santa Anna's forces had defeated the small American band. Davy Crockett and his fellow soldiers were all dead.

But those 13 days gave General Sam Houston enough time to build up a large army of his own. Houston's men attacked Santa Anna's men in April. Houston's men were angry about the deaths of Crockett and the others. During the battle, they cried out, "Remember the Alamo!" They fought hard and won. After Santa Anna gave up, Texas first became an independent republic. Then, in 1845, it became part of the United States.

# Questions

1. **Circle the vocabulary word that best fits the sentence.**

    *His father was (furious/frontier) when he heard what happened.*

2. **Mark each statement as T (true) or F (false).**

    ___ Legends are stories told about people that are known to be true.

    ___ Davy Crockett graduated high school and went to college.

    ___ Davy Crockett served in the Tennessee legislature and in Congress.

    ___ Davy Crockett lost his life fighting in the Battle of the Alamo.

3. **Number the following events in the order in which they took place.**

    ___ Davy Crockett learned to read and write.

    ___ Davy Crockett worked as a farmhand and cowboy.

    ___ Davy Crockett traveled from Tennessee to Texas.

    ___ Davy Crockett became a businessman.

4. **What was the author's purpose in including the third paragraph in the section titled** *"Davy Crockett: Frontiersman and Statesman"*?

    A. To explain why Crockett lost a congressional election

    B. To explain how Crockett got involved in politics

    C. To explain how Crockett was killed in the Battle of the Alamo

5. **Why did Crockett become so popular?**

    _____

    _____

    _____

# Stop Bugging Me! Ladybugs and Spiders

*A ladybug crawling on a leaf*
**Credit:** *Sander Lamme, Wikimedia*

Did you ever say, "stop bugging me"? Many people think bugs, also called **insects**,[1] are yucky. They climb all over, sometimes running past **unexpectedly**.[2] People seem to put a lot of effort into killing bugs. But some bugs are helpful to people. Even though they are tiny, there are certain things only they can do.

## How Ladybugs Look

Ladybugs are among the prettiest bugs. They are often shiny red. They crawl around slowly, step by step, on their six legs. Ladybugs are harmless to people. They are sometimes called ladybird beetles, because they are in the beetle family.

There are thousands of different types of ladybugs. Not all are red. Some are yellow or orange. Most ladybugs have dark spots on their wings. Some are striped, but some don't have markings on them. Ladybugs lay lots of eggs at once, and leave them on a leaf to **hatch**.[3] These little bugs can live in many different places, including cities, forests, or grasslands. They are often found along rivers, as well.

---

1 **insects** – small creatures with an outer shell instead of a backbone, three pairs of legs, and pairs of wings
2 **unexpectedly** – without any warning; suddenly; by surprise
3 **hatch** – be born; come out

Did you ever notice that ladybugs are only around in the summer? That's because they hibernate all winter. They look for a dark, warm place to gather in large groups and sleep through the cold season.

Many different kinds of birds, frogs, and spiders would like to eat ladybugs. But don't worry, the ladybug has several tricks to keep its predators away. Ladybugs can stay very still, pretending to be dead, so that others won't want to eat them. They can also let out a smelly and bad-tasting oil whenever they think there is danger around. Their bright red color helps the bigger bugs remember this if they ever forget. In that way, their red color protects them.

Ladybugs' bright, red color reminds other bugs to stay away!

## How Ladybugs Are Useful

Ladybugs are helpful to farmers. There are tiny bugs called aphids that often eat from plants while they are still growing. The ladybugs swoop in to save the day! They feast on the aphids, sometimes even 75 in one day. That can add up to 5,000 aphids gone in a ladybug's lifetime! Ladybugs also eat other tiny plant-eating bugs, like scale insects, leafhoppers, worms, and mites. That keeps the plants healthy and bug-free. Some farmers don't have ladybugs living **naturally**[4] on their farms. Sometimes they buy bags of ladybugs and spread them around. In this way, they keep their farm free of the bugs that are bad for their plants.

A ladybug creeps toward a group of aphids.

4 **naturally** – by nature; happening by itself

## Spiders

*Most spiders look scarier than they really are.*

Many other types of little creatures are also helpful in a garden. You might be surprised to hear this, but one of them is the spider. A lot of people are afraid of spiders.

That is because certain types of spiders can bite you. But most spiders can't really hurt you.

There are many types of spiders, and most are dark-colored. They don't have ears but can **detect**[5] sound through their eight legs. All spiders spin silk thread from their bodies. Most spiders spin webs to catch their food. Some spiders can spin several different types of silk. Spiders like to snack on other insects, and some big spiders can even eat lizards!

So, spiders are helpful to have around. If you have one in your house, it can eat all the moths, flies, and mosquitoes that get stuck on its web. It can even eat insects that carry diseases. On a farm, spiders do the same job, killing all the small creepy crawlers that want to eat the **crops**.[6]

Now that you know more about these little creatures, you won't try to run away if you see one. You might even thank it for coming!

---

5 **detect** – notice; sense
6 **crops** – plants grown for food

 # Questions

1. Circle the vocabulary word that best fits the sentence.

   The car stopped (**unexpectedly/naturally**) and almost caused an accident.

2. Mark each statement as T (true) or F (false).

   ___ Ladybugs and spiders are helpful to farmers.

   ___ Ladybugs and spiders both have eight legs.

   ___ All ladybugs are red and have markings.

   ___ Ladybugs hibernate all winter.

3. Place a check mark next to each statement that correctly describes spiders.

   ___ They can detect sound through their eight legs.

   ___ They are usually shiny red and crawl around slowly.

   ___ They are helpful to have around because they eat other bugs.

   ___ They hibernate all winter.

4. Which sentence in the lesson supports the statement that we only notice ladybugs in the summertime? Circle the correct answer.

   A. *These little bugs can live in many different places, including cities, forests, or grasslands.*

   B. *Some farmers don't have ladybugs living naturally on their farms.*

   C. *That's because they hibernate all winter.*

5. What do you think would happen if there were no spiders in your house?

   _____

   _____

   _____

160  Lesson 34: Stop Bugging Me! Ladybugs and Spiders

# Zookeepers: Keeping the Animals Happy

*A zookeeper shows an eagle to visitors.*
**Credit:** *William Warby from London, England, Wikimedia*

Have you ever heard someone say, "It's like a zoo in here!"? Usually, when people say that, they mean that things are very messy or confusing. But really, zoos are very well-run, organized places where the animals are well-cared for. People often don't realize what hard work it is to be a zookeeper. Today we're going to read some things about zookeepers that may surprise you.

## How Does a Person Become a Zookeeper?

For people who love animals, being a zookeeper is a dream job. A lot of people want to become a zookeeper. There are certain things you must do to **qualify**.[1] Most zoos will only accept those who have at least a high school education. A college **degree**[2] in **zoology**[3] or another life science is usually also needed. Experience is also very important. Zoos want their zookeepers to know as much as possible about dealing with animals. The best way to know is to practice! That's why many zookeepers start out by volunteering at a local zoo, **veterinarian's**[4] office, or animal shelter.

---

1 **qualify** – be fit to do something
2 **degree** – certification that one receives from a college after studying a certain topic
3 **zoology** – the study of animals
4 **veterinarian** – an animal doctor

161

## What Do Zookeepers Do?

The answer is: Lots of things! A zookeeper has many responsibilities, and every day brings something new! Here are just some of the things that zookeepers are busy with:

*Cleaning enclosures:* Being a zookeeper isn't just about petting cute animals. Zookeepers have to get right into dirty animal enclosures and give them a good clean. You don't **relish**[5] the idea of shoveling up lots of animal droppings? Then zookeeping may not be for you!

*A zookeeper feeds a giraffe.*
**Credit:** *Kmajiks, Wikimedia*

*Feeding the animals:* Zookeepers try to feed animals the food they would eat in the wild. This is a big job. Every animal needs different foods. Elephants, for example, usually get fed carrots, apples, and bananas. Bears, on the other hand, are commonly fed salmon, rabbit, and chicken. Feeding animals is an expensive business. Huge amounts of meat, fruit, and grain need to be provided every day.

*Training the Animals:* Animals can be trained to do all sorts of things. For example, monkeys can be trained to use new toys for enjoyment. Sometimes animals are trained to do things for visitor shows. Usually, animals are trained with food rewards. Have you ever watched a seal show? Did you notice what happened every time the seal did what the zookeeper asked it to do? The zookeeper would feed it a fish! These rewards encourage the animals to do what the zookeeper wants them to do.

*A zookeeper encourages a seal to perform.* **Credit:** *User:Piotrus, Wikimedia*

5 **relish** – enjoy greatly

Lesson 35: Zookeepers: Keeping the Animals Happy

## A Day in the Life of a Zookeeper

Zookeepers can work all hours of the day, sometimes even through the night. For example, suppose an animal is being born—someone needs to be there to help!

Zookeepers don't know exactly what time they'll get home from work each day. Animals can be **unpredictable**[6] at times. For example, it's not always easy to get the animals into their enclosures for the night.

*A tiger posing with his front paws on a log*

On a hot day, the animals are not **keen**[7] to go indoors. On a cold day, the animals might just want to cuddle up inside. If they don't do what the zookeeper wants them to do at the right time, it can interfere with the zookeeper's schedule.

Often, out of all the animals in the zoo, at least one will be sick. The zookeeper will look after it and give it the medication it needs. What happens, though, if the animal doesn't like the medicine? In that case, the zookeeper will hide it in a delicious treat! If it's a tiger, that might mean **concealing**[8] it in a piece of cheese—a tiger's favorite!

---

6 **unpredictable** – unreliable; not dependable
7 **keen** – eager; excited
8 **concealing** – hiding

 # Questions

1. Circle the vocabulary word that best fits the sentence.

   *They wanted to enter the race, but they didn't **(qualify/relish)**.*

2. Mark each statement as T (true) or F (false).

   ___ Zookeepers always know ahead of time what will happen at work that day.

   ___ The one thing zookeepers never do is clean the animals' enclosures.

   ___ Many zookeepers start out by volunteering at a local zoo, veterinarian's office, or animal shelter.

   ___ All animals like to take their medicine.

3. What is the main reason zookeepers feed treats to animals?

   A. They don't want the animals to be hungry between meals.

   B. They want to encourage the animals to do certain actions.

   C. They don't know what else to do with the leftover food.

4. Which of the following statements best summarizes the first two sentences in the section titled *"A Day in the Life of a Zookeeper"*?

   A. Animals would rather be indoors than outdoors.

   B. A zookeeper can't always count on going home on time because sometimes unexpected things happen.

   C. Animals always give birth at night.

5. Have you ever seen a zookeeper at work? What were they doing?

   _____

   _____

   _____

# Are You Afraid of Heights?

Would you jump off a cliff attached only to a cord? Thousands of thrill seekers do so each year.
Credit: Chmouel, Wikimedia

Have you ever climbed up a tall mountain or rode to the higher floors of a skyscraper? How does it feel to see the world from so high up? There are thrill seekers who enjoy being high up. Some like riding and jumping down from these heights as well.

## Thrill Seekers

Daniel has jumped out of an airplane with a parachute. He's walked from one building to another while balancing on a thin tightrope. Daniel owns a motorcycle. He sometimes uses it to jump in the air over tires. Daniel is a thrill seeker. A thrill seeker is a person who likes to do scary things that are sometimes dangerous. Thrill seekers enjoy the feeling of being afraid and then overcoming their fears. They like the feeling of going super-fast or being super high up.

## Bungee Jumping

Since Daniel is a thrill seeker, he likes extreme sports. Extreme sports are dangerous sports that give thrill seekers their excitement. One of Daniel's favorite sports is bungee jumping. Bungee jumping is when people jump off a high platform, attached to it only with a rubber rope around their feet. The bungee jumper falls toward the ground really fast. At the last moment, just before the jumper hits the ground, the rope snaps back, and the jumper bounces back up in the air. Daniel travels a lot. Wherever he goes, he looks for a bungee jumping location. He also looks for zip lines. Both are thrill-seeking activities that can be ridden by visitors, trained or not.

## Zip Line

Ziplining is another extreme sport. Like bungee jumping, zipline riders start from high up. And like bungee jumping, zipline riders go really fast. But bungee jumping and ziplining aren't really that similar. A bungee jumper free-falls to the ground. Free-falling means falling quickly without anything to slow the fall. But a zipline slides along a rope or wire stretched between platforms, like a tightrope. Usually, the first platform is higher than the second one. The rider wears a harness that is attached to a **pulley**[1] by a clip, called a carabiner. The pulley slides along the rope or wire, pulling its rider with it.

*Thrill seekers enjoy extreme sports such as skydiving.*
**Credit:** *Simonsanely, Wikimedia*

## Thrills and Scenic Views

When Daniel looks for a bungee jumping experience, he looks for one that is high up off the ground. Daniel bungee jumps for the thrill. Bungee jumpers can fall at speeds up to 75 miles per hour! When Daniel looks for a zipline, sometimes he looks for a thrilling one. Some zip lines also go as fast as 75 miles an hour.

But sometimes, Daniel rides ziplines for the views. Ziplines can be built above **scenic**[2] locations. Daniel rode his favorite zip line over the top of a rainforest. Daniel got to see the rainforest from above, the way monkeys, birds, and other animals see it. Riding the line with his arms outstretched, Daniel felt like he was flying. He rode across the forest **canopy**[3] with his body outstretched, laying flat. He even pulled the rope to brake and slow down the ride, so he could see more.

*A bungee jumper leaping off a platform with a stretchy cord attached to his legs.*
**Credit:** *Ellywa, Wikimedia*

---

1 **pulley** – a wheel and cord machine, often used to lift heavy weights
2 **scenic** – pretty; attractive
3 **canopy** – top layer of a forest

## Equipment

Daniel likes to get to the area early and watch the crew of workers set up. The bungee jumping crew inspects the entire bungee rope by hand every day. They check to make sure nothing is fraying. Bungee jumping rope is usually made of strong rubber and has many strands. Each rope is used for only about 500 to 1,000 jumps before it is replaced. After inspecting the rope, the crew tests that the course is ready. One of the crew members puts on a harness and clips it on the rope. Then he jumps off the platform. Ziplining crews also test their equipment. They make sure the carabiners are strong and aren't damaged. They look at the zipline and make sure it is strong. A zipline is usually made of steel, with several strands twisted together.

*This zipliner is wearing a harness. Attached by a carabiner to his harness is an orange pulley system. The pulley system is attached to a wire. As the pulley system slides across the wire, the rider is pulled along at high speeds.*

*Bungee jumpers usually fall headfirst. Zip liner riders can ride in different positions, depending on the ride.* **Credit:** *İbrahim Yıldırım, Wikimedia* **Credit:** *Costaricapro, Wikimedia* **Credit:** *Hayk.arabaget, Wikimedia*

## Are They Safe?

Bungee jumping and ziplining look dangerous. They can be dangerous as well. But if the place has good equipment and a trained crew, these sports are usually safe. Never use a bungee jumping or ziplining location that doesn't follow the safety rules.

*A zipline is usually made from a strong, braided metal rope.*

# Questions

1. Circle the vocabulary word that best fits the sentence.

   *The construction workers used a **(pulley/canopy)** to lift the load of bricks.*

2. Place a check mark next to each statement that correctly describes bungee jumping.

   ___ It is an extreme sport.

   ___ It is almost the same as ziplining.

   ___ Bungee jumpers usually wear a harness.

   ___ Bungee jumpers free fall toward the ground.

3. Which of the following checks does a bungee jumping crew NOT do?

   A. Inspect the entire rope by hand

   B. Replace the rope after 500 to 1,000 uses

   C. Test that the course is ready

   D. Make sure the carabiners are strong and aren't damaged

4. What was the author's purpose in including the section titled *"Thrills and Scenic Views"*?

   A. To explain that ziplining can be done for thrills or to enjoy scenic views

   B. To explain how fast bungee jumpers can fall

   C. To explain how bungee jumping and ziplining are similar

5. Would you rather go bungee jumping or ziplining? Explain your answer.

   _____

   _____

   _____

168   Lesson 36: Are You Afraid of Heights?

# Yellowstone National Park

The Earth is a beautiful place. Look around. See if you can spot something amazing. It can be as small as the wings of a fly. Now let's go bigger. Think of the most beautiful place you have ever been. What was there? Tall mountains? Gushing waterfalls? Breathtaking scenery? Yellowstone National Park has all of this and more. Together we will explore this extraordinary **pocket**[1] of nature.

*A picture of the Grand Canyon in Yellowstone National Park.* **Credit:** *Grastel, Wikimedia*

## The History of Yellowstone National Park

Yellowstone National Park is a national park in the United States. Most of the park is located in Wyoming, although it also reaches into Montana and Idaho. In 1872, Yellowstone became the very first national park! A national park is an area set aside to protect nature, including its landforms, vegetation, and animals.

People have appreciated Yellowstone for a long time. Besides being beautiful, Yellowstone has many natural resources. Natural resources are things found in nature that people can gain from. Trees are one example of a natural resource. Trees provide people with wood for building, fuel for warmth and cooking, and more. People lived in Yellowstone for thousands of years, even before North America was settled by Europeans. Archaeology allows us to have a glimpse into the lives of these ancient people. We can learn how they lived off the land.

1 **pocket** – a small section of something

## Yellowstone's Hydrothermal Features

There are so many incredible places to visit in Yellowstone. It can be hard to choose where to visit first. There are lakes, waterfalls, mountains, and valleys. But one thing is certain. You cannot visit Yellowstone without enjoying its hydrothermal **features**.[2] *Hydro* means "water," and *thermal* has to do with "heat." *Hydrothermal* refers to water that is heated under the surface of the Earth. The hot water that comes up from underground creates many of Yellowstone National Park's wonderful attractions. Grand Prismatic Spring and "Old Faithful" are two very famous ones.

One of the beautiful views in Yellowstone National Park

## Grand Prismatic Spring

Springs are places where water flows out of the ground. The Grand Prismatic Spring is another one of Yellowstone's hydrothermal features. It is a stunning hot spring, and it is as colorful as a rainbow. Bacteria living in the hot spring are the reason for its magnificent colors. Not only is the Grand Prismatic Spring beautiful, but it is big. It is the third-largest hot spring in the world. It is bigger than a football field! Remember, this hot spring is good for looking but it is too hot for swimming.

## "Old Faithful"

Geysers are exciting for everyone. A geyser is a kind of hot spring, meaning that the spring water boils from time to time. A fountain of water and steam shoots into the air after the boiling water builds up enough pressure underground. In fact, the name geyser comes from an Icelandic word meaning "gush."

Old Faithful erupting
**Credit:** Grahampurse, Wikimedia

---

2 **features** – noticeable details

*A view of Grand Prismatic Spring.* **Credit:** *Brocken Inaglory, Wikimedia*

You want to be sure you will be able to watch this show. You cannot visit Yellowstone just to stare at a geyser, hoping it will **erupt**.[3] That is why you visit a geyser like Old Faithful. Old Faithful erupts every 60 to 110 minutes. It has erupted this often for years. No wonder this geyser is called "Old Faithful." Just pack a picnic and wait for the fun to begin. There are viewing areas and boardwalks where you can thrill at this natural wonder and still stay safe.

## Other Attractions

A canyon is a deep, narrow valley. Many canyons, like the Grand Canyon of Yellowstone, have a river running through them. The Yellowstone Grand Canyon is awe-inspiring. It is a massive 20 miles long. Its flowing river and giant waterfalls are breathtaking.

There are many more activities and places to see in Yellowstone. Visit gurgling **mudpots**[4] to watch how they bubble like soup on the stove. Water lovers can enjoy canoeing and kayaking on Yellowstone Lake, North America's largest high-elevation lake. Or, they can swim and wade in the river sites. Animal fans will also get a treat. Yellowstone is **teeming**[5] with wildlife like bears, bison, wolves, sheep, and deer.

So, pick your **destination**,[6] grab a pair of binoculars, and let's go!

> 3 **erupt** – explode; spurt up
> 4 **mudpots** – hot springs filled with mud that bubbles
> 5 **teeming** – full of
> 6 **destination** – the place a person is going to

# Questions

1. Circle the vocabulary word that best fits the sentence.

   We had to drive for miles until we reached our (**destination/features**).

2. Mark each statement as T (true) or F (false).

   ___ Yellowstone's land is all level and flat.

   ___ Yellowstone was the first national park.

   ___ A national park means that only American citizens can visit there.

   ___ Yellowstone has many beautiful plants but no animals.

3. Make a check mark next to each statement that correctly describes geysers.

   ___ They are hot springs that boil from time to time.

   ___ There are many geysers in the Yellowstone's Grand Canyon.

   ___ They shoot steam and hot water into the air.

   ___ They often shoot hot mud into the air.

4. Which of the following statements best summarizes the lesson?

   A. Yellowstone was the world's first national park.

   B. Yellowstone is a national park with many fascinating things to see and do.

   C. A national park is an area set aside to protect nature and the animals living in it.

5. How did "Old Faithful" get its name?

   _____

   _____

   _____

Lesson 37: Yellowstone National Park

# *Woodpeckers: Pecking All Day*

*A woodpecker sitting on a tree*

Have you ever heard something that sounded like a **rhythmic**[1] hammering or tapping when you were playing outside or walking through the park? You might not have realized it, but what you heard was probably a woodpecker hard at work high up in a tree. "Woodpecker" is a very fitting name for these fascinating birds because that is exactly what they do—they **peck**[2] at wood. Let's read more about why and how they do this.

## Woodpeckers

Woodpeckers are small birds that break down the wood inside trees. That's how they find their food. They search between the parts of the trees for carpenter ants, beetle **larvae**,[3] and other insects to eat. Eating these bugs is helpful to the trees because some of the bugs can harm trees.

There are about 180 different species of woodpecker, and they can be found in almost every country around the world. Most woodpeckers live where there are many trees, such as in forests. The birds are usually between six and ten inches long, but some species can grow up to 20 inches. They come in a variety of colors and patterns.

---

1 **rhythmic** – having a steady beat
2 **peck** – strike; tap
3 **larvae** – newly-hatched baby bugs

Besides for hunting, woodpeckers drill holes in trees for **roosting**[4] and building their nests. They make bigger holes if they want to lay eggs. They usually lay four eggs at a time. After the eggs are laid, the mother and father take turns sitting on them. The father usually sits on the eggs at night. After a couple of weeks, the eggs hatch.

## Special Bodies

Because woodpeckers are different from other birds, they need special bodies. Each part of their body helps them in a different way. Just on their faces alone, they have many features that protect and help them. For one thing, woodpeckers have very sharp beaks that they can use to break wood. Their tongues are long and sticky, so they can stick them into holes in the tree to check for food inside. Woodpeckers' eyes have special covers that come down as they tap on the tree.

The covers protect their eyes from small **splinters**[5] of wood that can fly into them. Their nostrils also have special protection, with narrow openings and feathers blocking them, so the wood doesn't enter them. Pretty amazing, don't you think?

*Woodpeckers make holes like these in trees.*
**Credit:** *M. Rehemtulla, Flickr*

*This father woodpecker is watching his babies.*
**Credit:** *Alastair Rae, Wikipedia*

4 **roosting** – resting; sleeping
5 **splinters** – little pieces; slivers

That is not all that is special about a woodpecker's body. You might wonder how they survive without injuring their brains with all that hammering and shaking their heads back and forth. The answer is that woodpeckers' brains are protected from injury in several ways. Their brains are small and deep in their heads. There is a thick, **spongy**[6] piece around the brain to keep it safe. There are also strong bones keeping the brain in place, so that it doesn't move when the woodpecker quickly shakes its head.

Woodpeckers have interesting feet, designed especially for wood pecking. They have four toes on each foot, with two toes facing forward and two facing backward. That arrangement helps them climb trees easily and hang on tight.

If you think that is all, then listen up. Woodpeckers' tails are also special. The tails help with their food hunting. After landing on the tree, woodpeckers need a place to sit while they break apart the wood, looking for food. Their tails are so strong that the woodpeckers can rest on them while they peck away on the wood. How **convenient**[7] to bring a comfortable chair along wherever they go!

*This woodpecker is about to break the tree apart with its sharp beak.*

*This woodpecker is leaning on its tail. You can also see how its interesting toes clutch the tree.*

6 **spongy** – soft; cushiony
7 **convenient** – handy; useful

# Questions

1. Circle the vocabulary word that best fits the sentence.

   *It is very (**spongy/convenient**) having a store so close to our house.*

2. Place a check mark next to each statement that correctly describes woodpeckers.

   ___ They can be found in almost every country.

   ___ They hunt for food underground.

   ___ They have sharp beaks for breaking wood.

   ___ They have four toes on each foot.

3. What do the special covers over woodpeckers' eyes do?

   A. They block out the sunlight.

   B. They keep them from being distracted while they're working.

   C. They help them fall asleep more easily.

   D. They prevent splinters of wood from flying into their eyes.

4. Which of the following sentences from the section titled *"Special Bodies"* supports the idea that woodpeckers' bodies are different from other birds?

   A. *For one thing, woodpeckers have very sharp beaks that they can use to break wood.*

   B. *Because woodpeckers are different from other birds, they need special bodies.*

   C. *How convenient to bring a comfortable chair along wherever they go!*

5. Some workers protect their eyes with special covers, just like woodpeckers have special covers over their eyes. Can you think of an example of a worker who does this?

   _____

   _____

   _____

# 'Listen, My Children, and You Shall Hear of the Midnight Ride of Paul Revere'

*Paul Revere is an American legend known for his brave midnight ride.*

Henry Wadsworth Longfellow was a poet who lived in the 1800s. Longfellow's country, the United States, was on the **brink**[1] of war. Longfellow and many others in the Northern states thought it was wrong to own slaves. People living in the Southern states needed enslaved workers to support their economy. The economy was largely based on crops such as cotton and tobacco. It took much human labor to plant, tend, and harvest these crops.

Longfellow wanted to **inspire**[2] people to fight for what he believed was right. How could he do this? He thought about his **ancestors**.[3] He remembered how his ancestor, Peleg Wadsworth, had fought for freedom from Britain. Peleg Wadsworth was commander of a brave man named Paul Revere during the Revolutionary War. Longfellow thought Revere's story could be that inspiration. He wrote a poem called "The Midnight Ride of Paul Revere." The poem became so famous that many American schoolchildren memorized it. It turned Paul Revere into a legend. Let's explore what the poem was about.

---

1 **brink** – on the verge; when something is about to happen
2 **inspire** – get people excited about
3 **ancestors** – relatives who one descends from

## The Sons of Liberty

*Listen, my children, and you shall hear
Of the midnight ride of Paul Revere*

Paul Revere lived in Boston, Massachusetts, a colony ruled by England, in 1775. Revere seemed like an ordinary man. However, Revere was a silversmith. But he also had a secret job. He belonged to an underground group called the "Sons of Liberty." The word *liberty* means "freedom." The Sons of Liberty planned to fight for freedom from Britain. Its members didn't want to be ruled by the British king anymore. They wanted to make their own rules.

*Paul Revere worked as a silversmith. Silversmiths craft useful objects out of silver. This tea set is an example.*

## Weapons in Concord

The Sons of Liberty hid weapons in many secret places. They had to be very careful not to let the British soldiers find out. If the British soldiers caught them hiding weapons or planning a **rebellion**,[4] they could be killed.

*Paul Revere lived in a house in Boston. Today, tourists can visit his home and see how he lived.*

In April 1775, the British soldiers discovered that the Sons of Liberty had hidden weapons. They were in the city of Concord. Concord was a small city north of Boston. The British soldiers made plans to travel from Boston to Concord to **seize**[5] the weapons. The Sons of Liberty wanted to warn the people living in Concord that the British were coming. They needed a messenger who could ride there quickly on horseback.

---

4 **rebellion** – refusing to follow authority
5 **seize** – take by force

# Paul Revere's Ride

*Hang a lantern aloft in the belfry-arch
Of the North-Church-tower, as a signal-light—
One if by land, and two if by sea;
And I on the opposite shore will be*

Two men were chosen to spread the alarm—Paul Revere and William Dawes. They needed to tell the people in Concord where the British soldiers would come from. They **arranged**[6] for a friend, Robert Newman, to go to the Old North Church. That was the tallest building in Boston. Newman would hang up signal lanterns in the tower. One lantern meant that the British planned to travel by land. Two lanterns meant that they planned to travel by sea.

*In 1933, an artist painted this picture of Paul Revere's ride.*

Revere and Dawes waited in the dark on April 18th. Finally, they saw the signal. Two lanterns! The British were coming by sea! Dawes jumped on his horse and sped toward Concord. Revere silently rowed past the British ships to the city of Charlestown. He let the people of Charlestown know that the British were on their way. Then, he borrowed a horse and **galloped**[7] toward Lexington as fast as he could.

In Lexington, Revere stopped at the homes of other **patriots**.[8] (Not everyone was against Britain!). He woke up the men and told them to get their guns. It was time to fight! After warning the people of Lexington, Revere, Dawes, and a third man, Samuel Prescott, headed for Concord. Shortly after taking off, the three men ran into a British army **patrol**.[9] "Stop right there!" the British soldiers called after them. Dawes, Revere, and Prescott tried to **flee**.[10] Prescott jumped his horse over a wall and escaped. He rode toward Concord and warned the men there.

6 **arranged** – planned in advance
7 **galloped** – rode at a fast pace
8 **patriots** – people who love and support their country
9 **patrol** – guards keeping watch on an area
10 **flee** – run away

Dawes also tried to escape. As the British chased him, he fell off his horse. He wasn't caught, but his ride ended there.

## The Battle of Lexington and Concord

*You know the rest. In the books you have read,*
*How the British Regulars fired and fled—*

Paul Revere, on the other hand, was caught by the British. They asked him many questions. Finally, they let him go—without his horse. Revere walked, through the night, towards Lexington. As he walked, he heard gunfire.

Revere reached Lexington just as the sun was rising. There he found a battle taking place. British soldiers were under fire from all the men Revere had warned. The British were outnumbered, and they fled. This battle was the first in the Revolutionary War. After years of fighting, the Americans won the war. They established the United States of America. America is a country thanks to brave men like Paul Revere.

*The city of Boston put up a statue in honor of Paul Revere.*
**Credit:** Kenneth C. Zirkel, Wikimedia

*Through all our history, to the last,*
*In the hour of darkness and peril and need,*
*The people will waken and listen to hear*
*The hurrying hoof-beats of that steed,*
*And the midnight message of Paul Revere.*

# Questions

1. **Circle the vocabulary word that best fits the sentence.**

   *Our teacher gave us an assignment to write about one of our **(ancestors/brink)**.*

2. **Mark each statement as T (true) or F (false).**

   ___ Robert Newman hung two lanterns because the British planned to travel by land.

   ___ Paul Revere walked towards Lexington on foot in the middle of the night.

   ___ Paul Revere stopped at homes in Lexington to warn the people.

   ___ Paul Revere's ride ended when he fell off his horse.

3. **Number the following events in the order in which they took place.**

   ___ Paul Revere first let the people of Charlestown know that the British were on their way.

   ___ Paul Revere and William Dawes were assigned to warn the people about the British.

   ___ Paul Revere was caught by the British.

   ___ Robert Newman hung signal lanterns in the tower of Old North Church.

4. **Which of the following sentences from the section titled** *"Weapons in Concord"* **supports the idea that the Sons of Liberty had to be careful not to let the British soldiers find out they had hidden weapons?**

   A. *The Sons of Liberty hid weapons in many secret places.*

   B. *If the British soldiers caught them hiding weapons or planning a rebellion, they could be killed.*

   C. *The British soldiers made plans to travel from Boston to Concord to seize the weapons.*

5. **What was the effect of the colonists winning the Revolutionary War?**

   _____

   _____

181

# The North Pole and the South Pole

The Aurora Australis can be seen in the South Pole's night sky. The North Pole has a similar display of colorful lights.

If you live in New York City or another northern area, you may have heard about "going south for the winter." Some people visit places in the southern United States, like Florida, to escape the cold winters in the North. Places in "the South" are usually much warmer than in the North. Some birds and other animals **migrate**[1] south for the winter as well.

Did you know that even though we think of the South as warmer than the North, if you go all the way to the southernmost point on Earth, you will find the coldest temperatures ever recorded? Let's read about the North and South Poles.

## Polar Nights and Midnight Sun

It's September at the North Pole. The sun rises, but its highest point is lower and lower with each passing day. It rises in the morning, stays near the horizon during the afternoon, and sets early. Then, one day, the sun doesn't rise at all. Its shining disc can't be seen. However, its rays peek over the horizon. It looks like the time just before dawn. The sky is a lighter blue during the "daytime" hours.

1 **migrate** – travel; journey

For the next six months, until March, none of the walruses, polar bears, fish, birds, or foxes in the North Pole will see the sun. In two of those months, December and January, the sun won't even come close enough to the horizon to lighten the sky. The sky will be pitch black, except for the stars. Colorful green, yellow, and blue flashes, called the *Aurora Borealis* or Northern Lights, will light up the sky like fireworks. The days with no sun are called polar nights.

*Even though the sun doesn't rise above the horizon during polar nights, it is close enough to the horizon to lighten the sky up to a bluish color. Credit: Bjørn Christian Tørrissen, Wikimedia*

While the North Pole has its polar nights, the South Pole has the exact opposite. It is summer at the South Pole. The sun doesn't set from September to March. Sometimes it gets closer to the horizon, and the sky becomes darker, but it never sets completely. When the sun shines in the sky in the middle of the night, it is called the "midnight sun." It is the warmest time of the year at the South Pole.

*Can you believe it was midnight near the South Pole when this picture was taken? The sun gets close to the horizon but doesn't sink below it during the months of the "midnight sun." Credit: Jason Auch, Wikimedia*

From March to September, the exact opposite happens. The North Pole has six months of sun. The South Pole has polar nights and six months without sun. From March to September, it will be summer at the North Pole and winter at the South Pole. During its polar nights, the South Pole also has green and blue lights, called the *Aurora Australis* or Southern Lights.

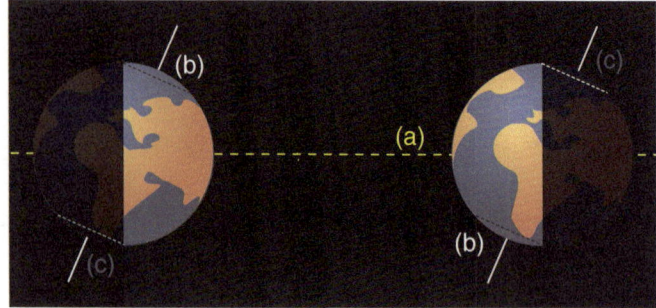

*Why do the polar nights and midnight suns happen? It has to do with the way the Earth is tilted. Because of Earth's tilt, during half of the year, the North Pole and the area around it is tilted towards the sun. During the other half of the year, it is tilted away. Credit: Mike Run, Wikimedia*

Lesson 40: The North Pole and the South Pole

*This map shows the continent of Antarctica. The South Pole is near the middle of the continent. Parts of the Southern Ocean around the continent are frozen year-round.*

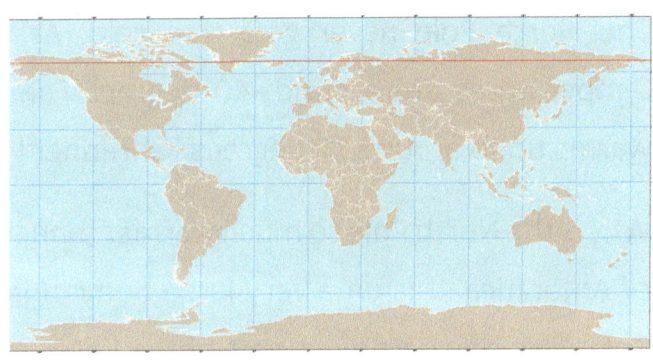

*On the map on the top, the red line is called the Arctic Circle. (It is circle-shaped on a sphere, such as a globe or planet Earth). Within the Arctic Circle is land and ocean. The ocean is called the Arctic Ocean. The picture below shows the Arctic Ocean and the Arctic Circle from a different viewpoint. It also shows the North Pole, marked with a "+."* **Credit:** *Thesevenseas, Wikimedia*

## Polar Weather

The South Pole is the southernmost point on Earth. It is located on the continent of Antarctica. Antarctica is so cold that even in the summer, the temperatures are still around -18 degrees Fahrenheit. Harsh winds blow on the edges of the continent. Antarctic winds are some of the most powerful on Earth. The winds pick up snow and blow it all around. The snow gets packed in layer after layer and turns to ice. It also rarely snows in Antarctica, and it certainly hardly ever rains— it's too cold. The snow that does fall stays on the ground without melting. Even though we usually think of a desert as a hot place, a desert is just a place with very little **precipitation**.[2] Since Antarctica has so little precipitation, it is a desert. During Antarctica's polar nights from March to September, temperatures drop to about -76 degrees Fahrenheit!

> 2 **precipitation** – rain, snow, sleet, or hail that falls from clouds

The North Pole never gets that cold. At the northernmost point on planet Earth, the temperatures are around -40 degrees Fahrenheit in the winter. In the summer, the pole warms up to around 32 degrees Fahrenheit!

Why is the North Pole so much warmer than the South Pole? The South Pole is on the continent of Antarctica. It is on a very large body of land. But there is no land underneath the North Pole. This northernmost part of the Earth sits on top of the Arctic Ocean. Warmer water in the ocean heats the air. Even though parts of the Arctic Ocean are frozen all the time, only the surface is ice. Underneath the ice, **currents**[3] carry the cold polar water south and bring warmer waters to the North Pole.

## Who Lives at the Poles?

Because the North Pole has water underneath it and not land, there are no people living at the Pole itself. But the **region**[4] around the North Pole is called the Arctic. The Arctic has land and water, and there are people living there. Tribes like the Saami in Norway and the Inuit in Alaska have lived in the Arctic for thousands of years. They have learned how to deal with the freezing cold weather. Some build houses

*This picture shows a member of an Innuit tribe building a traditional ice home (igloo) while wearing a warm parka coat.*

of snow or ice. They hunt animals and use the skins and furs to make warm clothing. They fish by walking onto the thick ice and cutting holes in it. Then they spear the fish swimming in the water underneath. Some people in the Arctic have special dogs used for pulling sleds.

For most of history, nobody lived at the South Pole itself either. There were no humans on the entire continent of Antarctica. Humans started exploring Antarctica a little over 100 years ago. They set up **research**[5] stations there. Today, about 4,000 people live in Antarctica in the summer and about 1,000 in the winter. Most people only stay for a few months or years before returning home.

---

3 **currents** – streams; flows
4 **region** – area of land
5 **research** – scientific investigation and exploration

## Animals Living at the Poles

Just because there are only a few humans in Antarctica doesn't mean there are no animals. The **coasts**[6] and oceans around Antarctica are teeming with wildlife. There are herds of majestic penguins. There are huge, fat, blubbery seals. Giant whales swim in the water off the coast. At the South Pole itself, away from the coast, it is much quieter. Although seals and penguins visit Antarctica's land, only one animal lives on the continent itself. The Antarctic midge is a tiny black bug. It keeps from freezing by **burrowing**[6] under the ice. It lives on the edge of the continent.

*Antarctica is famous for its penguins! But the South Polar region also has other animals, like the strange-looking icefish swimming in the Southern Ocean and the tiny Antarctica midge.*
**Credit:** *Marrabbio2, Wikimedia*

Many animals also live in the waters of the North Pole. They even live near the Pole itself. Seals, walruses, and whales swim in the icy water. Polar bears, arctic foxes, and rabbits live on the lands within the Arctic Circle. During the winter, they can travel over the solid ice of the frozen ocean. Other Arctic land animals include reindeer, musk ox, and lemmings.

*The narwhal is one of the strange Arctic creatures. Like a unicorn, this whale has a long horn coming out of its face.*

From the Northern Lights to the penguins to the superfast winds, the polar regions have things that can be found nowhere else on Earth. Where do you want to visit?

6 **coasts** – edges of the land near the sea
7 **burrowing** – making holes or tunnels underground

## Exploring the Poles

Nowadays, we know a lot about the North and South Poles. There are even research stations and people living at the South Pole.

But for most of history, these places were unreachable. In the 1800s and 1900s, explorers tried to reach these unexplored parts of Earth. Their journeys were dangerous. The freezing temperatures and harsh winds made the explorers sick. In some places, finding food and water was difficult. The frozen seas also made traveling by ship dangerous.

Many men died trying to reach the Poles. For example, three explorers from Sweden tried to take a hot air balloon to the North Pole in 1895. All three died sometime after their balloon crashed, trapping them in the freezing Arctic.

Finally, in 1909, American Robert Peary led a party of men. He claimed he reached the North Pole, but not everyone agrees that he found the correct spot. A year before, American Frederick Cook also made the same claim. In 1926, Roald Amundsen was the first to prove that he had reached the North Pole.

Attempts to reach South Pole were just as dangerous. Many men died trying to reach it. In 1909, after many years of trying, two voyages set out for the South Pole. Roald Amundsen of Norway left with a large group of men and dogs in 1909. Robert F. Scott, a British man, also headed for the South Pole in 1910 on a ship carrying sleds, dogs, ponies, and a crew of hundreds of men.

Newspapers around the world were excited about the two groups. They called it the "race to the Poles." People around the world followed the progress of the voyages. They wanted to see who would be the first to explore the unexplored.

After spending the polar nights on board his ship in the Southern Ocean, Amundsen's crew started for the Pole in the summer. They climbed over the tall transatlantic mountains and reached the South Pole a few weeks later. Amundsen left a note there for Scott's crew. Scott's crew was still about a month behind.

A month later, Scott's crew reached the Pole. But getting there was only half the battle. They were running low on supplies. Many crew members were suffering from frostbite. Others were starving. Scott was supposed to have a rescue team meet him and give him additional supplies. But the team never showed up. Scott and his men died on the march back from the South Pole to their ship. When the news reached the world in 1913, Scott was praised as a hero.

In 1914, another explorer, Ernst Shackleton, tried to reach the South Pole. He and his crew ran into trouble on the way. His ship became trapped in ice. Later, the ice crushed the ship. They were stuck in the coldest area on Earth, with no one to rescue them.

The crew managed to survive in the South Pole region for three years. Once the ice melted a bit, the crew took small lifeboats to frozen islands. Eventually they managed to find rescuers.

# Questions

1. **Circle the vocabulary word that best fits the sentence.**

   We watched the dog **(migrate/burrowing)** a hole to bury its bone.

2. **Mark each statement as T (true) or F (false).**

   ___ The North and South Poles have their polar nights at the same time.

   ___ The midnight sun is when the sun shines in the sky in the middle of the night.

   ___ The North Pole has six months of sun from September to March.

   ___ Antarctica is a desert because it is very hot.

3. **How have the people living in the Arctic learned to deal with the freezing cold weather?**

   A. They build houses of snow or ice.

   B. They use animal skins and furs to make warm clothing.

   C. They fish by cutting holes in the ice.

   D. All of the above

4. **Which of the following sentences from the lesson supports the idea that just because there are only a few humans in Antarctica, it doesn't mean there are no animals?**

   A. *For most of history, nobody lived at the South Pole itself either.*

   B. *The coasts and oceans around Antarctica are teeming with wildlife.*

   C. *The Antarctic midge is a tiny black bug.*

5. **How are the North Pole and South Poles similar? How are they different? Give a few examples.**

   _____

   _____

   _____

# Wet and Thrilling: Go with the Flow

Feel the breeze, smell the damp air, and get ready to get soaked. We are having a day out on the water. Let's hear about kayaking and white-water rafting. Then, choose your sport, grab your oars, and dive in!

## What are Kayaking and White-Water Rafting?

Kayaking and white-water rafting are both water sports. They are a perfect day out for you if you enjoy being outdoors, feeling a thrill, and having a great time. Kayaking and white-water rafting both take place on the water and both use a type of boat, but they are not **identical**.[1] They use different types of boats and oars and can fit a different number of passengers. Both sports are fun in different ways.

*Kayaking on a lake*

## Boats

Kayaks are narrow and sit close to the water. They look a lot like canoes. Kayaks usually fit only one person. Some kayaks can **accommodate**[2] two people. Kayaks that seat more than two people are not easy to find. A kayak is often covered. A small opening allows you to slide your legs into the kayak and sit down. Your legs are now protected from splashing water. White-water rafting, as the name suggests, uses rafts. Thankfully, our rafts today are a bit sturdier than an armful of logs tied together with twine.

> 1 **identical** – exactly the same
> 2 **accommodate** – have space for

Specially designed rafts are strong and fit lots of people. Rafts are wider and **steadier**³ in the water than kayaks. Join this sport for a fun group activity.

## Oars

A boat by itself is fabulous for floating, but it is uncontrollable. Along come oars. Kayaking and white-water rafting both use old-fashioned oars, so these sports are a great all-body exercise as well as being exciting. Kayakers hold one oar that has a paddle at each end. They first dip the oar into the water on one side of the kayak before lifting and repeating on the other side. White-water rafts use an oar with one paddle, the **traditional**⁴ oars we easily picture in our mind.

*A white-water raft. Notice the size of the raft, the oars, and the number of people onboard.*
**Credit:** *Royroydeb, Wikimedia*

## Water

Do you enjoy looking at sparkling lakes and beautiful landscapes? People usually kayak on lakes, ponds, and canals. You can relax, take it easy, and enjoy the **spectacular**⁵

*Look at the kayak's shape and the type of oars used.*

scenery as you slowly work the oars. If you like to make your heart pump, paddle hard and move the kayak quickly. However, kayaking is not only done in gentle pools. You can go white-water kayaking, which is much like white-water rafting. White water is **shallow**,⁶ fast-flowing water that **froths**⁷ and splashes so much that it looks like white foam.

---

3 **sturdier** – stronger
4 **steadier** – more stable or balanced
5 **traditional** – regular; standard; usual
6 **spectacular** – splendid; magnificent; remarkable
7 **shallow** – not deep
8 **froths** – foams; sprays

Traveling on white water makes a thrilling outing. Gather your family or friends and enjoy a breathtaking ride down the stream. Try to stay on the raft! Beginners, don't worry. This sport can be enjoyed by everyone, even if it sounds extreme. There are different difficulty levels of white-water rafting. Some are easier, and some are more dangerous or tricky. Pick what works for you and enjoy the ride.

Rafting in white water.

Kayaking can also be an extreme sport.

## Safety

Knowing how to be safe is always important. It is normal to fall overboard in these sports. Learn how to swim before you go kayaking or white-water rafting. Also, wear a life jacket. You may be the strongest swimmer. But always wear a life jacket. It can save your life.

Will you take your boat near rocks? If so, it is sensible to wear a helmet. You do not want to spoil your day by hitting your head. So, while kayakers in the middle of a lake do not need a helmet, white-water rafters do.

## Other Equipment

Here is the reality: Kayaking and white-water rafting are water sports, and you will probably get wet. Soggy[9] clothes are not fun. Wear a wetsuit to keep warm and dry. Wetsuits are made of strong rubber. They cover the whole body and will protect you from the water.

Pack a drink and a snack. Watersports can be tiring, so you will need the energy. Just be sure to pack them in something waterproof.

Grab your wet suit and head down to the lake. Which sport do you prefer?

9 **soggy** – wet; soaked

# Questions

1. Circle the vocabulary word that best fits the sentence.

    Watching the sun rise over the mountains was a **(spectacular/traditional)** experience.

2. Mark each statement as T (true) or F (false).

    ___ Kayaking and white-water rafting use the same kind of boats.

    ___ White-water rafters use an oar with one paddle.

    ___ It is normal to fall overboard while kayaking and white-water rafting.

    ___ White water is white because it is frosty.

3. Which of the following are ways to stay safe while kayaking or white-water rafting?

    A. Learning how to swim

    B. Wearing a life jacket

    C. Packing a drink and a snack

    D. All of the above

4. Which of the following sentences from the section titled *"Water"* supports the idea that kayaking is not only done in gentle pools?

    A. *People usually kayak on lakes, ponds, and canals.*

    B. *If you like to make your heart pump, paddle hard and move the kayak quickly.*

    C. *You can go white-water kayaking, which is much like white-water rafting.*

5. Why is white water called that?

    _____

    _____

    _____

# Shipwrecked at Sea: The Story of Robinson Crusoe

What do you do in your free time? What are your favorite hobbies? Reading is a hobby that many people enjoy. People like to read all sorts of different things. One type of writing that many people enjoy is the **novel**.[1] Let's read about what novels are, how they became popular, and about one of the first novels that got people excited about reading.

*A monument in England honoring Robinson Crusoe.*
**Credit:** *Steve F-E- Cameron, Wikimedia*

## A Recent History of Books

Today, most people you meet know how to read and write. Children learn to read in school from a young age. If you go back 500 years, though, that was not the case. In the 1500s, fewer than one in five people in Europe knew how to read.

But things didn't stay that way for long. New inventions changed Europe very quickly. In the 1400s, Johannes Gutenberg invented the printing press. Before this, books and documents had to be hand-written. There was no way to make copies of them quickly. The printing press let people make many copies of writing very quickly. Books became a lot cheaper, but there were still not many who were able to read them.

---

1 **novel** – a long fiction story

But people who could read now found it easier to share ideas. Powered by books, scientists and **philosophers**[2] began changing the world from the 1600s through the 1800s. New inventions made it easier for people to get food, water, and other necessary items. People had more free time to study and learn. Over time, these changes led to more and more people learning how to read.

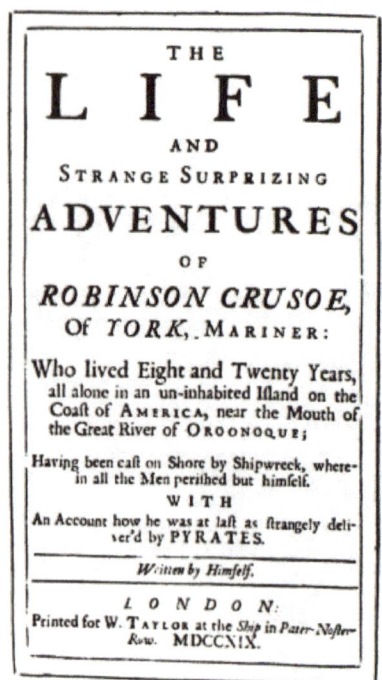

*This was the front cover and picture of the book Defoe published.*

You might think that as people learned to read, they enjoyed books with exciting tales of adventure. This wasn't true until the early 1700s when Daniel Defoe wrote the first European novel. A novel is a long **fiction**[3] book that tells an exciting story. Today, there are millions of novels, written in hundreds of languages. However, in Defoe's time, most books were meant for sharing information, not stories.

## The First European Novel

Defoe changed this when he wrote his book in the year 1719. He called the novel *The Life and Strange Surprizing Adventures of Robinson Crusoe, of York, Mariner: Who Lived Eight and Twenty Years, All Alone in an Un-inhabited Island on the Coast of America, Near the Mouth of the Great River of Oroonoque; Having Been Cast on Shore by Shipwreck, Wherein All the Men Perished but Himself. With an Account how he was at last as Strangely Deliver'd by Pyrates. Written by Himself.* However, most people used the shorter title *Robinson Crusoe*.

Defoe's novel became very popular very quickly. Not only did thousands of copies sell, but people started writing their own novels. They copied Defoe's style and his plots.

> 2 **philosophers** – scholars who think about life and the world
> 3 **fiction** – not true; a made-up story

These novels were called robinsonades. *Robinson Crusoe* and the robinsonades made novels popular and got people excited about reading. Fast-forward to today, where there are whole sections of bookstores and libraries that contain novels. Defoe changed the world by **publishing**[4] his book.

*This map from Defoe's book shows Crusoe's strange island and some of the things that happened there.*

## What Is Robinson Crusoe About?

Defoe's story, *Robinson Crusoe*, must have been really good to have been able to change the world. What is it about?

As the title suggests, *Robinson Crusoe* is about a man named ... Robinson Crusoe! As a boy, Crusoe dreams of being a sailor. His father tells him that going on a ship is too dangerous. He tells Crusoe to pick a different type of work. Crusoe doesn't listen to his father. He sets sail, hoping to become a rich man. Instead, his ship runs into a storm. The storm destroys the ship. Luckily, Crusoe isn't killed. The waves push him to the shore of an island. Crusoe learns that he is alone on the island. Without a boat, Crusoe is trapped on the island. He is **shipwrecked**.[5]

Crusoe builds a shelter on the island. He also finds goats there that he can eat, and he plants crops. Crusoe tries to build a boat, but he cannot escape the island. However, after a few years alone on the island, Crusoe sees a footprint in the sand. He realizes that he is not alone anymore. Crusoe is frightened. He thinks there may be someone dangerous there.

---

4 **publishing** – preparing books to be sold
5 **shipwrecked** – stuck on an island after a ship becomes too damaged to use

Soon, Crusoe learns that he is right. He sees a group of **cannibals**[6] and their **victims**.[7] Crusoe is able to rescue one of the victims and kill the attackers. He names the man he rescued Friday because he rescued him on a Friday. Friday becomes Crusoe's loyal servant. The two have many adventures on the island together.

In the end, after 28 years of being shipwrecked, a ship reaches Crusoe's island. The crew wants to harm their captain. Instead, Crusoe rescues the captain. Then he asks the captain to bring Friday and himself back to England. When he returns home, Crusoe learns that he has become a wealthy man, just as he had wanted. His property has become more valuable over the past 28 years.

*Some historians think Defoe got the idea for his story from the story of Alexander Selkirk. Selkirk was a real-life sailor. He was trapped on an island for four years. Pictured above is a statue of Alexander Selkirk, which stands at the site of his original home in Scotland.*
**Credit:** *SylviaStanley, Wikimedia*

Stories inspired by *Robinson Crusoe* are still being written today. In some **versions**[8] of the story, the hero is shipwrecked on Mars instead of on an island. *Robinson Crusoe* changed the world when it was written. And its **plot**[9] continues to entertain people around the world 300 years later!

---

6 **cannibals** – people who eat human flesh
7 **victims** – people harmed by an accident or crime
8 **versions** – different forms; variations
9 **plot** – story; storyline

# Questions

1. **Circle the vocabulary word that best fits the sentence.**

   *The **(cannibals/victims)** of the hurricane didn't have any electricity for a week.*

2. **Number the following events in the order in which they took place.**

   ___ Robinson Crusoe rescued Friday.

   ___ Robinson Crusoe was shipwrecked on an island.

   ___ Robinson Crusoe rescued the ship's captain.

   ___ Robinson Crusoe found a footprint in the sand.

3. **Why was the printing press such an important invention?**

   A. It made it possible to make books more quickly.

   B. It gave philosophers something to think about.

   C. It made sea travel less dangerous.

   D. It made Defoe famous.

4. **Which of the following sentences from the section titled *"A Recent History of Books"* supports the idea that in Defoe's time people did not read for entertainment?**

   A. *Over time, these changes led to more and more people learning how to read.*

   B. *Books became a lot cheaper, but there were still not many who were able to read them.*

   C. *However, in Defoe's time, most books were meant for sharing information, not stories.*

5. **Why do you think most people called the book *Robinson Crusoe* instead of what Defoe named it?**

   _____

   _____

   _____

# LEGO: Building a Business Brick by Brick

Lego bricks.
**Credit:** Benjamin D. Esham, Wikimedia

What toy entertains both a four-year-old and a 12-year-old? Small blocks carry you to a place of imagination. You can create new worlds and test your construction skills. Instruction **manuals**[1] help you make complicated and impressive models. Hours of joy. Days of fun. Have you figured it out? Yes, we are describing Lego. We will see how one man's idea became one of the world's most favorite toys.

## Childhood Years

Ole Kirk Kristiansen was born in Denmark. He was the tenth child in his family. Although his parents were poor, Ole Kirk attended school two days a week. When he was six years old, he began working as a **farmhand**[2] and became fascinated with **whittling**[3] wood. When he was about 20 years old, Kristiansen left Denmark for Germany, where he did carpentry work for five years.

## Early Business Days

Kristiansen stepped into his new workshop. He had bought The Billund Woodworking and Carpentry Shop. He was ready for success.

---

1 **manuals** – booklets
2 **farmhand** – farm worker
3 **whittling** – carving an object out of wood

His workshop made wooden items, from doors to cabinets—and even buildings. Whatever he made, Kristiansen **guaranteed**[4] one thing: that it would be of excellent **quality**.[5] Then, in 1929, disaster struck. The Great Depression began. People lost their jobs, and businesses closed. The Great Depression affected the entire world. It even affected the farmers in Denmark. They could not afford to buy things from Kristiansen. It was a tough time. Kristiansen had the difficult **task**[6] of telling his workers they could no longer work at his shop.

*A picture of Ole Kirk Kristiansen.*

## The Beginnings of Toy Making

This **crisis**[7] forced him to think of other ways to make money. Kristiansen began to make wooden toys. He made toys he knew would sell, like wooden cars and even yo-yos.

*The Lego logo.*

Kristiansen organized a competition to find a new name for his company. He chose himself as the winner. He liked his idea of using the phrase LEG GODT which means "play well" in Danish, the language spoken in Denmark. The first two letters of each word form the **brand**[8] name LEGO. As well as a new name, the company had a motto. This **motto**[9] was not new. Kristiansen's motto was "only the best is good enough." Kristiansen expected that anything coming out of his workshop would be of the best quality. Each toy was constructed with care. This helped him build the high-quality toys we enjoy today. World War II started in Europe in 1939. Kristiansen still managed to sell toys.

---

4 **guaranteed** – gave official assurance that something would happen
5 **quality** – how well made something is
6 **task** – duty
7 **crisis** – emergency; disaster
8 **brand** – company name or identification
9 **motto** – expression; saying

In fact, he sold more than ever. But a fire destroyed the workshop in 1942. He had to rebuild. At this point, he made a brave decision. This decision helped to make Lego the success it is today. He decided to put all his energy into making toys. He stopped making anything else in his workshop.

## Plastic Bricks

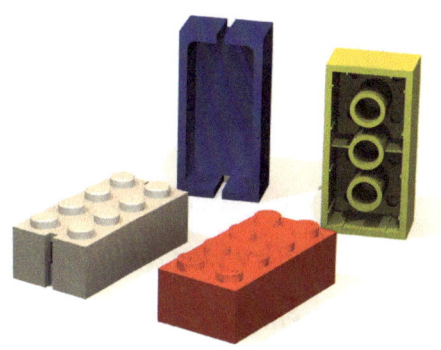

A comparison of the first and current Lego bricks. Notice how the first brick did not have the tubes underneath.
**Credit:** ruizo, Wikimedia

World War II ended in 1945. Now, Kristiansen managed to get a machine that would mold heated plastic into different shapes. This special machine allowed him to make plastic toys. In 1949, he made the first Lego brick. He called it an automatic binding brick. No one could imagine how successful Kristiansen's Lego would be. Even his family did not think a plastic brick would become popular.

## Lego Development

Kristiansen developed his idea. He was **convinced**[10] that children would enjoy playing with Legos. He added more machines to his workshop. More machines meant he could make more toys. In 1953, he changed the bricks' name to Lego bricks and stamped the company name Lego onto the **studs**[11] of each brick. Have a look—the design is still the

Lego sets on display at a store in London. **Credit:** Simeon87, Wikimedia

same today. Then, in 1958, he perfected the brick design. He added tubes to the bottom. Each Lego brick could now properly click into the one underneath. Your Lego bricks can attach to the Lego bricks your parents played with. Lego's **popularity**[12] spread throughout the world. Children loved this great toy. More and more Lego sets were developed. Even today, Lego is constantly inventing new sets. Lego is a success story. I challenge you to find a child who does not enjoy playing with Lego!

10 **convinced** – sure; certain
11 **studs** – projections; pieces that stick up
12 **popularity** – being well-liked

 # Questions

1. Circle the vocabulary word that best fits the sentence.

   *The student was **(whittling/convinced)** that joining the photography class would be time well spent.*

2. Mark each statement as T (true) or F (false).

   ___ Kristiansen guaranteed that whatever he made was of excellent quality.

   ___ Once World War II started, no one bought toys anymore.

   ___ The farmers in Denmark weren't affected by the Great Depression.

   ___ Lego's design has not changed since 1958.

3. Number the following events in the order in which they took place.

   ___ Kristiansen bought The Billund Woodworking and Carpentry Shop.

   ___ A fire destroyed Kristiansen's workshop.

   ___ World War II started.

   ___ The Great Depression began.

4. Which of the following sentences from the section titled *"The Beginnings of Toy Making"* supports the idea that Kristiansen's decision to start putting all his energy into making toys was wise?

   A. He made toys he knew would sell, like wooden cars and even yo-yos.

   B. This helped him build the high-quality toys we enjoy today.

   C. This decision helped to make Lego the success it is today.

5. What do you think might have happened if a fire hadn't destroyed Kristiansen's workshop?

   _____

   _____

# Electric Eels: Hunters of the Amazon!

Electric eels like to swim in murky water.
**Credit:** G. Garitan, Wikimedia

People use a lot of electricity throughout the day. Lights inside the house, air conditioning, and telephones are just a few examples. What are some ways that you use electricity in your daily life? Long before people learned how to use electricity, some fish were already using it for hunting. Let's read about how the electric eel uses electricity in its daily life.

## A Calm Day in the Amazon

It's a beautiful day in Brazil's Amazon rainforest. Even though the forest usually gets a lot of rain, today is sunny. There is a light **breeze** blowing over the Amazon River. The Amazon River is a very long, winding river. It twists its way through the Amazon rainforest. Many animals in the rainforest need the river to stay alive.

Underneath the calm surface of the river, a little fish is hiding. The fish swims under a pile of **rocks** on the bottom of the river. The rocks disguise it. They keep predators from spotting the little fish. Predators are animals that eat other animals. Safely hidden, the small fish searches for **tasty** insects and shrimp. The little fish feels safe. The dirty, cloudy water makes it hard to **see**. But danger hides around the corner. The fish doesn't know it, but its beating heart is sending signals through the water.

## Eli, The Electric Eel

Eli the electric eel **slithers**[1] along in the Amazon River too. Although his long, thin body makes him look like an eel, Eli is actually a knifefish. Knifefish are not eels. They are a type of fish similar to catfish. Unlike other fish, they cannot breathe underwater. Eli has to hold his breath as he slides through the river. Eli's long, scaly body is eight feet long. That is longer than a human. Most electric eels grow to be between six to eight feet long.

The Amazon River is the longest river in South America.

Eli is hungry. He usually eats small reptiles, fish, mammals, and birds. However, knifefish have poor eyesight. They can't find **prey**[2] using their eyes alone. Luckily for Eli, he has a special hunting power. The small fish hiding under the rocks is about to learn what it is. The small fish feels a weird **sensation**[3] in the water. It hides in the shelter of the rocks. The feeling gets stronger and stronger. What could it be?

## On the Hunt

The little fish doesn't realize it, but Eli is on the hunt. Although Eli cannot see well, he has something inside him called Sach's organ. Sach's organ sends out small bursts of electricity. By sensing how these bursts move through the

A scientist holding an electric eel shows how long it is.
**Credit:** Marat Orbel, Wikimedia

water, Eli can "see" objects around him. He can also sense the prey's heartbeats and muscle movements under the Amazon River's cloudy surface. The grey rocks and muddy water don't help the small fish to hide. Eli can still sense it **quivering**[4] inside the shelter. He knows exactly where it is hiding.

> 1 **slithers** – moves by sliding
> 2 **prey** – animals hunted by other animals for food
> 3 **sensation** – feeling
> 4 **quivering** – shaking

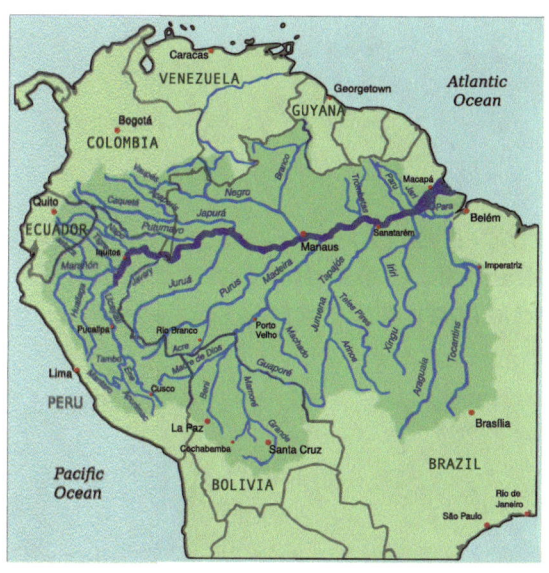 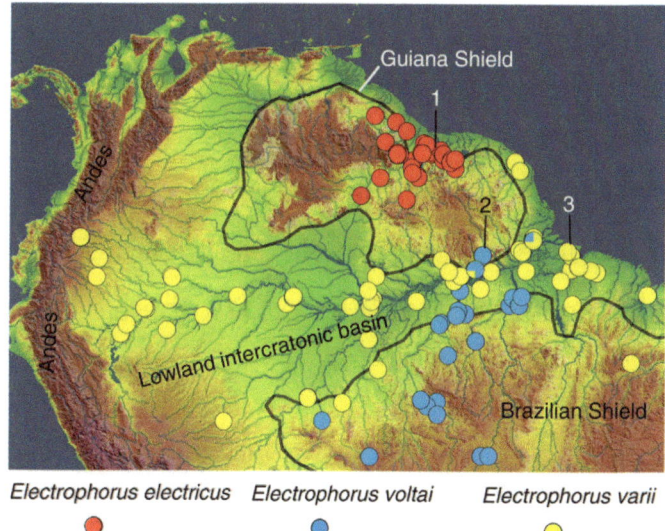

*Scientists have identified three species of electric eel. The first map shows the area around the Amazon River. The second map shows where three different species of electric eel live near the river.*
*Credit: Kmusser, Wikimedia*
*Credit: Carlos David de Santana, William G. R. Crampton, Casey B. Dillman, Renata G. Frederico, Mark H. Sabaj Pérez, Raphaël Covain, Jonathan Ready, Jansen Zuanon, Renildo R. de Oliveira, Raimundo N. Mendes-Júnior, Douglas A. Bastos, Tulio F. Teixeira, Jan H. Mol, Willian Ohara, Natália Castro e Castro, Luiz A. Peixoto, Cleusa Nagamachi, Leandro Sousa, Luciano F. A. Montag, Frank Ribeiro, Joseph C. Waddell, Nivaldo M. Piorsky, Richard P. Vari et Wolmar B. Wosiacki, Wikimedia*

## The Attack

Eli swims right next to his prey. He curls his body up like a C. Inside Eli's body are **cells**[5] called electrocytes. These cells store electricity

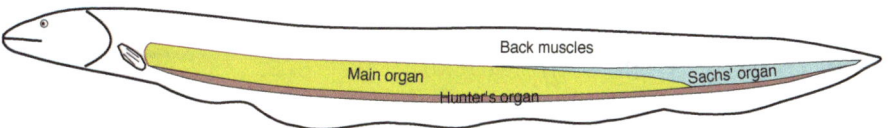

*An electric eel has three organs that store electricity. Sach's organ can deliver a small burst of electricity which the electric eel uses to "see." The Main organ and Hunter's organ are used to shock prey.*
*Credit: Chiswick Chap, Wikimedia*

like a battery. When Eli is near his prey, the electric **charges**[6] jump from his tail. He can release up to 600 **volts**[7] of electricity. Six hundred volts is five times as much as what comes out of your wall socket. It is more than enough to **stun**[8] prey. Eli shocks the small fish with electricity. The fish cannot move. It cannot escape Eli's powerful jaws as he swallows it up.

5 **cells** – small units
6 **charges** – energy stored as electricity
7 **volt** – unit for measuring strength of an electric current
8 **stun** – numb; temporarily paralyze

Although his shock is large enough to stun fish, Eli himself doesn't get harmed by it. Scientists are still not sure exactly why electric eels don't shock themselves. Some think they have special proteins in their bodies that protect them. Others think the electric eels are so big that they are not affected.

## Eli Builds a Nest

With his stomach full, Eli finds a safe area on the bottom of the river. It is time to build a nest. Eli spits on the rocks. His saliva turns into foam. Eli uses the foam to build a safe nest. A female eel will lay about 1,200 eggs there. The male eel guards them until they hatch a few months later. The electric eel babies, called larva, will grow up. They will learn to use their own shocking powers. Someday, Eli's children will be the electric hunters of the Amazon River.

The electric eel isn't the only fish that can shock other fish. The electric catfish can also stun and kill prey with electricity.

The electric eel isn't the only fish that can shock other fish. The electric catfish can also stun and kill prey with electricity.

## Alessandro Volta Invents the Battery

*Did you know that if not for electric eels, people may never have learned to harness the power of electricity? Alessandro Volta, who lived in the 1800s, is known for inventing the first battery. How did he do it? Volta wanted to find a way to produce and store electricity. He knew that electric eels could do that. Volta wondered if people could learn from them.*

*Volta studied the inside of electric eels' bodies. He learned that the electrocytes that powered the eels' shocking powers were stacked inside the body. They looked like a roll of stacked-up coins. Volta decided to try stacking coin-like materials. He experimented many different times. He used different metals.*

*Finally, Volta added saltwater-soaked disks to his stack. It worked! The stack of disks produced and stored electricity. Volta called his "battery" invention an "artificial electric organ." Artificial means something not found in nature but rather produced by humans.*

*Volta was not the last person to learn from the electric eel. Scientists are still working on making a better battery by copying the electric eel's body. They hope to make a soft battery that can move and also bend. Some scientists even want to make a battery that is powered by the human body. This is also like the electric eel. This could help people who need electronic devices inside their bodies for medical reasons.*

# Questions

1. Circle the vocabulary word that best fits the sentence.

   *The water was so cold that their bodies were **(quivering/slithering)** and shuddering when they came out of the pool.*

2. Mark each statement as T (true) or F (false).

   ___ The male eel builds the nest and guards the eggs.

   ___ Electric eels are known to have very sharp eyesight.

   ___ The knifefish is a type of eel.

   ___ Most electric eels grow to be between six to eight feet long.

3. What is the purpose of the electrocytes in electric eels' bodies?

   A. To help them sense when their prey is nearby.

   B. To store electricity like a battery.

   C. To supply material for building their nests.

4. What was the author's purpose in including the section titled *"The Attack"*?

   A. To explain how electric eels capture their prey.

   B. To tell us how much electricity comes out of our wall sockets.

   C. To warn us to be careful of getting electric shocks.

5. Why is "electric eel" a good name for this animal?

   _____

   _____

   _____

# Funny Visitors: Medical Clowns

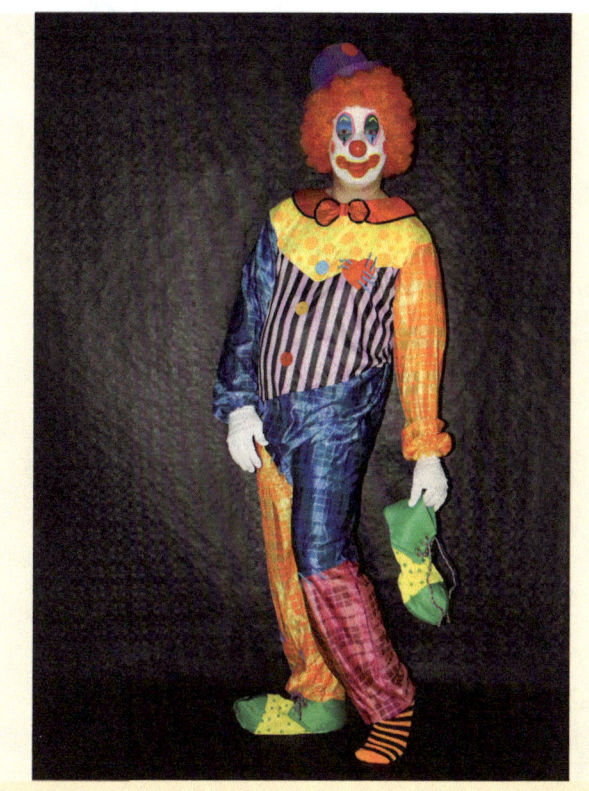
*Clowns are always exciting.*

Have you ever seen a clown perform? It may have been at a birthday party or at some other event. But did you know that clowns also perform in hospitals? Let's read more about these entertaining clowns and their special audiences.

## What is a Clown Doctor?

Have you ever visited someone in the hospital? It may look exciting. You might notice a hospital room full of presents and balloons. You might notice kind, cheerful nurses. But for a sick child, the hospital is not much fun. Often, patients are bored and lonely. They miss their friends and family. Patients get woken up in the middle of the night for all different reasons. They have many check-ups, blood tests, and **procedures**[1] every day. They may feel sick and weak. Although they often receive gifts, children in the hospital can be sad, bored, or afraid. Often, people visit them and try to make them happy. Some people visit very often. They add cheer to a hospital **ward**[2] and break up the long days. These visitors are known as hospital clowns, medical clowns, or clown doctors.

Medical clowns come to the hospital wearing funny costumes. They may have big, red noses and funny hats, ties, and suspenders. Their clown costumes add to the fun while they do all kinds of tricks. They perform and tell jokes.

---

1 **procedures** – ways to get something done
2 **ward** – hospital room or unit

211

The clowns add magic, music, and storytelling to the patient's day. Many of them have trained in **theatrical**[3] arts. They know how to act, sing, and do cool acrobatic tricks.

*A group of clowns entertaining patients during World War I*

Sometimes, a patient has to start a new **treatment**[4] or medicine. A clown doctor can visit and act out the new procedure in an entertaining way. That can be a fun way for the patient to get used to new **routines**.[5]

Clown doctors try to make the patients forget their pain for a while. They make the children happy. Doctors report that medical clowns do help patients feel a bit better. They say that the clowns help the patient feel calmer before **surgery**.[6] They help the patient manage with less pain medication. Laughter makes a person feel better and stronger.

*Medical clowns entertaining a patient in the hospital*

Some medical clowns are also studying medicine. They want to understand what the patient is going through. They want to follow what is going on. The medical clowns might even be in the middle of becoming doctors themselves. They volunteer as clowns when they have free time. This way they can spend time in the hospital learning all about sicknesses and treatments.

Some hospital clowns were sick when they were kids. They understand the pain and loneliness of being stuck in the hospital. They are familiar with the fear and worry that patients have. Those clowns come to the hospital to make things better for the children who are unwell. They understand what the children are going through.

---

3 **theatrical** – having to do with acting or the theater
4 **treatment** – way to deal with medical issues
5 **routines** – ways of doing things
6 **surgery** – operation

## Becoming a Medical Clown

Usually, someone who is interested in becoming a medical clown first goes to a medical clown **academy**[7] or college. It will take them about eight weeks to learn all the skills they need. After that, the college might help them find places to **audition**.[8] If the place likes their act, they might hire them. Other times, medical clowns can find jobs by advertising on their own. Sometimes they start out by performing at birthday parties or other small events. In some cities, it is necessary to get a license to be a clown.

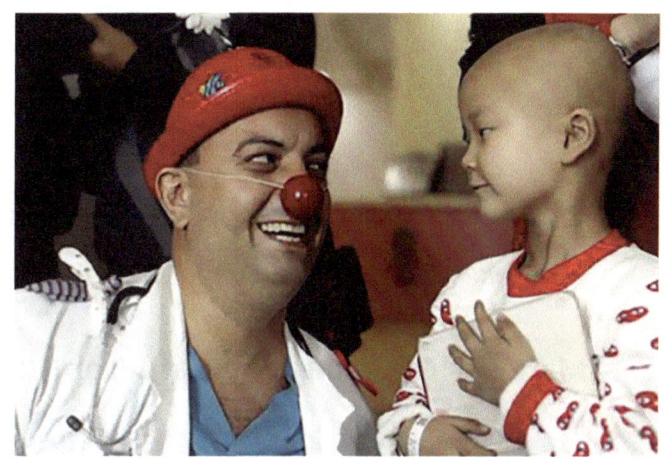

*A medical clown entertaining a patient*
**Credit:** *Sarhan mahamed, Wikimedia*

## The Important Rule of Helping

One important rule when helping others is to respect their **boundaries**.[9] Clown doctors know how important good social skills are when helping another person. They must be **sensitive**[10] to the patient's needs. They must always ask the patient if it is a good time for a visit. Of course, they must also get permission to visit from the patient's parents. The clowns are careful to respect the patient's privacy. They never talk about the patient to others.

---

7 **academy** – school
8 **audition** – try out
9 **boundaries** – limits
10 **sensitive** – thoughtful of; aware of

 **Questions**

1. Circle the vocabulary word that best fits the sentence.

   *He broke his arm so badly that he had to have **(routine/surgery)** to fix it.*

2. Mark each statement as T (true) or F (false).

   ___ It's always a lot of fun for children in the hospital.

   ___ Some medical clowns also study medicine.

   ___ Someone who is interested in becoming a medical clown usually goes to a medical clown academy or college first.

   ___ Medical clowns can visit patients without getting permission from anyone.

3. How do medical clowns cheer patients up?

   A. They wear funny costumes

   B. They do acrobatic tricks

   C. They tell them stories

   D. All of the above

4. What was the author's purpose in including the section titled *"The Important Rule of Helping"*?

   A. To explain how someone becomes a medical clown

   B. To explain how medical clowns help patients feel better

   C. To explain how medical clowns must be sensitive to the patient's needs

5. Why do you think people who were sick when they were children make good medical clowns?

   _____

   _____

   _____

# Buffalo Bill and the Wild West

*A portrait of William F. Cody, known as Buffalo Bill*

Buffalo Bill was a man who lived in the 1800s. No, his parents did not name him after a buffalo. His actual name was William Frederick Cody. How did he earn his nickname? Read on!

Buffalo Bill–William Cody–was born in 1846. The world then was hugely different from the world we live in today. For one thing, jobs were different. There were no computer jobs, bus drivers, or airplane pilots. There were buffalo hunters and Pony Express riders, among others. Buffalo Bill worked these jobs and more. His interesting life fits well with his interesting name.

## Early Life

When young William Cody's father died, he was left with little choice. His family needed money, so he went to work at nine years old. In his first job, he worked for a company that **transported**[1] things across the American West. Cody was an excellent rider, so this job suited him perfectly.

*A buffalo (American bison)*

1 **transported** – transferred; moved

At age 14, William Cody started his next job. He was a Pony Express rider. The Pony Express was a mail delivery service. In the 1800s, American postal workers faced many more difficulties than bad weather. Delivering the mail was an incredibly dangerous job. Riding through harsh landscapes or meeting unfriendly Native Americans or **bandits**[2] was normal. And Pony Express riders often rode for hours. Cody once rode for 22 hours straight! Remember, he had to be awake enough to stay on his horse!

*A U.S. postage stamp honoring the 80th anniversary of the Pony Express*

Cody's trips were action-packed. Roads were not safe. On one ride, he was fleeing Native American **warriors**.[3] He managed to reach the Pony Express station. There, he found that the station manager was dead, and the horses had been stolen. Cody got back on his horse and galloped to the next station. He quickly gathered a group of men. Together they chased the Native Americans and found the stolen horses.

On another day, Cody had to deliver money. He knew that there were thieves on the road. He decided to hide the money under his **saddle**[4] blanket and stuffed his money bag with paper instead. That was a wise choice. When the bandits stopped him, Cody threw the paper-stuffed bag at them and escaped with the money.

## Other Jobs

The American Civil War began. Cody went from Pony Express rider to soldier. When the war ended, he needed a job. He found one. A massive railway was being built across the United States, and the hungry railway builders needed to eat, of course. So, Cody became a buffalo hunter. He killed over 4,000 buffalo in one year. No need to guess where his nickname Buffalo Bill came from!

---

2 **bandits** – robbers; outlaws
3 **warriors** – fighters; soldiers
4 **saddle** – seat on the back of a horse or other animal

Buffalo Bill continued to work for the U.S government as a **scout**.[5] He also worked as a guide, showing people the way through new land. The difference between a scout and a guide is that a scout goes by himself, and a guide leads others. These journeys were extremely unsafe. Other guides refused to make some of the trips that Buffalo Bill agreed to.

*A poster showing Buffalo Bill's Wild West show*

## Entertainer

Buffalo Bill led a **thrilling**[6] life. People read about his adventures in newspapers and novels. Buffalo Bill was now a hero. This was the perfect time for Buffalo Bill to try a different skill. He became an actor. Buffalo Bill performed on stage in the winter and worked as a scout in the summer. Slowly he changed from ordinary William Cody to the famous Buffalo Bill.

*A photograph of Buffalo Bill's Wild West show in Italy*

In 1883, Buffalo Bill organized his own Wild West show. It was full of exciting scenes. He acted out buffalo hunts and exciting Pony Express rides. Buffalo Bill was still acting when he was 71, even though he did need help getting on his horse. In 1917, just two months before he died, Buffalo Bill still brought joy to the stage.

5 **scout** – person or soldier sent out to gather information
6 **thrilling** – very exciting

 # Questions

1. Circle the vocabulary word that best fits the sentence.

   *They threw him into jail along with the other thieves and **(bandits/warriors)**.*

2. Mark each statement as T (true) or F (false).

   ___ Buffalo Bill's parents named him that because they raised buffalo.

   ___ Working for Pony Express was a very boring job.

   ___ Cody worked as a scout for the U.S. government.

   ___ Buffalo Bill was still acting at the end of his life.

3. Number the following events in the order in which they took place.

   ___ Cody became a buffalo hunter.

   ___ Cody transported things across the American West.

   ___ Buffalo Bill became an actor.

   ___ Cody worked for Pony Express.

4. Which of the following sentences from the section titled *"Early Life"* supports the idea that being an American mailman was a very dangerous job?

   A. *Cody once rode for 22 hours straight!*

   B. *However, in the 1800s, American postal workers faced many more difficulties than bad weather.*

   C. *Riding through harsh landscapes or meeting unfriendly Native Americans or bandits was normal.*

5. Why did the other scouts refuse to make some of the trips Buffalo Bill made?

   _____

   _____

   _____

218  Lesson 46: Buffalo Bill and the Wild West

# The Suez Canal: Gateway to Trade Between Europe and Asia

A container ship is a ship with boxes and boxes of goods being transported or sold stacked on it. This container ship is passing through the Suez Canal in Egypt. **Credit:** Maersk Line, Wikimedia

Look around your home. Do you see clothing, furniture, toys, and books? On their journey from where they were made to your home, it's very possible that they traveled through the Suez Canal. What is the Suez Canal, and why is it so important?

## Trade Routes

Naftali Mizrahi can't wait to see his family in the city of Salonika again. He is a **merchant**[1] and trader living in what today is Greece. But in Naftali's time, in the 1800s, Salonika was part of a huge **empire**[2] called the Ottoman Empire.

Naftali's job is very dangerous. He makes his money by bringing goods from far away India and selling them in Europe. Naftali travels to India to buy spices and silk. Then, he needs to make the dangerous journey back home from India. The long trip keeps Naftali away from his family most of the time. To travel back home from India, Naftali has three choices. He can travel by land. That means crossing deserts and mountains, fighting bandits, and trying to keep his **caravan**[3] together. He can travel by ship. But Naftali's crew would have to stay on board their ship for months to get from India back home. This means braving storms, pirates, and rough seas.

---

1 **merchant** – someone who trades goods
2 **empire** – kingdom; territory
3 **caravan** – a group that travels together across a desert

Naftali's third choice combines land and water travel. He can get on board a ship heading from the Arabian Sea, off India's coast, headed for the Red Sea. The Red Sea reaches as far as Egypt's Sinai Desert. Then, Naftali will need to get off the ship with all his goods. He will need to hire a caravan to cross part of the desert. Once he reaches the Mediterranean Sea, Naftali will need to load his goods onto another ship. Then he can set sail again for his home in Salonika.

When he is away from his family and traveling in dangerous areas, Naftali wishes there was a way to sail directly across Egypt. If he didn't have to switch from ship to caravan to ship again, traveling would be much faster and safer.

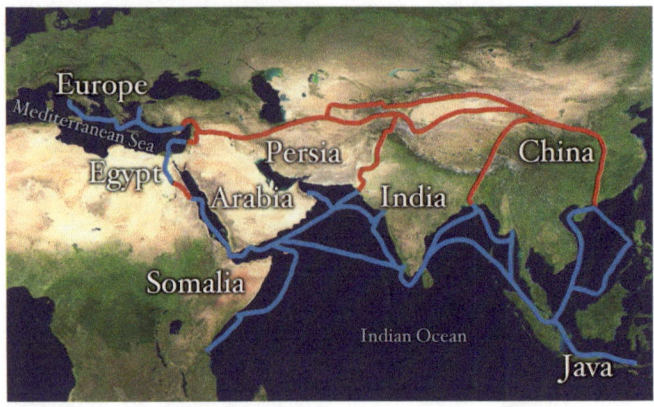

This map shows part of the Asia-Europe trade routes. From India, a trader can travel through Persia and Arabia by land. One can go by sea towards Somalia and from there around the entire African continent. The last option is heading toward Arabia by sea, getting off the ship in Egypt, and then reloading cargo back onto a ship at the coast of the Mediterranean Sea. **Credit:** Wikiality123, Wikimedia

## The Idea to Build a Canal

As it turned out, Naftali wasn't the only one wishing for a new **route**.[4] Many people in European countries wanted a safer shipping route for goods from Asia. They wanted to construct a canal across Egypt. A canal is like a small, man-made river. It would connect the Red Sea with the Mediterranean Sea. It would turn part of the Sinai Desert into a river, allowing ships to cross it. This would change world trade and trade routes forever! The problem was that the Ottoman Empire ruled Egypt. It didn't want a canal built. In 1854, French-born Ferdinand de Lesseps saw his chance to act. His friend, Said (pronounced Siy-ed) Pasha, became the governor of Egypt. Lesseps got permission from Pasha to start on the project. He borrowed millions of francs (French money) to **finance**[5] it. Finally, the canal diggers were breaking ground.

This drawing shows the canal under construction. Trains are bringing materials to be used in building it.

4 **route** – passageway

Lesson 47: The Suez Canal: Gateway to Trade Between Europe and Asia

*Dredgers pulled sand out of the canal space, which made the construction go faster.*
**Credit:** H. (Hippolyte) Arnoux, Wikimedia

*An old postcard showing the office of the Suez Canal Company in Port Said, Egypt*
**Credit:** Cairo Postcard Trust, Wikimedia

*There used to be a huge statue of Ferdinand de Lesseps, the Frenchman who was involved in building the canal. After Egypt nationalized the canal, it took down the statue to show that the canal was Egyptian and not French.*

## Working on the Canal

Working on the canal in the desert was very difficult. It was hot. Workers didn't always have enough food or water. In the beginning, Egyptian slaves were forced to dig the canal. Many died while digging. The workers dug by hand, using shovels and picks.

After Said Pasha died and Ismail Pasha took over, the Suez project stopped using slaves. Instead, workers were brought in from all over the world. These workers built themselves new cities along the canal. Lesseps also brought in heavy machinery, like steam shovels and dredgers. These machines dug out millions of feet worth of sand.

## The Completed Suez Canal

In 1869, the canal was completed! Over time, more and more ships began using it. Today the Suez Canal is part of one of the busiest shipping routes in the world. Nearly 50 ships cross the canal each day, and the canal brings in billions of dollars a year.

5 **finance** – pay for

*These photos show a birds-eye view of the canal and its opening to the Mediterranean Sea.*

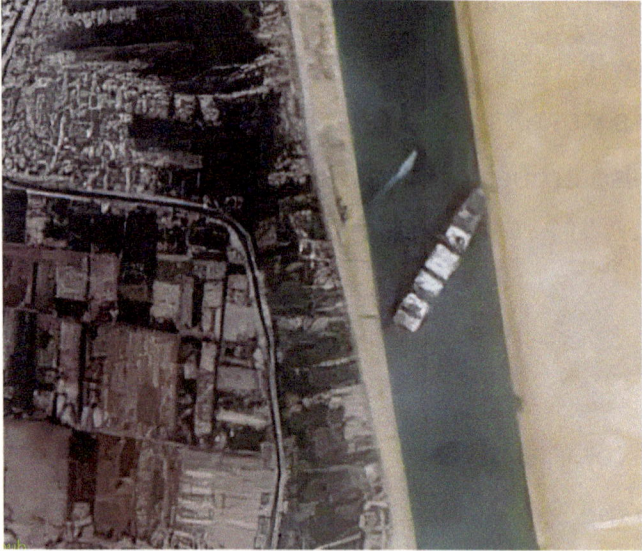

*The container ship Ever Given got stuck in the canal in 2021. It blocked traffic and created a miles-long backup. Countries couldn't get their goods until the blockage was cleared.*
**Credit:** *Pierre Markuse, Wikimedia*

Lesson 47: The Suez Canal: Gateway to Trade Between Europe and Asia

# Questions

1. Circle the vocabulary word that best fits the sentence.

   *There were many horse-drawn wagons in the **(caravan/merchant)**.*

2. Number the following events in the order in which they took place.

   ___ Egyptian slaves were forced to dig the canal.

   ___ Ferdinande de Lesseps got permission from Said Pasha to start on the canal project.

   ___ Many European countries wanted to build a canal across Egypt.

   ___ Lesseps brought in heavy machines, like steam shovels and dredgers.

3. Why was working on the canal in the desert very difficult?

   A. It was hot.

   B. Workers didn't always have enough food and water.

   C. The workers dug by hand with shovels and picks.

   D. All of the above

4. What was the author's purpose in including the section titled *"The Idea to Build a Canal"*?

   A. To tell us why Naftali Mizrahi wanted a canal to be built

   B. To tell us what a canal is

   C. To tell us why many people wanted a canal

5. What was the effect of the Suez Canal being built?

   _____

   _____

   _____

# Elephant Building of Bangkok, Thailand and Other Skyscrapers

A view of skyscrapers in New York City
**Credit:** Pedro Szekely, Wikimedia

Most of you have probably heard of skyscrapers, and many of you may have visited one. Skyscrapers are sometimes called high-rise buildings. Some of the more famous skyscrapers in the United States are landmarks in Manhattan, New York. These are the Empire State Building and the Freedom Tower. (The Statue of Liberty is also **considered**[1] a famous New York landmark, although it is not a skyscraper.) There are many skyscrapers throughout the world. Some are very serious and official-looking. Some are **sleek**[2] and very modern-looking. And some, well... just look weird. Let's tilt our heads way back and have a look at some of the more unusual skyscrapers in the world.

## What Is a Skyscraper?

Before we begin, let's pin down exactly what skyscrapers are. We know they are tall buildings, but not every tall building is a skyscraper. To be considered a skyscraper by today's standards, a building must be at least 492 feet tall. It must have at least 40 **stories**[3]. Skyscrapers must have people living or working in them on a steady basis.

> 1 **considered** – counted as
> 2 **sleek** – graceful; elegant
> 3 **stories** – floors; levels

225

They must have elevators so that people can travel between floors easily and quickly. There are a few other **requirements**[4] that buildings must have to be skyscrapers. Most of them have to do with how the buildings are **constructed**.[5]

## The Elephant Building

There are thousands of skyscrapers in the world, so it would be impossible to discuss them all here. Instead, we'll read about just a few of them. Let's start with a skyscraper that has been named one of the 31 ugliest skyscrapers in the world.

*The Elephant Building*
**Credit:** *Ong-ard architects, Wikimedia*

The Elephant Building of Bangkok, Thailand, stands 335 feet high. Although today a skyscraper must be at least 492 feet tall, when the Elephant Building was built, that rule did not apply. The building was made to **resemble**[6] an elephant, the country's national animal. The building's "ears" are balconies built on several stories. The "**tusks**"[7] are the building's offices. The Elephant Building is **comprised**[8] of three towers. Two of them **represent**[9] the elephant's legs. The third tower represents the elephant's trunk. About 32 of the building's stories consist of shops, offices, and **luxury**[10] apartments. The Elephant Building is also known as the Chang Building. Look at the picture of the Elephant Building above. Does it look like an elephant to you?

## The Robot Building

The Elephant Building isn't the only strange skyscraper in Bangkok. Another one is the Robot Building. Why do you think it's called the Robot Building? If you guessed that it looks like a robot, you are right! The designer of this skyscraper got the idea to make it that way when his son walked into his office carrying his toy robot.

---

4 **requirements** – necessary things
5 **constructed** – built
6 **resemble** – look like
7 **tusks** – long, pointed teeth of some animals, such as elephants and walruses
8 **comprised** – made of
9 **represent** – symbolize; stand for
10 **luxury** – grand; magnificent

He had been trying to come up with an idea for quite a while without any luck. But when he saw his son's robot, it seemed to be just what he was looking for.

The Robot Building is 20 stories high. Again, although skyscrapers today must have more than 40 stories, when the Robot Building was built, that rule did not apply. The walls of the upper floors are set back further from the street than those of the lower floors. They create the robot's "body." The top section is the "head." It has two round windows resembling eyelids over eyeballs. These give the robot a slightly sleepy appearance. Antennas on the roof add to the "roboty" look. There are large nuts on both sides of the head.

*The Robot Building.*
**Credit:** *Sumet Jumsai, Wikimedia*

(Not the kind of nuts you eat; the kind used to hold things together.) The nuts look like the robot's ears. The Robot Building cost $10 million to build. It is used as the main office of a large bank. Sumet Jumsai, the designer, won a **prestigious**[11] award for the Robot Building. Look at the photo. What do you think of that robot?

## The Turning Torso

Let's leave Bangkok for now and visit Malmo, Sweden. Here we can find what might well be the first modern twisting skyscraper. The Turning Torso is 623 feet tall and has 54 stories. It is Sweden's tallest skyscraper. It contains 147 apartments for people to live in and is the third-tallest building in Europe where people live. Besides the apartments, it also has a special room for storing wine. People living in the Turning Torso enjoy its spa, which is used for resting and relaxing.

*The Turning Torso.*
**Credit:** *Väsk, Wikimedia*

Look at the picture of the Turning Torso. Now let's take a vote. Which of these three skyscrapers is your favorite?

11 **prestigious** – very important

# Questions

1. Circle the vocabulary word that best fits the sentence.

   Most people think I **(resemble/represent)** my brother because we are the same height and have the same color hair.

2. Place a check mark next to each statement that correctly describes the Robot Building.

   ___ It is located in Malmo, Sweden.

   ___ Its floors get smaller as they move upward.

   ___ It has round windows that resemble eyes.

   ___ It has been named one of the 31 ugliest skyscrapers in the world.

3. Which of the following is NOT something a building needs to be considered a skyscraper?

   A. Must be at least 492 feet tall

   B. Must have people living or working in it on a steady basis

   C. Must have more than 1,000 windows

   D. Must be at least 40 stories high

4. Which of the following statements best summarizes the lesson?

   A. It can be hard to think of ways to design a skyscraper.

   B. Some of the world's many skyscrapers are strange and unusual.

   C. Not every tall building is a skyscraper.

5. If it had been up to you, would you have called the Elephant Building one of the 31 ugliest skyscrapers in the world? Why or why not?

   _____

   _____

# Deep in the Sea: Deep Sea Divers

*Divers under the water*

Do you like to swim? Some people swim almost every day. Divers spend a lot of time underwater, and they get paid to do it. Most divers spend time in the ocean, very deep down. However, some work in other places, like lakes or pools.

## Becoming a Deep-Sea Diver

People who become divers are usually fantastic swimmers. But they are still required to take diving classes and exams. Divers also take classes to learn about the equipment and **gear**[1] they will use, what to do in an emergency, and all other information that they must know. Altogether, they are in class for 100 hours! Different divers have different jobs, and each job has its own **training**.[2] Divers that do underwater work need training in that area. They may need classes in construction or metalwork if they will be doing underwater construction.

Certain divers also study different types of **marine**[3] science. Divers can study different topics about the sea, such as animal life in the ocean or the plants and rocks found on the ocean floor. Divers need to stay calm—always. They need to know how to focus when another diver needs help under the water or if a piece of equipment breaks in the middle of a job. It wouldn't be a good idea to panic at that time!

---

1 **gear** – special outfit for a certain job
2 **training** – classes and instruction in preparation for a certain job
3 **marine** – having to do with the sea

## Diving Jobs

Many people like to dive for fun. But when diving is a job, the diver must dive in assigned places.

*Divers practicing in a pool*

A research diver is one type of diver. Some research divers explore everything that is under the water, like seaweed, fish, and giant squids. Other research divers collect plants and animals to bring back to a laboratory so that others can study them. Research divers may travel to distant locations to study life beneath the ocean's surface. They might travel all the way to Antarctica, where there aren't too many people around and it is very cold. These divers dig holes in the ice on the ocean and then dive in. They have to bring along all their equipment, food, and supplies to Antarctica—there are no stores there.

*Animals and plants in the sea*

Sometimes divers stay underwater for a long time—even up to a month! They travel with a team of divers, and they all stay in a special cabin, deep underwater. The divers take turns going out of the cabin and into the sea. It can be hard for such divers to be away from their families for so long, but they usually get a long break when they get back home.

## Other Types of Divers

Some divers work closer to home. They are called inland divers because they work further inland, not in the ocean. They work wherever there is deep water, such as big lakes, rivers, or on bridges or docks. They can set up and fix pipes. Sometimes, they measure underwater spaces.

*Divers in their gear, ready to go!*

Inland divers also dig for tunnels and paint anything that is under the water. They can build or repair bridges, gas lines, and sewers. They can search for lost objects. Inland divers have work schedules according to the weather because if a lake freezes, they can't dive in it.

Some lucky divers get to work in waterparks. When slides and pools need fixing under the water, a diver is needed to do the work. The diver paints, repairs, and sets up everything that is needed in the waterpark.

Aquariums need divers to take care of all their underwater needs. In an aquarium, the divers dive into deep fish tanks. They clean the inside of the glass and all the rocks and plants. Divers set up the lights inside the tank. They check on the fish and feed them.

There are many other diving jobs, including diving for the army, the police, and for newspapers. All diving jobs are interesting and always very wet!

 # Questions

1. Circle the vocabulary word that best fits the sentence.

   *Astronauts have to wear special **(gear/marine)** when they are on a space mission.*

2. Mark each statement as T (true) or F (false).

   \_\_\_ Divers who work in Antarctica have to bring all their own equipment, food, and supplies.

   \_\_\_ People who are good swimmers can become divers without taking any classes or exams.

   \_\_\_ Some divers learn how to do construction or metalwork.

   \_\_\_ Inland divers live underwater year-round.

3. Place a check mark next to each statement that correctly describes research divers.

   \_\_\_ They collect plants and animals to bring back to a laboratory.

   \_\_\_ They work in laboratories, studying plants and animals.

   \_\_\_ They sometimes travel to far locations.

   \_\_\_ They work further in on the land and not in the ocean.

4. Which of the following sentences from the section titled *"Other Types of Divers"* supports the idea that the work of inland divers depends on the weather?

   A. *Sometimes, they measure underwater spaces.*

   B. *Inland divers also dig for tunnels and paint anything that is under the water.*

   C. *Inland divers have work schedules according to the weather because if a lake freezes, they can't dive in it.*

5. If you were a deep sea diver, where would you like to work and why?

   _____

   _____

   _____

# Welcome to Anchorage, Alaska

What is your favorite vacation experience? **Seeking**[1] new adventures? Exploring old cities? Relaxing under shady palm trees? Today we will visit mountains, snow, and possibly see a bear. Welcome to Anchorage, Alaska.

## Where is Anchorage?

*A ship leaving Anchorage port. Behind the ship are the city of Anchorage and the Chugach mountains.*
**Credit:** *Jack Connaher, Wikimedia*

Anchorage is a city in Alaska, a **constituent**[2] state of the United States. It is much further north than you would expect. Travel up through the lower 48 states, then up through Canada, and you will reach Alaska. Not many people live in Alaska, but there are still more people than polar bears. Anchorage is the largest city in the state. It is a port city surrounded by mountains. A **port**[3] is an area where ships can load or unload.

The Arctic Circle is an **imaginary**[4] line far north of the equator. The region north of this imaginary line is called the Arctic. Parts of Alaska are north of the Arctic Circle, although Anchorage is not. However, it is close. In fact, it is so close that Anchorage is a great place to stay if you want to brave a visit to the Arctic's frozen world.

---

1 **seeking** – looking for
2 **constituent** – part of a whole
3 **port** – dock; harbor
4 **imaginary** – not real; existing only in the imagination

## History

Native Americans lived in the area long before Anchorage became a city. Anchorage was **established**[5] in 1914 as the **headquarters**[6] of the company building the Alaskan railway. It started as a tent city, an area of people living in temporary structures. Anchorage slowly developed from a set of campsites into a proper city. Today you can visit Oscar Anderson's house. Anderson said he was the 18th person to arrive at the tent city. He owned one of Anchorage's first houses. Disaster struck in 1964 when a powerful earthquake hit Anchorage. People died, and houses **collapsed**.[7] However, Anchorage was rebuilt and became the city it is today.

*A mountain peak near Anchorage.*
**Credit:** *Nathan Searles, Wikimedia*

Anchorage is Alaska's main port, but this is not the only important thing about this place. The United States has an army base in Anchorage, where soldiers are trained to help defend the country.

## Weather and Climate

When we think of Alaska, most people picture freezing snow and **blustery**[8] winds. This is true for some of the year. But Anchorage is not always snowy. It can have pleasant and even warm weather in the summer.

Sleeping during the Anchorage summer can get interesting. Anchorage is near the Arctic Circle.

*A moose resting on a lawn in Anchorage during the summer.*

---

5 **established** – set up; formed; started
6 **headquarters** – main office
7 **collapsed** – fell down
8 **blustery** – gusty; strong; forceful

That far north, it is mostly light outside during the summer. It will probably be light when you try to go to bed after a busy day out and about. However, the days are very short in the winter. The shortest day will only give around five and a half hours of daylight. Lunchtime could look like a midnight feast!

### Things To Do

Anchorage is a great city to explore. The city is packed with fun outdoor activities. You can enjoy them on your own or with family and friends.

Oscar Anderson's house.
**Credit:** 61north, Wikimedia

There are numerous biking and hiking trails. Visitors can enjoy a gentle walk around the city. Do you want a bigger challenge? Then come prepared with energy and equipment. The nearby mountains can be tough to climb, but many people do. Be ready for beautiful views on whichever trail you choose.

Boating is a fun way to explore the nearby sea, rivers, and lakes. Kayaks are perfect for enjoying a peaceful day on the water. Travel past **glaciers**[9] and paddle around **icebergs**.[10] Spot sea animals like otters, dolphins, and even whales. Animal lovers, listen closely. Besides the sea creatures, there are many land animals. Bears, wolves, and even moose live in and around Anchorage.

Portage Glacier is about 50 miles from Anchorage. **Credit:** Frank K., Wikimedia

If you are lucky enough to be in Anchorage at the right time, you may notice something beautiful and strange up in the night sky. **Shimmering**[11] curtains of light dance in the sky. These are the famous Northern Lights.

---

9 **glaciers** – massive blocks of slow-moving ice
10 **icebergs** – big blocks of ice floating in the sea
11 **shimmering** – sparkling; glittering

When you need a rest after all the hiking and kayaking, Anchorage has the answer. Take a helicopter ride to view the stunning area from above. Visit art galleries and museums. And, of course, a trip to Alaska would not be complete without dog sledding!

*Northern Lights in Alaska.*

# Questions

1. **Circle the vocabulary word that best fits the sentence.**

   *Looking at the shapes of clouds, one can sometimes see **(established/imaginary)** beings.*

2. **Mark each statement as T (true) or F (false).**

   ___ Anchorage started as a tent city before it developed into a proper city.

   ___ The United States has an army base in Anchorage.

   ___ Anchorage is north of the Arctic Circle.

   ___ In Anchorage, summer days are short and winter days are long.

3. **Who was Oscar Anderson?**

   A. The person who discovered Alaska

   B. The owner of one of the first houses in Anchorage

   C. The person in charge of building the Alaskan railway

   D. The head of the army base in Anchorage

4. **Which of the following sentences from the section titled *"Where is Anchorage?"* supports the idea that Alaska is much further north than you would expect?**

   A. *Anchorage is a city in Alaska, a constituent state of the United States.*

   B. *Not many people live in Alaska, but there are still more people than polar bears.*

   C. *Travel up through the lower 48 states, then up through Canada, and you will reach Alaska.*

5. **Would you rather visit Anchorage in the summer or winter? Explain your answer.**

   _____

   _____

   _____

237

# Winemaking: From Vineyard to Market

You probably drink grape juice more often than wine, but the two are close cousins. Wine is grape juice that has gone through a process to increase its alcohol level. Let's read about the wine-making process, from vineyard to market.

Bottles of wine for sale.
Credit: Prayitno / Thank you for (12 millions +) view from Los Angeles, USA, Wikimedia

## History of Winemaking

Winemaking has existed since ancient times, especially in the Middle East and Eastern Europe. Archaeologists have found vines, seeds, and **fragments**[1] of pottery jugs in the ruins of ancient civilizations. After **analyzing**[2] the **residue**[3] on the jugs, they have concluded that these vessels were used to store wine. The wine may not have been made from grapes, though. The ancient Chinese made wine from fruit, honey, and rice. China is also one of the earliest known places where wine was made from grapes. The ancient Greeks and Romans also made wine from grapes. Greece is thought to be one of the first places that produced wine for sale, not just for home use. The Greeks even **exported**[4] wine to be sold in other places.

---

1 **fragments** – broken pieces
2 **analyzing** – examining; inspecting
3 **residue** – matter that is left over after a process is finished
4 **exported** – sent to another country for sale

## What Fruits Can Be Used to Make Wine?

Wine can be made from many different kinds of fruit. Apples, plums, berries, pomegranates, pumpkins , and kiwis can all be used to make wine. Believe it or not, those pesky yellow dandelions that pop up on your lawn every spring can also be made into wine! However, 99.9 percent of all wine is made from grapes, because grapes make the best wine.

*Fragments of pottery jugs.*
**Credit:** *The Portable Antiquities Scheme/ The Trustees of the British Museum, Wikimedia*

## Ingredients and Process

Wine has very few ingredients. In fact, if grapes are being used to make the wine, nothing else is needed. (Usually, though, other ingredients are added.) The process is simple. First, the grapes are picked. This can be done by having people cut them off the vines with scissors, or it can be done by machine. The stems are removed, and the grapes are washed well. Then the grapes are crushed. This step has been done in different ways over the years. In ancient times, grapes were crushed not by hand but by foot. Yes, that's right! People stepped on them with their bare feet. (Hopefully, they washed their feet well first.) Thank goodness, as time went on, crushing machines did the job. Today, **sophisticated**,[5] computer-controlled machines are used for crushing the grapes.  Then the crushed grapes are transferred to tanks or **vats**.[6] The type of container used depends on what type of wine the **manufacturer**[7] wants to make.

*Wine grapes on the vine.*
**Credit:** *Tomás Castelazo, Wikimediaw*

When the grapes are crushed, they release their juice. The juice comes in contact with yeast that is found naturally in vineyards.

---

5 **sophisticated** – complicated; complex; advanced
6 **vats** – containers
7 **manufacturer** – person or business that makes things for sale

240    Lesson 51: Winemaking: From Vineyard to Market

You have probably heard of yeast because that is what causes bread and other doughs to rise. When the yeast reacts with the sugar in the grape juice, the juice ferments, meaning it changes its natural sugar to alcohol. The process is called fermentation.

Vats for storing wine.

It can take a few days to a few weeks for the grapes to ferment completely. Sometimes the process even lasts a few months. How long it takes depends on the type of grapes used, the weather, and the amount of alcohol that the manufacturer **prefers**.[8] If the grapes do not have enough time to ferment properly, the wine will not taste good. The fermentation process must be complete for the wine's full flavor to be released.

Manufacturers may add extra sugar to the crushed grape mixture to increase the wine's alcohol level. They also add preservatives to keep the wine from spoiling quickly. Other ingredients are added to change the wine's appearance, flavor, and color.

## Aging

After the fermentation process is complete, the wine sits in barrels or stainless steel vats for a period of time. This is called the aging process. Once again, how long the wine is aged depends on the type of wine the manufacturer wants. Some wines are aged for many years. Once the wine has aged enough, it is bottled and shipped to stores, ready to be sold and enjoyed!

A wine store.
**Credit:** Dough4872, Wikimedia

8 **prefers** – likes better

 **Questions**

1. Circle the vocabulary word that best fits the sentence.

   *Our teacher **(exported/prefers)** that we write with a pen instead of a pencil..*

2. Number the following events in the order in which they take place.

   ___ The grapes are picked off the vines.

   ___ The wine is transferred to tanks or vats.

   ___ The grapes are crushed.

   ___ The wine is allowed to ferment.

3. Why are other ingredients usually added to wine?

   A. To change its color

   B. To change its appearance

   C. To change its flavor

   D. All of the above

4. Which of the following sentences from the section titled *"Ingredients and Process"* supports the idea that wine has other ingredients besides the crushed fruit?

   A. *Usually, though, other ingredients are added.*

   B. *In ancient times, grapes were crushed not by hand but by foot.*

   C. *The type of container used depends on what type of wine the manufacturer wants to make.*

5. What does the length of the fermentation process depend on?

   _____

   _____

   _____

# Amazon: From Mocked to Amazing

Amazon boxes are a familiar sight for most people today, but it wasn't always like that.

It's always exciting to get something in the mail. It's even more exciting if it's a package. These days, many packages come from a company called Amazon. People order gifts for each other, clothing, shoes, and home-decorating items. You can get toys, pet supplies, and food on Amazon. Amazon sells many other items, too. Amazon is a huge business that makes billions of dollars every year. It is easy to order items from Amazon. They can deliver items faster than most other stores, often for free. If you think Amazon was always around or that it started as a huge business everyone wanted to get involved with, you will soon be surprised. Read on to learn more about Amazon's unusual start.

## Jeff Bezos

Jeff Bezos is the person who **founded**[1] Amazon. Today he is one of the richest people in the world. Some rich people were born into wealthy families, where they got expensive presents, like apartment buildings and fancy cars. Such kids can grow up learning all about money and business. Bezos was not one of those kids.

---

1 **founded** – started; created

243

Bezos's family lived on a ranch when he was young. His father was an **immigrant**.² Jeff's parents worked hard, and Jeff helped out. The family moved to Florida when Jeff got older, and that's where he went to high school. He did well in school and loved to experiment with **electronics**³ at home. After high school, Bezos went to college and earned a degree. When he was 30 years old, Bezos decided to start a company in his garage. At first, Amazon only sold books.

Many people thought that Amazon would not work out. They said there were enough other bookstores. Some of those are huge businesses that sell books all over the world. Although buying online wasn't so common when Amazon started out, people thought that all the other book companies would start their own websites, and then Amazon would go out of business.

*A package at your door is always exciting.*

At first, it seemed like those people were right. For the first few years, Amazon did not make much money. All the money Amazon made through sales had to be spent on growing the company. Growing a company means making it bigger and more **profitable**.⁴

## "Get Big Fast"

But Bezos thought that Amazon could be different from other bookstores and businesses. He had some ideas on how to make Amazon easy and pleasant for people to use so that customers would come back after using it once.

*Jeff Bezos is one of the richest men in the world.*
**Credit:** *Seattle City Council from Seattle, Flickr*

> 2 **immigrant** – someone who moved from a different country
> 3 **electronics** – computerized devices
> 4 **profitable** – successful; making a lot of money

244    Lesson 52: Amazon: From Mocked to Amazing

From the start, Bezos knew that he wanted his company to grow big, famous, and successful. He chose the name Amazon because it starts with the first letter of the alphabet and because Amazon is the name of the largest river in the world. His motto was "Get Big Fast." He printed t-shirts for all his **employees**[5] with that motto on them.

It turned out that customers did like Amazon. Many people think Amazon is so popular because it is a company that focuses on making customers happy. The website has helpful features, like telling customers what products they might like based on what they bought in the past. Amazon also lets customers know if others have enjoyed a certain product. Other sellers can also advertise their **merchandise**[6] through Amazon, making it more convenient for people to find what they want to buy. Within two years, Amazon had a million customers.

Amazon also created many jobs. So many people work for Amazon, in offices, on delivery trucks, or in fulfillment centers.

Today, Jeff Bezos is a rich guy. His story can help us remember that if you have a good idea, you should go for it. Never mind the people who don't believe in you.

*At first, Amazon sold only books.*

*This picture shows part of the long Amazon River. Bezos wanted his business to be the biggest business.* **Credit:** *lubasi, Wikimedia*

*Today, Amazon has many fulfillment centers that send out orders.*
**Credit:** *Álvaro Ibáñez, Wikipedia*

5 **employees** – workers
6 **merchandise** – goods; products

 # Questions

1. Circle the vocabulary word that best fits the sentence.

   The clothing store has new **(immigrant/merchandise)** coming in every day.

2. Mark each statement as T (true) or F (false).

   ___ Jeff Bezos grew up in a rich family.

   ___ At first, Amazon only sold books.

   ___ Jeff Bezos named his company Amazon because it means "Get Big Fast" in Spanish.

   ___ Amazon focuses on making its website easy and pleasant to use.

3. Number the following events in the order in which they took place.

   ___ Jeff Bezos started a company in his garage.

   ___ Jeff Bezos became a rich man.

   ___ Jeff Bezos helped out on his family's ranch.

   ___ Jeff Bezos named his company Amazon.

4. Which of the following sentences from the section titled *"'Get Big Fast'"* supports the idea that Jeff Bezos had ideas about how to make customers use Amazon again after using it once?

   A. *He printed t-shirts for all his employees with that motto on them.*

   B. *The website has helpful features, like telling customers what products they might like based on what they bought in the past.*

   C. *So many people work for Amazon, in offices, on delivery trucks, or in fulfillment centers.*

5. What can the story about Jeff Bezos and Amazon help us remember?

   _____

   _____

   _____

Lesson 52: Amazon: From Mocked to Amazing

# How Dimes Defeated Polio

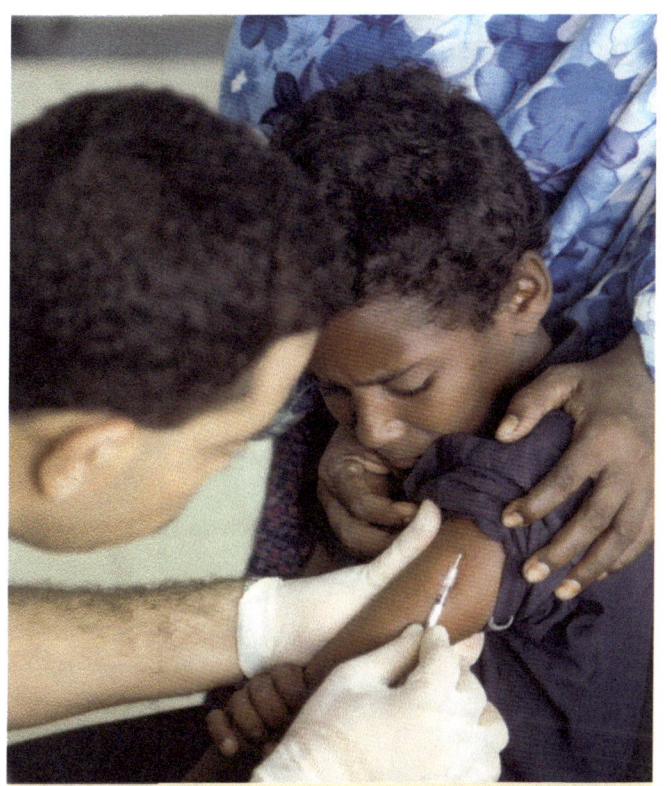

This boy is getting the polio vaccine. This will keep him from getting sick with the very dangerous disease.

Have you ever wanted to be a hero? If you picture a hero, you probably think of someone with superpowers. Or maybe you think of someone who saves a victim of drowning. Dr. Jonas Salk was a hero who saved the lives of millions of people. He did it all by studying diseases. Let's read about how he saved so many people and the national movement that helped him.

## Polio: A Frightening Disease

Franklin Roosevelt was living a happy life. At age 39, he had a good job in the government, a happy family, and a lot of money. Then, one day in 1921, Roosevelt set sail on his private ship. Suddenly, he lost his balance and fell into the water. Roosevelt didn't think much of it, but the next day, he felt sicker and weaker. He fell again. By the third day, he could no longer stand.

Roosevelt learned that he had polio, a terrifying disease. He was very concerned. Polio made many people ill in the 1900s. It usually affected children. Thousands of children died from polio every summer. Thousands became too weak to walk without crutches. Others could not walk at all, and needed a wheelchair to get around. Sometimes, their muscles became completely **paralyzed**.[1] The muscles that made their lungs work were paralyzed too. They needed a machine called an "iron lung" just to breathe.

---

1 **paralyzed** – unable to move

## The March of Dimes

Roosevelt did not die from polio, but he did become paralyzed. He learned to walk with **braces**,[2] and he also used a wheelchair. Still, Roosevelt was an important man. In fact, he later became the president of the United States. He used his fame and wealth to stop the spread of polio. Roosevelt started an organization and paid researchers to find a cure for the disease.

Many people gave money to Roosevelt's organization, the March of Dimes. Many were not wealthy. Some were even children. The March of Dimes asked people to give — even if it was just a dime. A dime is not a lot of money. But if thousands of people give, it adds up. And that's exactly what happened .

## Jonas Salk

Dr Jonas Salk developed a vaccine against polio.

Jonas Salk was born in 1914, long before Roosevelt got polio. Jonas's family did not have a lot of money. His mother urged him to go to school, learn a lot, and get a good job. Jonas became a doctor. When he saw many children getting sick from polio, he decided to act. Salk started writing about ways to defeat polio. The March of Dimes liked his ideas. They gave Salk money to develop a **vaccine**.[3] All those dimes that people across the country had collected were being put to use.

## A Killed Vaccine

Salk used the money to study vaccines. He knew that sometimes **injecting**[4] a virus into people could teach their bodies how to fight the disease. But injecting polio into a person could make them ill. Salk decided to try a new approach.

---

2 **braces** – supports for weak legs to help people walk
3 **vaccine** – shot; injection
4 **injecting** – giving medicine through a shot

**248** Lesson 53: How Dimes Defeated Polio

He killed the polio virus in his laboratory. He did this by mixing it with something that made it **inactive**.[5] The dead virus couldn't make people sick. Still, it might be able to teach their bodies how to fight polio. This would prevent them from getting sick with it.

## Testing the Vaccine

Dr. Salk didn't know if the vaccine would work. He decided to test it first by injecting it into his own children. That test was successful. His children were protected against polio. Dr. Salk tested his vaccine on another million children. It worked better than anyone could have imagined.

## Getting Rid of Polio

People were very excited! Dr. Salk was asked how much he wanted to sell his vaccine for. Dr. Salk explained that he couldn't **patent**[6] or sell it. It was paid for by the country's dimes and belonged to the world. Dr. Salk explained that patenting the vaccine to make money from it would be like "patenting the sun." Just like the sun "belonged" to everyone, so did the vaccine. Dr. Salk gave it away for free.

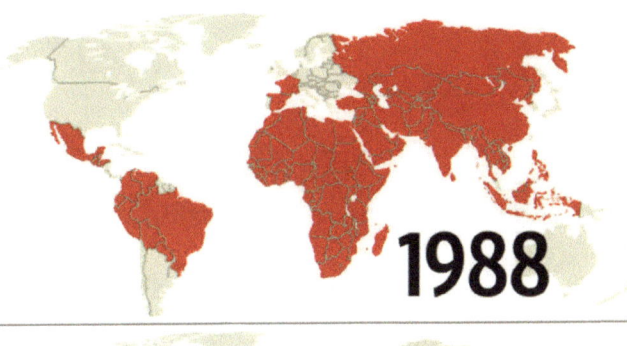

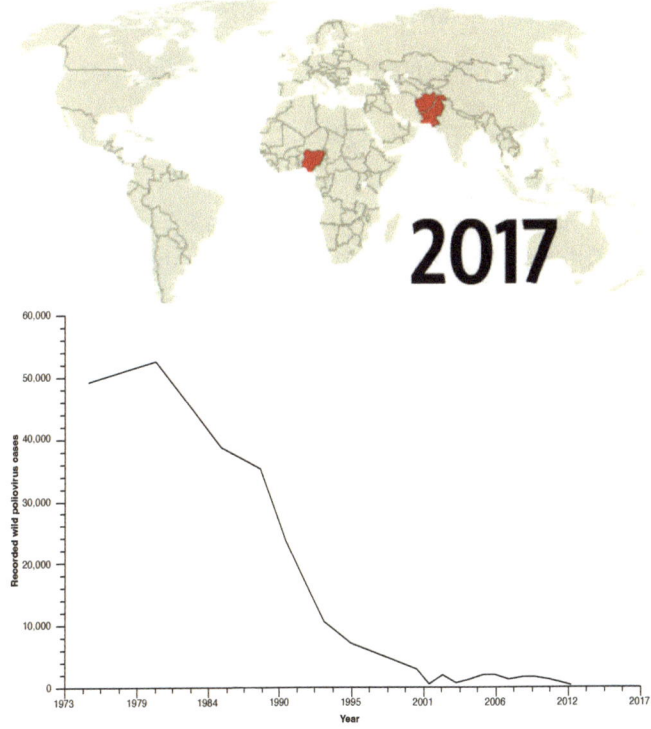

*The graph shows how there have been fewer and fewer polio cases thanks to the vaccine. The map shows how countries worldwide have gotten rid of polio. Only a few countries (the ones in red) still had polio cases as of 2017.*
**Credit:** *MicroChip08, Wikimedia*
**Credit:** *World Health Organization, Wikimedia*

Countries across the world rushed to use Dr. Salk's vaccine. Nowadays, there are only a few hundred cases of polio each year and almost none in America. Instead of fearing summers, children can enjoy swimming, running, and playing, thanks to Dr. Salk and the March of Dimes.

---

5 **inactive** – not active or alive
6 **patent** – the right to make or sell a product

## Dr. Albert Sabin

Surprisingly, even though Dr. Salk was the first to invent a polio vaccine, a different vaccine quickly became more popular. This vaccine was invented by Dr. Albert Sabin.

Unlike Salk's vaccine, Dr. Sabin's vaccine used live polio, not an inactive form. This meant that its benefits would last longer. Someone who got the vaccine invented by Dr. Salk would need to be vaccinated again a few years later to teach his body how to fight polio again. But someone who got Dr. Sabin's vaccine was protected for life. Dr. Sabin's vaccine was also cheaper to make.

Dr. Salk's vaccine had to be given by way of a shot. Dr. Sabin's vaccine was swallowed. Children liked the vaccine they could swallow from a spoon or lick off a sugar cube.

In the end, there were so many benefits to Dr. Sabin's vaccine that most countries started using it. After inventing the vaccine, Dr. Sabin led a worldwide fight to get rid of polio for good.

# Questions

1. Circle the vocabulary word that best fits the sentence.

   He walks so well that no one even notices that he wears *(braces/patent)*.

2. Mark each statement as T (true) or F (false).

   ___ Roosevelt himself paid Salk to find a vaccine to prevent polio.

   ___ The iron lung helped children learn to walk again.

   ___ Dr. Salk's vaccine used a killed virus.

   ___ The March of Dimes encouraged people to donate as little as a dime.

3. Place a check mark next to each statement that correctly describes Jonas Salk:

   ___ He came from a very rich family.

   ___ He wanted to help children who were sick with polio.

   ___ The first people he tested his vaccine on were his own children.

   ___ He charged a lot of money for using the polio vaccine.

4. Which of the following sentences from the section titled *"Getting Rid of Polio"* supports the idea that Dr. Salk could not sell or patent his vaccine? Circle the correct answer.

   A. *Just like the sun "belonged" to everyone, so did the vaccine.*

   B. *Dr. Salk was asked how much he wanted to sell his vaccine for.*

   C. *Instead of fearing summers, children can enjoy swimming, running, and playing, thanks to Dr. Salk and the March of Dimes.*

5. What was the effect of Roosevelt starting the March of Dimes?

   _____

   _____

   _____

# Something Fishy: The Fishing Industry

Many people fish, either for fun or to earn a living.

Fishing is a great hobby if you enjoy spending time outdoors.

When lots of stores and businesses make money from one type of thing, that is called an industry. You might be surprised to hear that almost two million people in the United States have jobs that have to do with fishing. Let's find out more about it.

## Making Money From Fishing

Do you know anyone who likes to fish? Many people fish as a hobby. They wear tall rain boots and maybe a sun hat. They bring lots of supplies along. They might know which lake is the best for fishing and even which spot in the lake. Other people fish for a **living**.[1] They make money from fishing. There are many other ways people make money from fishing besides actually catching fish.

The main people who fish are fishermen. Fishermen can make money from fishing in a few different ways. Some of them sell their fish to people who have fish tanks. Others give fishing lessons to children and adults who want to learn the tricks of the trade.

1 **living** – income; way to make money

253

Fishermen can make money by taking people along on their fishing trips and letting them catch some fish. They can even open fishing day camps, where kids can fish every day!

Pet shops pay fishermen to supply them with the fish they sell. Fishermen can work for companies that sell fish to many stores. Those fishermen earn money doing something they enjoy, but they also have to work hard. They have to catch a lot of fish every day. Such fishermen work many hours of the day, and sometimes it can be very cold or rainy. Most fishermen love to fish, but if it is their job, they have to do it every single day, even when the weather is not so enjoyable.

*Fishermen need lots of equipment.*

Some fishermen have lots of interesting stories about the places they went and the fish they caught. They write books or give speeches about their lives. Sometimes they take pictures of pretty or unusual fish. Then they sell their books or pictures.

There are many fishing contests that fishermen can enter. Some contests give prizes to whoever caught the biggest fish. Others give prizes to whoever caught the most fish. Some contests are open to fishermen from all over the country or even a few countries. Those contests can give huge prizes, but the fishermen also have to pay to travel there if it is not near their home. Of course, a fisherman can't **rely**[2] on the prize money from contests to live off. Winning a contest just gives the fisherman some extra money.

*Fishermen can get paid to give lessons to children and teens who are interested in fishing.*

2 **rely** – count on

Fishermen can enter contests to catch big or beautiful fish.

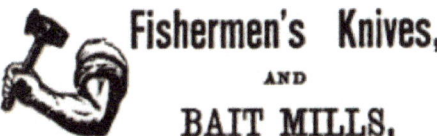

An 1870 advertisement for a producer and supplier of fishing supplies

Companies that sell fish to fish stores and aquariums hire fishermen to catch all the fish.

## Stores and Companies

Fishermen need lots of supplies and equipment. Some of their equipment is inexpensive, like the **bait**[3] they put on their fishing rods to **attract**[4] the fish. Other items that fishermen need can be very expensive, like boats. Anyone who owns or works in a fishing supplies store makes money from fishermen. Also, the companies and workers that design and **produce**[5] all the supplies make a lot of money from fishermen. There are also the truck drivers who deliver fishing rods, buckets, tall boots, and other supplies from the factories to the stores. Every fishing company has many people working for it, not only the fishermen. There are also managers, secretaries, deliverymen, and cleaners. Big companies also may hire people who are in charge of **advertising**[6] or in charge of hiring the other workers.

That adds up to many workers involved in the fishing industry!

3 **bait** – something put at the end of a fishing rod to attract fish
4 **attract** – tempt; pull towards
5 **produce** – make; create
6 **advertising** – letting people know about; announcing

# Questions

1. Circle the vocabulary word that best fits the sentence.

   *Sometimes stores have sales to **(rely/attract)** people to come and shop there.*

2. Mark each statement as T (true) or F (false).

   ___ Some fishermen write books or give speeches about their lives.

   ___ People who fish for a living can stay home when the weather isn't so enjoyable.

   ___ Fishermen's supplies are mostly very inexpensive.

   ___ There are not so many people involved in the fishing industry.

3. Fishermen sometimes win prizes for which of the following?

   A. Catching the biggest fish

   B. Traveling the most miles away from home

   C. Catching the most fish

   D. A and C

4. What was the author's purpose in including the section titled *"Stores and Companies"*?

   A. To explain why there are many workers involved in the fishing industry

   B. To explain how fishermen can win prizes

   C. To explain the best way to catch fish

5. Do you think you would like to go to a fishing day camp? Explain why or why not.

   _____

   _____

   _____

# Balloonists: Smooth Sailing

Did you ever see a hot air balloon soaring high above the land? Its bright, colorful design makes it noticeable and exciting to everyone down below. For the passengers, the ride in the hot air balloon is windy and fun, with a great view. Have you ever wondered who flies hot air balloons and what they need to know and do on the job?

*This picture shows two beautiful hot air balloons.*

## A Balloonist

The giant hot air balloon is filled with warm air. That makes the balloon rise in the cooler air outside it. A fire placed at the mouth of the balloon heats up the air inside it. Although it might look as if a hot air balloon just floats along, that is certainly not the case. Hot air balloons need someone in charge. Someone is up there, **adjusting**[1] the fire, raising and lowering it. The person who works on a hot air balloon is called a balloonist.

A pilot flies the hot air balloon. Before becoming a pilot, they need to take classes to learn everything they need to know. They study for a few months and then take some tests. If they pass, they become **certified**[2] as a hot air balloon pilot. Although pilots control the balloon, they can't control the weather. Strong winds can blow the balloon off **course**[3] or in the wrong direction. Clouds and fog can also affect it.

1 **adjusting** – changing; rearranging
2 **certified** – licensed; approved
3 **course** – planned path

Rain can make flying impossible because it can cool off the air inside the balloon too much. The pilot can raise or lower the balloon to **avoid**[4] certain problems, but sometimes, the balloon just has to stay on the ground.

## On the Job

There are different balloonist jobs. Some hot air balloon companies have many balloons and many crew members to do different jobs. They can have one person in charge of checking the balloons while another is the pilot.

*The fire in the hot air balloon heats the air inside it, causing it to rise.*
**Credit:** *Tiddly Tom, Wikipedia*

Before taking off, the balloonist has a number of tasks to complete. The balloon, basket, and **rigging**[5] must be carefully **inspected**.[6] A hole in the skin of the balloon can ruin the whole ride. If there is a rip, the balloonist can **patch**[7] it or use a different balloon altogether. A hole in the basket makes it unsafe for the riders. Also, all the parts of the rigging that keep the basket attached to the balloon must be in working order.

*The giant balloon has to be inspected carefully before sailing off.*

Another important job the balloonist has is to plan the ride. Before every trip, the balloonist has to check the weather report for the areas the balloon will fly through. Some balloon pilots **compete**.[8] They race other balloon pilots to see who can do certain things first, such as passing a certain spot.

---

4 **avoid** – keep away from
5 **rigging** – ropes that attach the basket to the balloon
6 **inspected** – checked; looked at carefully
7 **patch** – mend; repair
8 **compete** – have contests

Sometimes companies hire balloon pilots to advertise for them, as hot air balloons always attract lots of attention. They attach the name of their company to the balloon in big letters, and the balloon pilot flies over certain areas so people can see the balloon and learn about the company.

*It is fascinating to see many balloons floating together.* **Credit:** *Ivankazaryan, Wikipedia*

Some balloon pilots ride to entertain others who enjoy watching them. Other balloon pilots give people rides. These pilots have to be prepared to answer lots of questions. People are usually curious about how the balloon works and what the different parts of the balloon are. They want to understand how the pilot directs the balloon. Of course, they must understand safety **regulations**[9] for the hot air balloon ride before they take off. The pilot has to be patient with all the questions and comments and also entertain the crowds.

All in all, being a balloonist can be a fun job for someone who likes to have their head in the clouds!

*A pilot and riders are in the basket of this hot air balloon.* **Credit:** *HRae, Wikipedia*

9 **regulations** – rules

#  Questions

1. Circle the vocabulary word that best fits the sentence.

   *My sister loves to (**compete**/**course**) in the school spelling bee every year.*

2. Mark each statement as T (true) or F (false).

   ___ Balloonists take courses to learn how to control the weather.

   ___ Sometimes companies hire balloonists to advertise for them.

   ___ Balloonists can take people for rides no matter what the weather is like.

   ___ Hot air balloon pilots have to take tests to get certified.

3. Place a check mark next to each statement that correctly describes balloonists.

   ___ One of their jobs is to plan the ride beforehand.

   ___ They learn what to do on the job without taking any training classes beforehand.

   ___ They sometimes compete with other balloonists.

   ___ They must be able to answer questions that people ask them.

4. What was the author's purpose in including the last sentence in the section titled "A Balloonist"?

   A. To explain that sometimes weather conditions make it impossible to fly the balloon.

   B. To tell us that not all pilots are good at what they do.

   C. To tell us how some balloonists compete.

5. Did you ever see a hot air balloon? Write a little about it.

   _____

   _____

   _____

# Origami: Crafty Folds

*An origami crane.*

Origami is a peaceful activity. Time slows. Nothing matters except for the next crisply folded line. You can make anything you wish, from a simple flower to a complicated animal. Have you tried origami? Was it fun and relaxing? Or did it turn into a crazy wrestling match with the paper, surrounded by a sea of scrunched-up efforts? Is folding napkins the closest you get to origami? Beginners and experts, grab a paper and let's learn about origami!

## What Is Origami?

Origami is the art of paper folding. It is simple. Fold a piece of paper and create something beautiful. You have probably practiced origami without even realizing it. Yes, think about those paper airplanes you throw across the room. Origami is a Japanese word. It comes from the two Japanese words oru, which means "to fold," and kami, which means "paper."

## Japanese Origami Traditions

Origami is a big part of Japanese **culture**.[1] Many people believe that origami started in Japan. But no one is certain, because China also practiced a form of origami. Even in Europe, people practiced the art of napkin-folding.

We think origami is just a fun activity for children. However, history tells a different story.

> 1 **culture** – customs; way of life

Origami became popular in Japan at a time when paper was expensive. Paper was new and special – forget about phones and **drones**! Imagine that! This meant that origami was saved for special occasions like weddings and other **ceremonies**.[3]

*An origami decoration made from many papers*

## Basic Origami

There is more than one way to fold paper. Each type of fold has its own name. There is a mountain fold, a pleat fold, a squash fold, and more. There are loads of designs to choose from. One charming origami bird flaps its wings when you pull its tail. Another sends a frog leaping across the room. Some designs are easy, some are hard. It can take minutes, hours, days, or even months to finish.

Practicing origami is fun. Let's enjoy this art together. Choose your favorite color of paper. (Use A4 size.) Follow the origami instructions in the diagram. Well done! You have successfully filled your classroom with a **fleet**[4] of boats. Now, set yourself a challenge. What is the most complex design you can achieve?

*Gorgeous and delicate origami artwork.*
**Credit:** Ви́ктор Хе́лен, Wikimedia.

## Cool Origami Uses

Origami is useful in so many ways. It is art. It can decorate a wedding hall. It can entertain children on a rainy day. It can make a parent smile when their toddler hands over the crumbled gift. And that is not all. Origami is used in buildings, medicine, and space. That does sound strange, but here are two examples to prove it.

---

2 **drones** – remote-controlled flying machines
3 **ceremonies** – practices at religious or formal occasions
4 **fleet** – group of ships

Lesson 56: Origami: Crafty Folds

Imagine someone coming to the hospital for an operation one day. The **surgeon**[5] arrives and decides to use origami during the operation (hopefully not paper origami!). What are they doing? It may seem odd, but scientists are using origami to make **equipment**.[6] The small origami-style pieces can be helpful in operations. They can travel through the body to hard-to-reach places. After reaching their **destination**,[7] they unfold.

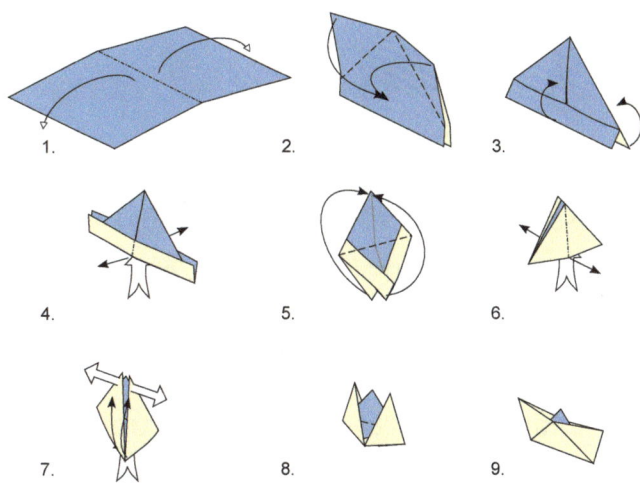

*Instructions for an origami boat*

It is a beautiful summer day. You head outside to play ball. Your friend throws the ball, but you cannot catch it. The sun is too bright, and you cannot see anything that is flying through the air! You put your hand up to block the sun. Now you can see and catch the ball. Problem solved. The game is on.

NASA is an American government agency that focuses on outer space. NASA has a problem that is similar to yours in the ball game. They want to photograph distant planets and other objects. However, something is stopping them: a star. The star's light is blinding. It is almost impossible to see anything around it. Space cameras need shade to block the star's light. NASA brought in origami experts to solve this problem.

*An image of the potential starshade.*

Origami experts helped them design a clever folding system to make a starshade. The shade will neatly fold away during takeoff and open up in space. Genius!

5 **surgeon** – a doctor trained to carry out operations
6 **equipment** – tools; supplies
7 **destination** – place where someone or something is going

 # Questions

1. Circle the vocabulary word that best fits the sentence.

   Remote-controlled **(drones/ceremonies)** can fly over places that larger aircraft cannot reach.

2. Mark each statement as T (true) or F (false).

   ___ Origami is a French word.

   ___ In origami, each type of fold has its own name.

   ___ Historians are certain that origami started in Japan.

   ___ Origami has even been used in outer space.

3. Place a check mark next to each statement that correctly describes origami.

   ___ It is the art of paper folding.

   ___ It is an important part of Japanese culture.

   ___ It is only used for entertainment.

   ___ It is one design repeated over and over.

4. Which of the following sentences from the section titled "*Japanese Origami Traditions*" supports the idea that origami is not just a fun activity for children?

   A. *Many people believe that origami started in Japan.*

   B. *Even in Europe, people practiced the art of napkin-folding.*

   C. *This meant that origami was saved for special occasions like weddings and other ceremonies.*

5. How are scientists using origami?

   _____

   _____

   _____

**Lesson 56:** Origami: Crafty Folds

# The Legend of Johnny Appleseed

Have you ever gone apple picking? If so, you probably know that apple trees grow in **orchards**.¹ In this lesson, we will read about a man who established apple orchards throughout the American Midwest in the 1800s. Let's meet Johnny Appleseed.

*A drawing of Johnny Appleseed*

## Who Was Johnny Appleseed?

He was known as Johnny Appleseed, but his real name was John Chapman. Not much is known about John Chapman's early years. He was born in Leominster, Massachusetts, on September 26, 1774. His father, Nathaniel Chapman, was a farmer who also served in the military. It is thought that John's father encouraged him to become an orchardist. An orchardist is someone who owns or manages an orchard. John worked as an apprentice to an orchardist named Mr. Crawford. By 1812, John was working and planting apple trees on his own.

## Career

Chapman traveled through many states. He traveled through Ohio, Pennsylvania, Indiana, Illinois, and what is now West Virginia. He established **nurseries**² as he traveled. Chapman built fences around the trees in each place to protect them from animals. Then, he left the nurseries in the care of a neighbor and **resumed**³ his travels. Every year or two, he returned to care for his nurseries.

---

1 **orchards** – areas of land planted with fruit trees
2 **nurseries** – places where plants or trees are grown for sale
3 **resumed** – continued; began again

The apples in these orchards were not **edible**.⁴ They were small and **tart**.⁵ They were mainly used to make drinks called hard cider and applejack. Establishing the orchards also gave Chapman ownership of the land they were planted on. In this way, Chapman owned around 1,200 acres of valuable land by the time he died.

Besides his business of growing apple trees, Chapman also sold apple **seedlings**.⁶ He charged about six or seven cents apiece for them. Chapman was kind to the poor **settlers**⁷ he met as he traveled. If they didn't have much money, he would **barter**⁸ with them. They would take his seedlings and give him something in exchange. Chapman would take just about anything they offered him, even old clothing. If a family had nothing to trade, Chapman gave them seedlings for free. This way they could still grow their

A memorial plaque on a fence around Johnny Appleseed's grave. **Credit:** Charles W. Chapman, Wikimedia

An apple orchard. **Credit:** A Somerset Apple Orchard by Mr Eugene Birchall, Wikimedia

own apples. Sometimes he also gave them money to help them out. One grateful settler gave Chapman the nickname "Johnny Appleseed." Chapman also tried to establish peaceful **relationships**⁹ between Native Americans and settlers.

Once, when Chapman was picking some apples from a tree, he fell. His neck got stuck in the fork of the tree. The fork of a tree is where its **trunk**¹⁰ divides in different directions.

---

4 **edible** – able to be eaten
5 **tart** – sour
6 **seedlings** – young plants
7 **settlers** – people who move with others to live in a new area
8 **barter** – trade; exchange
9 **relationships** – connections; friendships
10 **trunk** – a tree's main, woody stem

Chapman could not get himself free. Fortunately, his eight-year-old helper, John White, found him in time. John couldn't get Chapman out of the tree. Instead, he cut it down, saving Chapman's life.

## Becoming a Legend

Chapman was not a poor man, but he dressed in old, worn-out clothing. He did this because he wanted to, not because he couldn't afford to buy new clothes. He often walked barefoot, even through the snow. Sometimes, he wore a tin hat. Chapman lived a rough life and sometimes slept in the woods.

*A stone marker near John Chapman's birthplace*

The exact date of Chapman's death isn't known for sure. Most people believe that he died on March 18, 1845. After he died, he became a legend. Stories, plays, and books were written about Johnny Appleseed. They all describe his unusual way of dressing and living. Johnny Appleseed is also remembered for his kindness and **generosity**.[11] He is remembered for his fondness for nature and the outdoors.

There are two museums named after Johnny Appleseed. A stone marker was placed near where his family's home stood. The street it is on is now called Johnny Appleseed Lane. March 11 and September 26 are sometimes celebrated as Johnny Appleseed Day. (March 11 is during crop-planting season, and September 26 was his birthdate.) In 1966, the United States Post Office printed a stamp in honor of Johnny Appleseed.

*The five-cent postage stamp printed in honor of Johnny Appleseed*

It is said that one tree planted by Johnny Appleseed is still growing. It grows on a farm in the city of Nova, Ohio. The seedlings from this tree are often called "Johnny Appleseed" plants.

---

11 **generosity** – giving to and sharing with others

# Questions

1. Circle the vocabulary word that best fits the sentence.

   *Going to sleepaway camp is a good way to form new (relationships/nurseries*

2. Mark each statement as T (true) or F (false).

   ___ John Chapman served in the military before becoming an orchardist.

   ___ John Chapman dressed in old, worn-out clothing even though he was not poor.

   ___ The apples John Chapman grew were sweet and tasty.

   ___ It is said that one of the trees that Johnny Appleseed planted is still growing.

3. What other business did John Chapman engage in besides growing apple trees?

   A. Making hard cider and applejack

   B. Selling old clothing

   C. Selling apple seedlings

   D. Repairing broken fences

4. Which of the following sentences from the section titled *"Career"* best supports the idea that Chapman was kind to the poor settlers he met as he traveled?

   A. *Then, he left the nurseries in the care of a neighbor and resumed his travels.*

   B. *If a family had nothing to trade, Chapman gave them seedlings for free.*

   C. *One grateful settler gave Chapman the nickname "Johnny Appleseed."*

5. How did establishing apple orchards benefit Chapman?

   _____

   _____

   _____

# Bicycles, Unicycles, and Tandem Bikes

Policemen on bicycles.

It's a beautiful spring day, not too hot and not too cold. Just perfect for a ride through the park, enjoying all the sights and sounds around us. How should we travel—by bicycle, unicycle, or tandem bike? First let's read a little about each of them. Then we'll decide the best way to go!

## Bicycles

None of you need to be told what a bicycle is! But you probably don't know that bicycles have existed since the 1400s. They didn't look the way bicycles look today. But they were two-wheeled **vehicles**[1] used for transportation.

The first, more familiar-looking bicycle was produced in Europe in the 1800s. It was called the velocipede. The velocipede was used to help farmers plow their fields without using horses. It was made entirely of wood and had no pedals. Instead, the rider had to push off the ground with their feet to move forward.

Slowly, improvements were made to the velocipede's design. Pedals were added, and tires replaced the wooden wheels. These changes led to the invention of the "Boneshaker." Can you guess why it was called that? This **contraption**,[2] made in France, caused terrible **vibrations**[3] when ridden on bumpy roads.

---

1 **vehicles** – methods of transportation
2 **contraption** – device; invention
3 **vibrations** – shaking; trembling

A British inventor, James Starley, created the Penny Farthing around 1870. This bicycle had a giant front wheel and a very small back one. Riding it wasn't such a bone-shaking experience, but it was far from easy to climb aboard and balance on it! The Penny Farthing was also not cheap. It cost what the average person earned in six months' time.

*A drawing of a velocipede.*

After that, many improvements were made in how bicycles were built. They began to look more like the bicycles we know today. They had pedals, brakes, wheels with **spokes**,4 and more. Some of these improvements were possible because of the Industrial Revolution. At that time, new machinery made it possible to produce parts more quickly and less expensively. Riding bicycles became more comfortable as roads were paved. Riding along a paved road was much smoother than riding on a dirt path.

## Unicycles

Unicycles were invented in the mid-1870s. An Englishman named James Bedford Elliott wanted to find a faster way than walking to travel. He thought that a one-wheeled vehicle would be more **efficient**5 than a horse and buggy, which was a common form of transportation then. He removed the back wheel of a Penny Farthing, and, ta-dah—the unicycle was born! Elliott made two styles of unicycles. One had a handlebar for steering, and the other had a seat above the wheel. However, the unicycle was not very **stable**6 or fast.

*A Penny Farthing*
**Credit:** Mike DeMille, Wikimedia

---

4 **spokes** – rods; bars; crosspieces
5 **efficient** – useful; effective
6 **stable** – steady; firm

*Riding a unicycle*
**Credit:** *Trammell Hudson from New York, USA, Wikimedia*

Today, unicycles are used mainly for exercise and for entertainment. There are different styles, depending on what they will be used for. Some have small wheels and high seats. These are used by people who perform tricks with them. Others are designed to be used in contests. They are strong and can withstand jumps over objects and heavy landings. Other unicycles have wider tires to travel over uneven grass or rocks. Some unicycles are designed to travel long distances more quickly.

## Tandem Bikes

*Riding a tandem bike*

Tandem bikes, sometimes called bicycles built for two, are built for two or more riders. Danish inventor Mikael Pedersen created the first tandem bike in 1898. Riding a tandem bike is a great way for friends or families to have fun together. It doesn't matter if one person can pedal more quickly than another; everyone travels at the same speed when riding a tandem bike. The front rider does all the steering and braking. People with disabilities who might not be able to ride alone can experience biking by riding together with someone else. For example, if a blind person bikes with a seeing person, he can enjoy the ride and the exercise even without being able to see.

Today, most tandem bikes are used for enjoyment, but some are built for racing. Two-seater tandems are most common, but some hold three, four, and even as many as more than ten riders! There's only one problem. Who decides where they're going to go?

 **Questions**

1. Circle the vocabulary word that best fits the sentence.

   *Jacob's system for sorting laundry is so **(efficient/stable)** that his family can finish the chore in half the time.*

2. Mark each statement as T (true) or F (false).

   ___ The Boneshaker was made entirely of wood and had no pedals.

   ___ The Penny Farthing was named that because it was inexpensive to buy.

   ___ Today, unicycles are used mainly for exercise and entertainment.

   ___ All tandem bikes are designed to hold two riders.

3. Who invented the first tandem bike?

   A. James Starley

   B. James Bedford Elliott

   C. Mikael Tandem

   D. None of the above

4. Which of the following sentences from the section titled *"Bicycles"* supports the idea that the Penny Farthing was far from easy to climb aboard and balance on?

   A. *It was made entirely of wood and had no pedals.*

   B. *This contraption, made in France, caused terrible vibrations when ridden on bumpy roads.*

   C. *This bicycle had a giant front wheel and a very small back one.*

5. What benefit do tandem bikes have for riders that bicycles and unicycles don't have?

   _____

   _____

   _____

Lesson 58: Bicycles, Unicycles, and Tandem Bikes

# Signatures and John Hancock

Have you ever heard someone say, "That's a no-brainer"? Or how about, "Go fly a kite!" Did you ever wonder how these and other expressions came into being? In this lesson, we will read about another expression, one you may not be familiar with. Let's join Yehoshua as he learns what this expression means and how it **evolved**.[1]

*This picture shows a ship named for John Hancock with his signature on it.*

## Putting on Your John Hancock

Yehoshua stood patiently near his mother while she paid for the groceries. The man behind the counter tore off the receipt and laid it neatly on the counter. "Put your John Hancock over here," he said to Yehoshua's mother. Yehoshua leaned closer to see what his mother would be giving the man. He was surprised when she simply took a pen and **scrawled**[2] her name.

As soon as they left the store, Yehoshua asked his mother curiously, "What did the man ask you for? And why did you sign your name?"

Yehoshua's mother laughed as she opened her car door and put down her bags. "When someone asks for your John Hancock, they are asking for your signature," she explained.

---

1 **evolved** – developed
2 **scrawled** – drawn in a lighthearted manner; scribbled

Yehoshua got into the car, but he still had more questions. "Who is John Hancock, and what does he have to do with signing your name?"

"Let me tell you about John Hancock's famous signature," his mother offered as she started the car.

## John Hancock

*John Hancock took over his uncle's business and became wealthy.*

John Hancock was a young boy who lived in Massachusetts many years ago. He was born in 1737 and was just seven years old when his father died. His mother continued to care for him and his brother and sister for a while, but soon John was sent to live with his aunt and uncle in Boston. John's Uncle Thomas was a wealthy man. He sold many different things, like cloth, **rum**,[3] and tea.

John went to university at a young age, and when he finished at age 17, he returned to work with his uncle. A few years later, his uncle died. John Hancock took over the business and became wealthy.

*This picture shows British troops arriving by ship.*

## Fighting the British

Great Britain controlled America at that time. One of the rules made by the British king was that Americans had to pay taxes on many items, including tea. Hancock didn't want to pay the **taxes**[4] because it made the tea more expensive. He always tried to get his tea shipped into the country without paying taxes. He also often spoke out against the British and the taxes. One time, the British accused him of sneaking some tea off a ship without paying the tax. They took away one of his ships as a **penalty**.[5]

---

4 **taxes** – money collected from citizens by the government
5 **penalty** – fine; punishment
6 **oppose** – act against

**274**   Lesson 59: Signatures and John Hancock

*Hancock is sitting on the right as the Declaration of Independence is being completed.*

When other people heard what happened, they were impressed that Hancock tried to **oppose**[6] the British. They **voted**[7] for him to be a part of the Massachusetts government.

John Hancock became more involved in opposing the British and speaking against them. Soon, the British soldiers wanted to catch Hancock and his friend, John Adams. Luckily, a man named Paul Revere came to warn Hancock and Adams, and they escaped in time. Soon after that, the American fight for **independence**,[8] the American Revolution, began. John Hancock was one of the revolution's **prominent**[9] leaders.

After many battles, the Americans **drafted**[10] the Declaration of Independence in 1776. It was a document declaring their independence from the British. It was their last step in becoming their own country.

*A memorial was put up where Hancock is buried.*

Many people signed it, but the first one to sign it was John Hancock. He signed his name in big, noticeable letters. People said that Hancock wanted the English king to be able to read his signature without using glasses! Although there are many signatures on the Declaration of Independence, John Hancock's signature is the most famous. Although Hancock had many other important accomplishments in his lifetime, his signature on the Declaration of Independence is what he is best remembered for.

---

7 **voted** – chose by election
8 **independence** – freedom; liberty
9 **prominent** – important; well-known
10 **drafted** – wrote; composed

 # Questions

1. Circle the vocabulary word that best fits the sentence.

   A birth certificate is a legal *(penalty/document)*.

2. Place a check mark next to each statement that correctly describes John Hancock.

   ___ As a young boy, he lived in Tennessee.

   ___ He didn't want to pay taxes on his tea.

   ___ He was a prominent leader in the American Revolution.

   ___ Signing the Declaration of Independence was his only important accomplishment.

3. Number the following events in the order in which they took place.

   ___ John Hancock signed the Declaration of Independence.

   ___ John Hancock was voted to be part of the Massachusetts government.

   ___ John Hancock and John Adams escaped before being caught by the British.

   ___ John Hancock lived with his aunt and uncle.

4. What was the author's purpose in including the story about John Hancock not paying tax on his tea?

   A. To give an example of how he opposed the British

   B. To explain how expensive the tea was

   C. To explain why the British took away one of his ships

5. Why did John Hancock's signature on the Declaration of Independence become so famous?

   _____

   _____

   _____

# Chess: A Thousand-Year-Old History

*Chess is a really old game! These king and queen pieces date back to the 12th century!*
**Credit:** *Andrew Dunn, Wikimedia*

Have you ever played chess? About 605 million people worldwide do, including millions of children. While most people today play for fun, this was not always so. In the past, people used to play chess to show that they were smarter, richer, or better than others. Sometimes chess games were used to befriend other **cultures**.[1] Chess has a long history. If you do play chess, you've probably heard the words check and checkmate. Some historians think check came from the Persian word shah, which means "king." Checkmate may have come from shah mat, meaning "the king is trapped." The word rook may have come from the Indian word ruk, which means "chariot." The names and shapes of the board pieces and how they move tell a story about the countries, cultures, and empires that were part of chess's history.

## Chaturanga: The Oldest Chess Game

About 1,500 years ago, there was no chess. But each country and culture had popular board games. The early Chinese had a game called xiangqi, which was a battle game played by moving pieces on a board. The goal was to capture the commander, Xiang. The ancient Greeks played a game called petteia, and the Jews of Babylonia had a board game similar to chess called nardshir.

> 1 **cultures** – civilizations; societies

These games were popular, but they probably didn't develop into chess. The earliest known **origins**[2] of chess are from India. Indians played a game called chaturanga. Chaturanga means "four parts," and there were four types of pieces on the board. Each had its own special moves. The four pieces were footmen, elephant riders, chariots, and horsemen. There was also a king on the board. The king needed to be protected by the other moving pieces. There was also an "advisor" who stood next to the king but couldn't move very far.

Chaturanga leaped from India to Persia when the Indian king wanted to prove to the Persian shah that he was wiser. He sent Shah Khusrau of Persia a game of chess and challenged him to learn the rules.

*These ancient Persian books show Shah Khusrau learning the game of chaturanga.* **Credit:** *Metropolitan Museum of Art, Wikimedia*

He said that only the "king of kings" would be wise enough to know how to play. After Khusrau won the challenge and proved he was indeed smarter, he made the Indian ruler pay him money.

## Chess Spreads Across the Muslim World

Less than 100 years after the game moved to Persia, Persia was taken over by Muslim Arabs. Now chess had a new empire to spread to. The Arabs loved the game and spread it across North Africa, Spain, and the Middle East. They called the game Shataranj.

*Muslim chess, called Shataranj, used pieces with different shapes that didn't look like animals or people.* **Credit:** *ZereshK, Wikimediat*

2 **origins** – beginnings

**Lesson 60: Chess: A Thousand-Year-Old History**

Muslims do not allow carvings or pictures that look like real people or animals. So they changed the look of the game pieces. They used different shapes and **notches**[3] instead of **carved**[4] horses, elephants, and soldiers. These changes traveled to Europe and affected the names and looks of different chess pieces.

## Europe Makes Changes

People loved the game, and it traveled with them through war, trade, and treaties. It seemed the world couldn't get enough of chess! People thought they could show how smart they were by playing chess. They also thought that chess taught important lessons. One lesson it taught is that everyone, from the lowly pawn to the ruling king, has a job to do.

In Europe, the names of some pieces changed. The elephant became known as a bishop. The shape of some pieces also changed. The Muslims gave the Indian *ruk* a triangular top instead. Europeans thought this looked like a castle. That's how the rook piece became **associated**[5] with a castle. Europeans also turned the weak "advisor" piece into a powerful queen piece that could move across the whole board! Some historians think this was because mighty female rulers wanted a strong queen. In modern chess, the queen is the most powerful piece on the board.

*Alfonso X. wrote a book in the 13th century translating into old Spanish the rules of games written in Arabic. His pictures of chess in the book show how many cultures loved the game. The picture on the left shows a Jewish man playing a Muslim. The picture on the right shows a European playing a North African.*

## A Standard Game

After the printing press was invented, people could make many copies of chess rule books. These books spread across the world, and the new rules and shapes and names of pieces became **standardized**.[6] This meant that all chess players worldwide used the same rules and pieces.

---

3 **notches** – cuts; nicks; grooves
4 **carved** – cut into a hard material; engraved
5 **associated** – connected
6 **standardized** – made the same way

Today, most people play the same game of chess. But chess is a game that has traveled around the world and witnessed all kinds of history.

Because chess has traveled the world, every culture has its own way of connecting to the game. This Mongolian chess board's pieces are shaped like animals that are important to Mongolian people. It dates back to the Qing dynasty, which lasted from 1644 to 1912.
**Credit:** BabelStone, Wikimedia

Chess is nicknamed "the game of kings" because it was a game played by royalty. This painting shows Tsar (Russian for king) Ivan IV, nicknamed Ivan the Terrible, playing chess on his deathbed. Tsar Ivan died in the middle of the game.

This picture illustrates a Jewish legend about chess in the Middle Ages. A scholar's son is kidnapped and raised as a Christian. He becomes important and makes a decree against the Jewish people in Mainz. The scholar comes to plead with him, and while the two are playing chess, he recognizes the man as his long-lost son!

**Lesson 60:** Chess: A Thousand-Year-Old History

# Questions

1. **Circle the vocabulary word that best fits the sentence.**

   *The boy (carved/associated) his initials in the wood with his pocketknife.*

2. **Number the following events in the order in which they took place.**

   ___ The Indian king wanted to prove to the Persian shah that he was wiser.

   ___ Chess spread to Europe and became popular there.

   ___ Indians played a game called chaturanga.

   ___ Persia was taken over by Muslim Arabs.

3. **Which of the following was NOT one of the four types of pieces on the chaturanga board?**

   A. Footman

   B. Pawn

   C. Chariot

   D. Elephant rider

4. **Which of the following sentences from the section titled** *"Chess Spreads Across the Muslim World"* **supports the idea that Muslims do not allow carvings or pictures that look like real people or animals?**

   A. *The Arabs loved the game and spread it across North Africa, Spain, and the Middle East.*

   B. *They used different shapes and notches instead of carved horses, elephants, and soldiers.*

   C. *These changes traveled to Europe and affected the names and the looks of different chess pieces.*

5. **Why do historians think Europeans changed the weak "advisor" piece into a powerful queen piece?**

   _____

   _____

281

# The Immune System: Fighting Foreign Invaders

A strong army stands ready and waiting for anyone who tries to invade.

Imagine a big, strong country. It has a strong government that ensures that no one makes any trouble or bothers others. Everyone feels safe walking around and going about their life because they know that the government is protecting them. One danger for every country is when **foreign**[1] armies **invade**.[2] Although many people come and go without harming anyone, if a foreign army comes in to fight, everyone will be in danger. So, any strong country also has a strong army. The army fights anyone who comes in uninvited to make sure none of the country's citizens get hurt. Your body is like a strong country. Many items enter your body because they should—like food, drinks, and air. However, your body needs to be protected against the harmful things that also come in. Luckily, it has a strong army protecting it. That army is called the **immune**[3] system.

## The Immune System

The immune system has many parts throughout your body. It protects you from foreign invaders, such as germs—viruses and bacteria.

> 1 **foreign** – from an unfamiliar place
> 2 **invade** – enter without permission; enter forcefully; attack
> 3 **immune** – protected from

Some parts of the immune system block the germs from entering the body in the first place. Other parts get rid of the germs that manage to come in. You can also become immune to certain germs.

Some ways that the body keeps out harmful germs might seem obvious. Your skin, for example, blocks dirt from entering your body. Your tears wash foreign materials out of your eyes. **Mucus**[4] keeps your nose and airways clear of germs. Dirt particles, bacteria, and other germs entering your body get stuck in the mucus and don't enter your lungs. The nose is also lined with little hairs called cilia that help trap unwanted visitors. Your stomach has special liquids inside it that kill or **deactivate**[5] any germs that come in with your food.

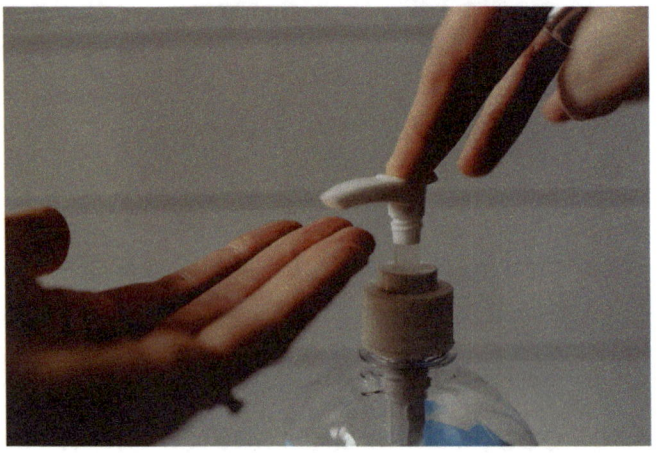

*The nose is lined with mucus and cilia that help prevent germs from entering.*

If an infection develops in your body, the body produces different types of blood cells to fight the germs. While that happens, your body is working hard and can develop a fever. Some people think that having a fever is a bad thing. Actually, it shows that the body is working to fight an infection.

*You should always wash your hands before eating and after spending time in a public place.*

It is wise to eat healthy foods, like fruits, vegetables, proteins, and whole grains. Such foods can make your immune system stronger. They give you the energy you need to fight foreign invaders.

You can also take vitamins, especially if you are **deficient**[6] in certain ones. Of course, you should always wash your hands before eating and after being out in a public place. Getting enough sleep and avoiding unnecessary stress also help to keep you strong and healthy.

---

4 **mucus** – a slippery substance lining the nose and other body passages
5 **deactivate** – stop from working
6 **deficient** – lacking; having too little

**Lesson 61:** The Immune System: Fighting Foreign Invaders

If something is bothering you, talking it over with a wise adult can help you to be less stressed.

## Acquired Immunity

If the flu or another virus tries to enter your body for the second time or more, your body does something fascinating. It "recognizes" these germs as something it already fought in the past and fights them very strongly so they can't harm you. This is called **acquired**[7] immunity because it is immunity you acquired, or obtained. You weren't born immune to chicken pox, for example. However, you became immune to it from having it in the past. Now if the virus that causes chicken pox tries to enter your body again, your immune system will fight it off strongly.

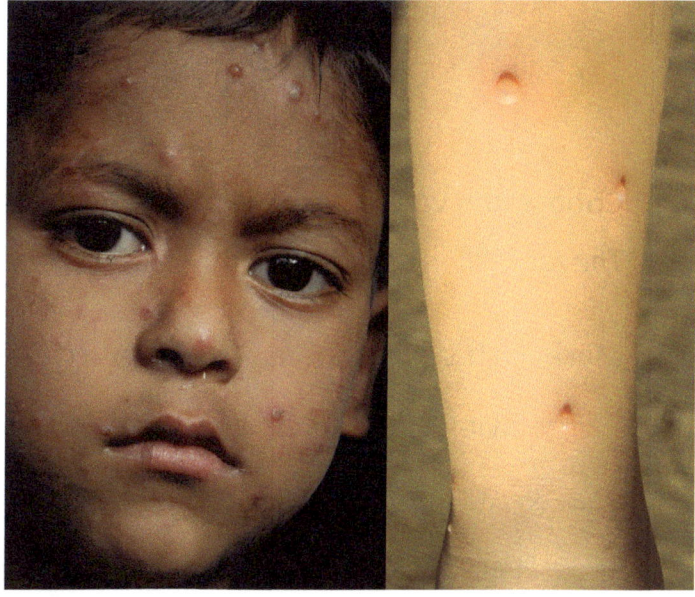

*This boy has chicken pox, but if the virus that causes it tries to enter his body again, his immune system will fight it.*
**Credit:** *Biswarup Ganguly, Wikimedia*
**Credit:** *Ronny Ager-Wick, Wikimedia*

## Vaccines

Vaccines, or "shots," work in a similar way. By giving you a small amount of the virus, they help you develop immunity to certain sicknesses, viruses, and flus. If any of these enter your body, you recognize it, and your immune system immediately swings into action to fight it off.

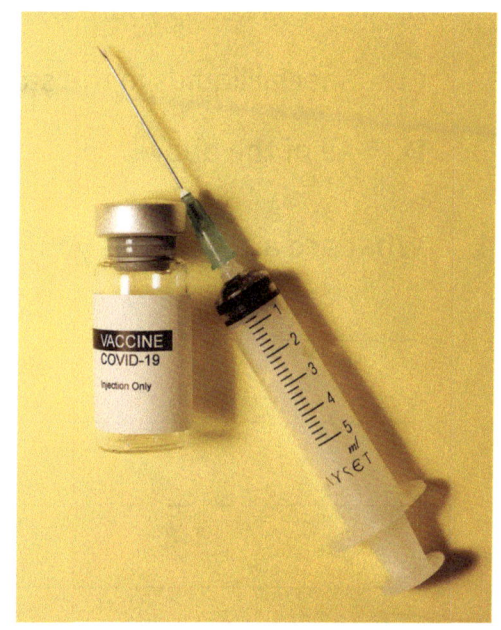

*Vaccines give you a small amount of a virus, and that helps your immune system fight off germs.*

When you think about your immune system, you can marvel at how fascinating your body is. You have a strong army inside you, fighting off those foreign invaders!

---

7 **acquired** – got; obtained

# Questions

1. Choose the vocabulary word that best fits the sentence.

   *The repairman couldn't fix our washing machine because it was a (foreign/deficient) brand.*

2. Mark each statement as T (true) or F (false).

   ___ Having a fever is a sign that the body is working to fight an infection.

   ___ Getting enough sleep is important for staying healthy.

   ___ Everyone is born immune to chicken pox.

   ___ Vaccines work after a person has had a disease at least one time.

3. Which of the following are ways the body keeps out harmful germs?

   A. The skin blocks dirt from entering the body.

   B. Mucus keeps your nose and airways clear of germs.

   C. Special liquids in the stomach kill germs.

   D. All of the above

4. What are a few things you can do to help stay healthy?

   _____

   _____

   _____

# Port Lockroy, Antarctica

*A iew of Port Lockroy on a summer evening.*
**Credit:** *Liam Quinn from Canada, Wikimedia*

Have you heard of Antarctica? It is Earth's fifth-largest continent and is almost totally covered in ice. No one lives there permanently because of the challenging weather conditions. About 1,000 people live in Antarctica during the winter months, mostly scientists doing research. During the summer months, the population can increase to up to 4,000. You may be wondering what there is to see in and around Antarctica. There are many whales, dolphins, penguins, and glaciers. And then there is Port Lockroy, which gets about 18,000 visitors a year. Let's read more about this fascinating area and what makes it such a popular visitor **attraction**.[1]

## The History of Port Lockroy

Port Lockroy is **located**[2] on Goudier Island, an area of Antarctica owned by Britain. Port Lockroy was first discovered by a French explorer named Jean-Baptiste Charcot. Charcot discovered Port Lockroy while exploring between 1903 and 1905. He named it after Étienne-Auguste-Édouard Lockroy, a Frenchman paying for his explorations.

---

1 **attraction** – thing or place of interest
2 **located** – found; situated

From 1911 until 1931, Port Lockroy was a whaling center. Fishermen went out to hunt whales and brought what they caught to ships waiting in the port for them. From there, the whales were taken to factories to be processed. This changed in 1944 when the British government built a building on Port Lockroy. They called the building by the code name Base A. During World War II, Base A was used for secret scientific research. It was used until 1962. Then, the research center was moved to a larger and more modern place, and Base A fell into **disrepair**.[3] Finally, in 1996, the building was rebuilt and renamed Bransfield House. Half of it was made into a museum where visitors can see displays and exhibits designed to look like the original science base.

*A sign in the museum exhibit commemorating Base A.* **Credit:** *Christopher Michel, Wikimedia*

## The Other Half of Bransfield House

The other half of Bransfield House contains a combined post office and gift shop. The post office is named the "Penguin Post Office." It is the most visited **site**[4] in Antarctica. Tourists love to buy postcards there and mail them to family and friends. Sometimes they even mail them to themselves, just for fun! After all, how often do you get a piece of mail with an Antarctica postmark on it? But don't expect the postcards to arrive anytime soon.

*All outgoing mail gets dropped into this red box in the Port Lockroy post office.* **Credit:** *Butterfly voyages Serge ouachée, Wikimedia*

3 **disrepair** – run-down; in poor condition
4 **site** – place

They can take as long as four months to come because of all the stops they make along the way. Each year, the post office sends out about 70,000 postcards to destinations in 100 different countries.

One of the most unusual things about the Penguin Post Office is that it is run by volunteers. Each year, the UK Antarctic Heritage Trust advertises for a team of volunteers to come to Port Lockroy. Besides running the post office and gift shop, the group is responsible for taking care of the museum and the historical items in Port Lockroy. Oh, and one other thing. They are also in charge of keeping track of how many baby gentoo penguins are born while they are there.

*The penguins feel very much at home around Bransfield House.*
**Credit:** *Liam Quinn from Canada, Wikimedia*

The volunteers are chosen based on how physically fit they are and how well they can get along with others. Getting along with others is especially important because they will live together for five months in a **confined**[5] space. The job lasts only from November to March, the Antarctic summer. During the rest of the year, sea ice makes it impossible for ships to travel to Port Lockroy. Believe it or not, hundreds of British people apply for the job, even though there is no running water or household electricity and the temperature is below zero, even in the summer! And did we mention that it is 11,000 miles away from home?

## Penguins

As was mentioned before, Port Lockroy also has gentoo penguins. A LOT of them! There were no gentoo penguins there when the research base was founded. It is believed that they came in around 1985. Gentoo penguins are the fastest underwater birds in the world. They can reach speeds of about 22 miles per hour. In body size, gentoos are the third-largest of all penguins, and weigh an average of 11 pounds. Adults can weigh as much as 19 pounds. The penguins build nests out of **pebbles**.[6] The male and female penguins take turns sitting on the eggs or on top of their chicks to keep them warm.

> 5 **confined** – small; cramped
> 6 **pebbles** – small stones

Baby penguins start to hatch by late December and grow to half their adult size within a few months. There are about 1,500 gentoo penguins in Port Lockroy. But even so, they are one of the most **endangered**[7] species of penguins. That is why the postal workers keep track of how many of them hatch.

So, what do you think? Is being a Port Lockroy postal worker something you'd be interested in doing?

7 **endangered** – at risk of becoming extinct

# Questions

1. **Circle the vocabulary word that best fits the sentence.**

   *The juggling act was the show's main (attraction/disrepair).*

2. **Number the following events in the order in which they took place.**

   ___ The British government built Base A.

   ___ Port Lockroy was a whaling center.

   ___ The building was rebuilt and renamed Bransfield House.

   ___ The research center was moved to a larger, more modern place.

3. **Which of the following are the volunteer workers NOT responsible for doing?**

   A. Running the post office

   B. Taking care of the museum

   C. Tracking how many baby penguins are born

   D. Helping the scientists with their research

4. **What was the author's purpose in including the sentence,** *"After all, how often do you get a piece of mail with an Antarctica postmark on it?"*

   A. To explain why it takes so long for the postcards to be delivered

   B. To explain why people send postcards even to themselves

   C. To explain how far away from home Port Lockroy is

5. **Why is it so surprising that hundreds of people apply to work in Port Lockroy every year?**

   _____

   _____

   _____

# Riding with Sally Kristen Ride

*The Challenger space shuttle*
**Credit:** Acroterion, Wikimedia

What do you think the chances are that a woman would be an astronaut? Well, you might be surprised to learn that there have been women who have traveled to space. In this lesson, we will read about the very first one.

## Early Years

Sally Kristen Ride was born on May 25, 1951, in the Encino neighborhood of Los Angeles, California. She lived there with her parents and younger sister, Karen. Their parents encouraged both of their daughters to **pursue**[1] whatever activities interested them. Sally enjoyed playing all sports, especially tennis. When she was ten years old, Sally took tennis lessons from a **former**[2] top tennis player. Before long, Sally was the 20th-best tennis player in Los Angeles among girls below 12. When she finished high school, Sally went to college. During her second year, Ride left college to become a professional tennis player. But after three months, she returned to college and changed her course of study so she could become an astrophysicist. An astrophysicist is a scientist who studies stars, planets, space, and the universe. Ride graduated college in 1978 with several English, science, and **physics**[3] degrees.

---

1 **pursue** – go after; follow
2 **former** – at one-time; was in the past
3 **physics** – the study of matter and energy

## Becoming an Astronaut

The National Aeronautics and Space Administration (NASA) is a government agency responsible for learning more about air and space. In 1977, NASA placed an ad in the newspaper. NASA was looking for someone who knew a lot about science to be part of a space program. Ride saw the ad and **applied**[4] for the job. Out of 8,000 people who applied for the job, only 35 were **selected**.[5] Of those 35, only five were women, and Ride was one of them.

*Astrophysicists study the stars and planets.*
**Credit:** *CactiStaccingCrane, Wikimedia*

Ride trained for one year. Some of the things she learned included parachute jumping, water survival, and radio **communications**. [6] She also had to learn about navigation, gravity, and weightlessness in space.

## Space Missions

In 1983, Ride was selected as one of five astronauts on board the Challenger space shuttle. This was a great honor for Ride. She was the first American woman and the third woman worldwide to travel to space. (Russia had already sent two women into space.) Ride was also the youngest American to have traveled to space at that time. Challenger spent six days orbiting Earth.

*NASA headquarters in Washington, D.C.*

In 1984, Ride participated in another Challenger mission. This time the Challenger carried seven crew members and stayed in space for nine days. After her second trip to space, Ride had several different jobs. She worked as a special assistant to one of NASA's managers. Ride also taught physics at the University of California.

> 4 **applied** – tried to get; bid for
> 5 **selected** – chosen
> 6 **communications** – giving and receiving information

Another job Ride had after finishing her second space mission was **investigating**[7] the 1986 Challenger disaster. This was a tragic space shuttle accident. The Challenger was making its tenth trip into space. It carried seven crew members on this mission, including two women. Only 73 seconds after launch, the Challenger exploded and broke apart 46,000 feet over the Atlantic Ocean. Sadly, all seven crew members were killed.

*The Challenger after takeoff*

## The *Challenger's* Tragic End

Many Americans were especially interested in the Challenger mission from its start. This was because one of the crew members on board, Christa McAuliffe, was a schoolteacher. How did a schoolteacher wind up aboard a NASA space shuttle? NASA and then-President Ronald Reagan held a contest called the Teacher in Space Project. Over 11,000 teachers applied. Of those 11,000, ten were selected as finalists, possible winners. Finally, 37-year-old Christa McAuliffe was

*The Challenger exploded 73 seconds after takeoff.*

chosen as the final winner. McAuliffe taught high school English and social studies for 15 years. After winning the contest, she, her family, and her students all became famous overnight. McAuliffe trained for six months before joining the Challenger mission. Her job was to help with experiments while in space. She was also supposed to give two lessons while onboard. The lessons would be heard in classrooms all across the country. Schools nationwide watched the Challenger's takeoff because of McAuliffe's presence onboard. Unfortunately, McAuliffe never had a chance to carry out her missions.

7 **investigating** – looking into; studying; examining

# Questions

1. Circle the vocabulary word that best fits the sentence.

   He was happy to be **(selected/applied)** for the new job.

2. Mark each statement as T (true) or F (false).

   ___ Sally Kristen Ride was the first American woman to travel to space.

   ___ Sally Kristen Ride was one of 35 women selected for NASA's space program.

   ___ Sally Kristen Ride taught at the University of California after her second trip to space.

   ___ Sally Kristen Ride was onboard the Challenger space shuttle when it exploded.

3. Number the following events in the order in which they took place.

   ___ Sally Kristen Ride left college to become a professional tennis player.

   ___ Sally Kristen Ride was selected as one of five astronauts onboard the Challenger space shuttle.

   ___ Sally Kristen Ride was the 20th-best tennis player in Los Angeles among girls below 12.

   ___ Sally Kristen Ride investigated the 1986 Challenger disaster.

4. Which of the following sentences from the section titled *"Space Missions"* supports the idea that it was an honor for Ride to be selected to be onboard the *Challenger* space shuttle?

   A. *She was the first American woman and the third woman worldwide to travel to space.*

   B. *In 1984, Ride participated in another Challenger mission.*

   C. *She worked as a special assistant to one of NASA's managers.*

5. Why were so many Americans interested in the 1986 Challenger mission?

   _____

   _____

   _____

# Geysers and Volcanoes: Eruptions From Deep Underground

Sometimes a volcanic eruption can cause lightning, like in this eruption of Mount Rinjani in Indonesia in 1994. *Credit:* Oliver Spalt, Wikimedia

Here's a simple experiment you can do at home. Find a sealed bottle of soda. Let it sit for about ten minutes. Now open it up. Do you hear a hissing sound? That's the sound of air inside the soda escaping. The drink has both gas bubbles and liquid inside it. A liquid is something that takes the shape of the container that it is in. But gas moves around and **expands**[1] to fill any space that it can. When the bottle is opened, the gas escapes and expands into the open air.

Now try shaking a sealed bottle of soda before opening it. When you do that, you make more gas bubbles. You also mix the gas with the liquid. Open the lid of the shaken bottle. The gas escapes as usual. Gas that was mixed with liquid pushes the liquid out too. Suddenly there are streams of soda coming out of the sides of the lid and a big puddle under your feet. In some ways, Earth acts like a giant bottle of soda. Geysers and volcanoes occur when trapped **magma**,[2] water, and gases underground escape to the surface and **erupt**.[3]

---

1 **expands** – grows; swells
2 **magma** – liquid rock under the Earth's surface
3 **erupt** – explode suddenly and dramatically

## Deep Underground

The center of the Earth, also called its core, is hot. Really, really hot. It reaches up to almost 10,000 degrees! We don't feel that heat because there are rocks between the center of the Earth and our feet. But underneath the surface, there are also liquids, solids, and gases.

As they get heated, they sometimes escape from underground. Think of a pot of soup on the stove. If you fill the pot up to the top and put a lid on it, it may start to bubble over. The liquid inside the pot escapes and makes a mess all over the stove. This also happens under the Earth, bringing what is underground up to the surface. These explosions take different forms. Sometimes they take the form of geysers. Other times they take the form of a volcano. What is the difference between a geyser and a volcano?

## Geysers

A geyser starts in a place where underground water gets trapped. These places are called **reservoirs**.[4] There are many reservoirs of water hidden underground. However, only a few become geysers. To become a geyser, the pool of water needs to be close to a heat **source**.[5] Sometimes this source can be magma. Magma is the superheated rock deep underground. Magma is so hot that it is partly liquid.

*The water in this geyser in Iceland came from deep underground.*

The water in the reservoir gets hotter and hotter. Steam is produced. The steam tries to rise up and move around. However, it is trapped underground by the cooler water that comes in from above. Eventually, the system overheats, and the steam and water rise up through cracks in the Earth's surface. The cracks are very narrow, so there isn't a lot of space to move. Then, the superheated gas and water finally reach the surface, where there is a lot of space. As soon as a little water and steam escape, the pressure pushing down on the water is broken.

---

4 **reservoir** – a place where water collects
5 **source** – where something comes from

The water starts to gush out very, very quickly. The gas expands, shooting the water high into the air. Sometimes the water can shoot up hundreds of feet into the air.

## Volcanoes

Just like geysers, volcanoes originate deep underground. But instead of water, the trapped pools of liquid are pools of magma. This reservoir of magma is called a magma chamber.

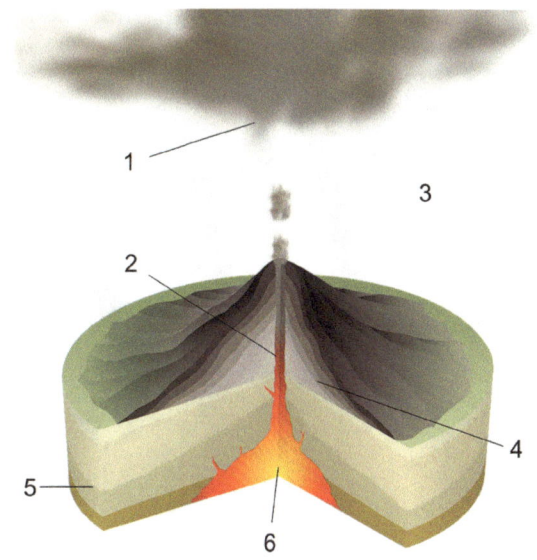

*This picture shows magma rising to the surface from a magma chamber underground.*
*1. Ash plume, 2. Magma conduit, 3. Volcanic ash fall, 4. Layers of lava and ash, 5. Stratum, 6. Magma chamber*
**Credit:** © Sémhur, Wikimedia

The magma is lighter than solid rock. So it slowly gets pushed up to the top of the mantle, the layer of Earth just below the crust. The weight of Earth's crust pushes down on the magma chamber. If the forces pushing up and pushing down are equal, the magma stays where it is.

However, when gas builds up, the force pushing the magma to the surface **increases**.[6] Sometimes an earthquake, landslide, or another event can also lessen the weight pushing down on the magma. These can also weaken the rock that is holding the magma underground. When there is a greater force pushing up than down or too

*Mount Pinatubo in the Philippines erupted in 1991. The ash cloud was 22 miles tall! Luckily there had been signs that the volcano was about to erupt, and people were able to flee the area beforehand.* **Credit:** *Mike Run, Wikimedia*

many cracks in the rocks, magma rushes up and erupts at the surface. (On the surface, magma is called lava.) The gases quickly expand into the air, sending **plumes**[7] of rock, gas, and boiling lava up into the air as a gas cloud. Lava also spills from the sides and runs along the ground.

6 **increases** – grows; becomes more
7 **plumes** – large puffs or clouds of smoke or ash

## Hazards

The lava shoots up in the air. It spills down the sides of the volcano. Sometimes it moves slowly and is easy to outrun. Still, it will destroy all houses and plants in its path. It will block roads. More dangerous is when the ash clouds or the mountain itself collapses. This can cause an event called a pyroclastic flow. In a pyroclastic flow, lava races down the mountain at 100 miles an hour or more. A pyroclastic flow carries rocks. These shoot out like bombs at anything that happens to be in their way. Anyone who is caught by the gases will get burned by their heat. They will be choked by the ashy air. Because they move so fast, pyroclastic flows are one of the most dangerous hazards of a volcano. Volcanoes kill about 500 people a year.

By contrast, geysers aren't really deadly. The water inside the geyser is hot. It is sometimes also **acidic**.[8] The chemicals and bacteria inside can turn the water into all sorts of beautiful colors. If a person falls into a geyser, they will be killed. But, if people stay away from the geyser's edge, there is no danger from it.

## Where Are They Found?

Another difference between geysers and volcanoes is where they are found. There are thousands of active volcanoes worldwide. Many are found in the places where the Earth's crust moves the most.

*Top: A pyroclastic flow sweeps down the Mayon volcano in the Philippines. Middle: A lava flow pours out of Mount Kilauea in Hawaii. Bottom: Slow-moving lava destroys homes and cities in Hawaii.*

*Bacteria and other microbes living in geysers can turn them different colors, like Rainbow Spring at Yellowstone National Park.*

8 **acidic** – sour; stinging

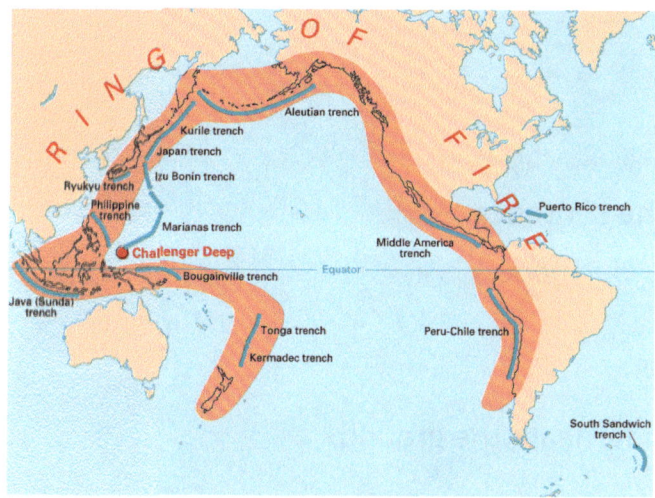

This map shows where the "Ring of Fire" is located.

This is a photograph of an underwater volcano. It is one of the hundreds of volcanic eruptions that take place deep under the ocean.

This area, surrounding the Pacific Ocean, is known as the "Ring of Fire." Even more volcanoes are deep underneath the oceans, where we can't see them erupt.

There are many fewer geysers than volcanoes. Worldwide, there are fewer than 1,000. About half are in the United States in Yellowstone National Park. Russia, Chile, New Zealand, and Iceland are other countries with geysers. The most famous geyser is called Old Faithful. It is in Yellowstone National Park. It is famous because it erupts on schedule. This makes it easier for tourists to plan to see the eruption.

Geysers and volcanoes are both heated from deep underground, but they are very different. Which would you prefer to see?

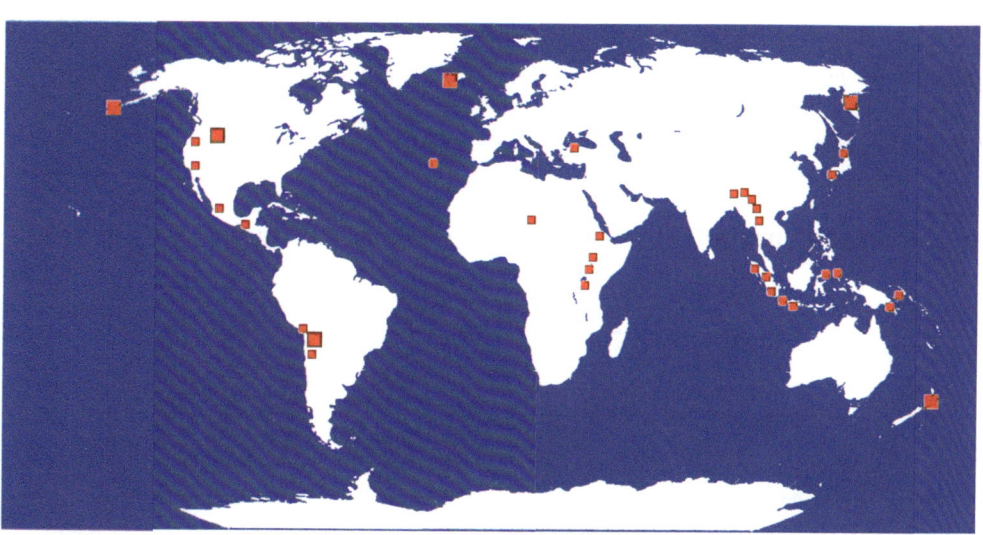

This map shows the main locations where geysers are found worldwide.
**Credit:** *World Traveller, Wikimedia*

 # Questions

1. Circle the vocabulary word that best fits the sentence.

   *They tried to find the **(source/reservoir)** of the loud noise.*

2. Mark each statement as T (true) or F (false).

   ___ There are liquids, solids, and gases underneath the ground.

   ___ Places where underground water gets trapped are called magma chambers.

   ___ Geysers and volcanoes both originate deep underground.

   ___ A pyroclastic flow is one of the most dangerous hazards of a volcano.

3. Number the following events in the order in which they take place.

   ___ Steam is produced.

   ___ Pools of water get trapped underground.

   ___ Water shoots out high into the air.

   ___ The water in the reservoir gets hotter and hotter.

4. Which of the following sentences from the section titled *"Hazards"* supports the idea that geysers aren't necessarily deadly?

   A. The water inside the geyser is hot.

   B. In a pyroclastic flow, lava races down the mountain at 100 miles an hour or more.

   C. But, if people stay away from the geyser's edge, there is no danger from it.

5. How are geysers and volcanoes similar? How are they different? Give a few examples.

   _____

   _____

   _____

   _____